Glory in Their Spirit

*How Four Black Women
Took On the Army
during World War II*

SANDRA M. BOLZENIUS

**UNIVERSITY OF
ILLINOIS PRESS**
Urbana, Chicago, and Springfield

Library of Congress Cataloging-in-Publication Data
Names: Bolzenius, Sandra M., 1959– author.
Title: Glory in their spirit : how four black women took on the Army
    during World War II / Sandra M. Bolzenius.
Other titles: How four black women took on the Army during World
    War II
Description: Urbana, IL : University of Illinois Press, [2018] | Series:
    Women, gender, and sexuality in american history |
    Includes bibliographical references and index.
Identifiers: LCCN 2017056073 | ISBN 9780252041716 (hardcover : alk.
    paper) | ISBN 9780252083334 (pbk. : alk. paper)
Subjects: LCSH: United States. Army. Women's Army Corps—
    History. | World War, 1939–1945—Participation,
    African-American. | Trials (Military offenses)—United
    States—History—20th century. | Strikes and lockouts—
    United States—History—20th century. | African-
    American soldiers—History—20th century. | Women
    soldiers—United States—History—20th century. |
    Race discrimination—United States—History—20th
    century. | Sex discrimination against women—United
    States—History—20th century. | World War, 1939–
    1945—Women—United States. | Fort Devens (Mass.)—
    History—20th century.
Classification: LCC D769.39 .B65 2018 | DDC 305.48/896073—dc23
LC record available at https://lccn.loc.gov/2017056073

ISBN 9780252050381 (ebook)

Negro Journal Of letters
212 S. 11th Ave.
Maywood, Ill.

A Negro's Prayer

Dedicated to the four WACS for their stand against discrimination

By Ruth M. Apilado

Dear God, at the close of every day
I kneel, not sure for what to pray-----
"The war," I could ask for this to cease
And pray with ardor for lasting peace.
But God, I don't know among the throng
Which one is right or which one is wrong.
England, Japan and Germany too
𝗫𝗫𝗫𝗫𝗫𝗫𝗫𝗫𝗫𝗫
Are aggressor nations through and through
America, land of the free
Denies Black folk their liberty.
You know, Oh God, the bad, the good-----
The men who practice brotherhood.
The verdict must be left to you;
We know that "Justice" you will do.
Dear God, before I close this prayer
I'd like to ask You, way up there,
"Isn't the spirit to be free
A God given right of humanity?"
For Patrick Henry, our thanks and then
For the four young WACS, thank God, Amen.

From the scrapbook of Alice Young Porter, courtesy of her daughter, Stacie Porter

To my mother, Lee, and my brother, Dan

Contents

List of Illustrations   xi

Acknowledgments   xiii

Historical Figures   xvii

Abbreviations and Definitions   xix

Timeline   xxi

Introduction   1

Chapter 1. The Army Diversifies: Fort Des Moines   13

Chapter 2. Fort Devens   40

Chapter 3. The Strike   66

Chapter 4. Trial and Verdict   83

Chapter 5. The Civilian Reaction   112

Chapter 6. Military Protocol   126

Conclusion: A Sociological Laboratory   152

Notes   167

Bibliography   195

Index   203

Illustrations

Figures (following p. 82)

The swearing-in of Oveta Culp Hobby as WAAC director in 1942
Black Wacs drill under the command of Captain Charity Adams at Fort Des Moines, Iowa
Mary McLeod Bethune and Dovey Johnson
Mary McLeod Bethune, Eleanor Roosevelt, and others, 1943
Waac mechanics Ruth Wade and Lucille Mayo, Fort Huachuca, Arizona, 1942
Private Annie Hawking, Halloran General Hospital, New York, 1943
Lieutenants Harriet West and Irma Cayton
Alice Young
Anna Collins (Morrison) at Fort Des Moines, Iowa
Tuskegee airmen, Selfridge Field, Michigan, 1943
Anna Morrison
Anna Morrison at Fort Devens
Advertising campaign photo depicting the WAC's ideal image of a female soldier, 1944
Pittsburgh Courier photo of the four court-martialed Wacs
Fort Devens headquarters building
Editorial cartoon by Oliver Harrington, *People's Voice*, 1945

Thurgood Marshall, lead attorney of the NAACP's Legal Defense Fund

Brigadier General Sherman Miles, 1941

Official WAC historian Mattie Treadwell

Tuskegee airman Lieutenant Lee Rayford

Commanding officer Charity Adams inspects the 6888th Postal
    Battalion, 1945

T/Sergeant Tommye Berry at Camp Shanks, New York, 1945

Tables

1. Comparison of White Wac and Black Wac Assignments,
    March 9, 1945   61
2. Comparison of White and Black Wacs' AGCT Scores, Fort Devens,
    April 17, 1945   143

Acknowledgments

Four World War II Wacs inspired this book, and an army of supporters brought it to completion. I am indebted to Judy Tzu-Chun Wu for her unfailing support, incisive commentaries that helped expose the multiple-identity contours so crucial to the story, and her graduate writing workshops that ensured numerous critical assessments for each chapter. Military and early modern European historian Geoffrey Parker lent his celebrated expertise in constructing seventeenth-century narratives to this twentieth-century American story, and his steadfast encouragement ensured the completion of this book. I first learned of the strike at Fort Devens through an anecdote in *The Home Front and Beyond: American Women in the 1940s*. Since then, its author, Susan Hartmann, has mentored me through the full story's development. I enjoyed sharing each breakthrough interview and exciting archival find. I am grateful for her readings of the various iterations of this project, her insight, and her guidance. This book would not have been possible without the collaboration of these three historians, with whom I had the opportunity to work with at the Ohio State University, and I thank them for their unwavering support, expertise, and generosity of time. I am also profoundly grateful to Tiyi Morris, Peter Mansoor, Kevin Boyle, Brigitte Soland, Stephanie Shaw, Paula Baker, Hassan Jeffries, Lilia Fernandez, and Mark Grimsley, whose scholarly commentaries, often their own publications, and their interest in the project aided its development. I appreciate the many hours that Aaron George, Peggy Solic, Adrienne Winans, Jeffrey Vernon, Leticia Wiggins, Delia Fernandez, Andrew Skabelund, Liz Perego, Brandy Thomas, and many others devoted to read lengthy drafts of unpolished chapters and they feedback they provided. While I have had the great privilege of this army of support, the final decisions were mine, and I take full responsibility for the contents of this book.

I also owe a debt of gratitude to those whose personal accounts of the Wacs who served during World War II have uniquely enriched the narrative. Anna Morrison, one of four Wacs court-martialed at Fort Devens, kindly revisited the episode for me. After her death, her friend Juanih Campbell helped fill in the gaps of Morrison's childhood and her life after military service. I appreciate the memories and photographs Juanih shared with me and her interest in ensuring that the historical record includes African women like her friend Anna Morrison. Stacie Porter, daughter of Fort Devens Wac Alice Young, had been trying to do the same long before I came along yet knew little about the strike. I shared my information with her, and she showed me her mother's scrapbook with related articles. She also introduced me to other family members, including her sister Elaine Tomlin who added her memories of her mother's thoughts about the strike. Mary Green's cousin Julia Leveston told me about Green's life in her later years and, along with longtime residents Walter Milo and Luzella Richard, provided insight into Green's Texas hometown. University of Illinois professor Teresa Barnes also generously shared the scrapbook and writings of her great-aunt and former Wac, Margaret Ellen Barnes Jones. Jones's accounts of her experiences often paralleled those of the Fort Devens women, thereby offering added context to the story I tell. I sincerely hope that this book meets the expectations of those who entrusted their loved one's memories and treasures to me.

I am also grateful to the organizations and individuals who have facilitated this project. The Ruth Higgins, Robert Bremner, and Bradley Foundation awards lent financial support for archival research. Ian Meisner and Kara Fossey at the Fort Devens Museum and Alexandra Kolleda at the U.S. Army Women's Museum, Fort Lee, Virginia, provided vital sources. Arlene Balkansky at the Library of Congress, and Sharon Culley at the National Archive College Park, Maryland, and many of their colleagues' relentless pursuit of materials was as helpful as it was impressive, as were the efforts of the archivists and librarians I consulted at the Mary McLeod Bethune House, Washington, D.C., and the Schomburg Center for Research in Black

Culture, New York. As custodians of national treasures, they lent essential assistance to this project. A special note of appreciation goes to the Dawn Durante, my editor at the University of Illinois Press. She has been a bedrock of support throughout the process. I also owe a debt of gratitude to the readers of my manuscript for their detailed reviews and suggestions. These include Elizabeth Escobedo, Deborah Oliver, and, in an earlier iteration, Leisa Meyer.

Friends and family have also been part of this endeavor through their interest in and support of my work. Foremost among them is my chief champion and mother, Lee Bolzenius. Whether I needed an editor or a meal while hunkered down on the book, she was there with practical and morale assistance. Dr. Ruth Staveley likewise read countless drafts and provided valuable feedback for this book. I also thank my older brother, Dan Bolzenius. His dramatic reenactments of historical tales when I was a little girl spurred my interest in history that has led to my own storytelling. Hailing from a large family, I could fill a page with the names of those who in some way had a part in this book. Whether family by birth or friendship, I thank you all.

Lastly, I acknowledge the first Wacs and other servicewomen who served during World War II and paved the road for the women who would follow them into the military. In early 1978, I was one of them as I headed to Fort McClellan, Alabama, one of just two army induction centers at the time for women. Shortly afterward, the army dissolved the WAC and—thirty-six years after inducting its first female soldiers—at last declared them regular soldiers in the regular army. Whether in the WAC or in the regular army, women in uniform still had their battles, yet only while investigating the Fort Devens strike did I realize that they were making their stand on far firmer ground than had their predecessors. All women serving during World War II forged a path where none had previously existed, yet the heavy lifting fell disproportionality on those who shared the labors of its construction and then had to fight for access to travel on it. As the Fort Devens strike illustrates, that burden fell most definitively on the African American women serving in the segregated WAC.

A Note on Archival Sources

The army conducted two investigations of the Wac strike, one authored by the First Service Command and the second by the War Department. The latter is far more extensive and includes the entire First Service Command's inquiry. I treat them as separate investigations, citing summaries, exhibits, and interviews as from either the First Service Command Investigation (FSCI) or from the War Department Investigation (WDI). Collectively, they fill three boxes at the National Archives, College Park, Maryland. Box 914 (part 1) contains the entire First Service Command's investigation and the first part of the War Department's probe beginning with its summary and first exhibits. Box 915 contains the remaining War Department's exhibits and transcripts of its first interviews. Box 916 (part 3) contains the remaining interviews.

Both investigations include a compilation of reports carrying different numbering systems. For example, the War Department numbered its summary's pages as well as its sections within those pages. I have defaulted to the page numbers. Additionally, its first interviews are grouped as one report with pages sequentially numbered while each of its latter interviews, that had not been typed out in time for the final report, are labeled separately and under inconsistent guidelines. These numbers feature dashes, decimals points, and parenthesis, often accompanied by initials, no doubt those of the typists. For the purpose of uniformity, I have defaulted to paginated whole numbers for the first group and to using decimal points for the second, thus transcribing, for example, page "(5)-2-ek" as "5.2."

File 291.1 refers to "Race" under the War Department's decimal system and is used across all military repositories for matter regarding racial matters, regardless of record group or collection.

In addition to citing interviews in the FSCI and WDI investigations, I cite interviews I personally conducted with Juanih Campbell, Jennie Hill, Julia Leveston, Walter Milo, Anna Morrison, Stacie Porter, Luzella Richard, and Elaine Tomlin.

Historical Figures

Charity Adams [Earley]   One of the first women to enlist in the WAC; served as commanding officer of the black WAC company at Fort Des Moines, IA, and of the 6888th Central Postal Directory Battalion in Europe.

Mary McLeod Bethune   Leading civil rights leader and the "surrogate mother" of the WAC

Col. Walter Crandall   Commanding officer of the Lovell General Hospital at Fort Devens, MA

Lt. Sophie Gay   Commanding officer of the black WAC detachment SCU 1127 at Fort Devens until her honorable discharge a month before the strike

Pvt. Mary Green   Defendant in the Fort Devens court-martial

Oveta Culp Hobby   Director of the WAC

Dovey Johnson (Roundtree)   Bethune protégé and WAC officer

Lt. Victoria Lawson   White commanding officer of Fort Devens WAC detachments

Thurgood Marshall   Chief attorney of the NAACP Legal Defense Fund; agreed to defend the Fort Devens Wacs in their appeal

Gen. Sherman Miles   Commanding officer of the First Service Command who ordered the orderlies on strike to return to their duties

Carolyn Moore   Executive secretary of the Philadelphia Branch of the NAACP who alerted Thurgood Marshall to the tinder-box conditions at Fort Devens

Pvt. Anna Morrison   Defendant in the Fort Devens court-martial; declared that she would take a court-martial if it would help her people

Pvt. Johnnie Murphy   Defendant in the Fort Devens court-martial; asserted that she would take death before returning to work

Martha Putney   Black Wac commanding officer of black WAC company at Gardiner Hospital in Chicago; historian of black Wacs who served during World War II

Julian Rainey   Civilian lawyer and NAACP member who defended the four defendants during their court-martial at Fort Devens

Henry L. Stimson   Secretary of War during World War II

Lt. Tenola Stoney   Supply officer of the black WAC detachment SCU 1127 at Fort Devens who took over as commander a month before the strike

Pvt. Harriet Warfield   Surgical technician whose reassignment to orderly duty sparked the letter that first alerted the NAACP to the problems at Fort Devens

T/Sgt. Harold Wicks   Supervisor of enlisted personnel at Lovell Hospital South

Pvt. Alice Young   Defendant in the Fort Devens court-martial; with nursing ambitions, she enlisted to work as a medical technician

Abbreviations and Definitions

AGCT	Army General Classification Test
AWOL	Absent without leave
Basic	(MOS 521) Recruit with no other assignment classifications beyond basic training
Cadre	Essential staff in a military unit responsible for its daily functions
KP	Kitchen Police, a traditionally unpopular military duty that enlisted personnel occasionally performed as assistants in mess halls
Law member	Military judge
LDF	Legal Defense Fund, the legal arm of the NAACP, which selected cases based on their potential to establish civil rights precedents and foster favorable legislation; chaired by Thurgood Marshall during World War II
Medical technician	(MOS 409) Personnel assisting medical staff in routine care of patients; technician duties included making beds to keeping records, sterilizing equipment, taking patient temperatures, and preparing bandages
Members of the Court	Officers assembled to hear military court cases and to render judgments
MOS	Military Occupation Specialty
MP	Military Police

NAACP	National Association for the Advancement of Colored People
NACWC	National Association of Colored Women's Clubs was established in 1896 and functioned until 1904 as the National Association of Colored Women (NACW). The umbrella organization was the nation's largest and most influential civil rights organization through World War I. Promoting feminine respectability as key to the success of African American communities, it adopted the motto "Lift as we climb."
NCNW	National Council of Negro Women was founded by Mary McLeod Bethune in 1935 to foster directly initiatives with the government in which to integrate African American women and their interests into national economic, educational, and political institutions
Orderly	(MOS 657) Personnel responsible for cleaning the hospital and assisting the staff and patients (also called aidmen)
PX	Post Exchange
SCU	Service Command Unit
Surgical technician	(MOS 861) Personnel assisting surgical professionals; duties included sterilizing operating equipment, preparing operating rooms, and preparing patients for surgery
T/4	Technician 4th Class, rank equivalent to a private class
T/5	Technician 5th Class, rank equivalent to a corporal
WAAC	Women's Army Auxiliary Corps
Waac	A member of the Army Auxiliary Corps
WAC	Women's Army Corps
Wac	A member of the WAC
Ward men	Enlisted service members responsible for keeping hospital wards supplied, cleaned, and running smoothly. Provided with a small staff of lower ranked personnel, they were also called ward masters.

Timeline

1940

October 9   The White House announces War Department policies
             that "Negroes will be utilized on fair and equitable basis,"
             albeit in a segregated force.

1942

May 15   Congress establishes the Women's Army Auxiliary Corps
             (WAAC).

1943

July 1   Congress converts the WAAC to the Women's Army
             Corps (WAC).

1944

January 3   The WAC activates the all-white SCU 1127 WAC Detach-
             ment for duty at Lovell Hospital, Fort Devens, MA, un-
             der the First Service Command.

May 24   Anna Collins (Morrison) enlists in the WAC, Cincinnati,
             OH.

May 25   Johnnie Murphy enlists in the WAC, Pittsburgh, PA.

May 31   Alice Young enlists in the WAC, Washington, DC.

June 6	Invasion of Normandy (D-Day).
June 12	The WAC activates Young for training at Fort Des Moines.
June 13	The WAC activates Morrison for training at Fort Des Moines.
June 20	The WAC activates Murphy for training at Fort Des Moines.
June 22	Mary Green enlists in Houston, TX.
June 28	The WAC activates Green for training at Fort Des Moines.
July 15	Lt. Victoria Lawson assumes command of the SCU 1127 WAC Detachment at Fort Devens.
September 21	First Service Command orders Col. Walter Crandall, Chief Administrator, Lovell General Hospital, Fort Devens, MA, to requisition black Wacs.
October	Black Wacs transfer to Fort Devens, SCU 1127, and placed under the leadership of Lt. Lawson and the black Wac detachment's assistant commander, Lt. Sophie Gay.
November 2	Lt. Tenola Stoney assumes her position as the black Wac detachment's supply officer.

1945

February 2	Lt. Gay discharged from the service; Lt. Stoney promoted to assistant commander of the black WAC Detachment at Fort Devens.
March 9	The Fort Devens strike begins.
March 10	Gen. Sherman Miles, commander of the First Service Command, orders the Wacs back to duty; Alice Young, Mary Green, and Anna Morrison opt for the court-martial.
March 12	Johnnie Murphy refuses Lt. Lawson's order to return to work.
March 19	Army convenes the court-martial of Young, Green, Morrison, and Murphy.

Glory in Their Spirit

Introduction

The Army is not a sociological laboratory.
—Col. Eugene R. Householder, December 8, 1941

On March 19, 1945, in the crowded makeshift courtroom in the headquarters building of Fort Devens, Massachusetts, Private Anna Morrison took the stand. Not two weeks had passed since she and her codefendants—Privates Mary Green, Alice Young, and Johnnie Murphy—had opted for the court-martial rather than return to their duties. Once the collective strike had collapsed, the four knew of no other way to capture their officers' attention to their detachment's grievances. The decision to be court-martialed, however, had exposed them to widespread castigation, dishonorable discharges, and imprisonment. Morrison had been among the strike's most vociferous proponents, yet the trial was proving all too traumatic. On the verge of a breakdown, she nevertheless held steady that first day. Facing military officers, black and white reporters, and curious onlookers crammed into the small room and awaiting her testimony, Morrison was determined to explain her reasons for disobeying the general's order to return to work.

"You testified," queried prosecutor Major Leon McCarthy, "that you would take a court-martial if it would help your people?" In a low but firm voice, Morrison replied, "I did."[1] McCarthy expressed puzzlement. "You were the one in trouble, weren't you?," he asked. "Your people had not done anything." Having primed the spectators, the prosecutor launched his accusation: "You were only looking out for yourself on that day, weren't you?"

Morrison replied, "exactly not for my own self."[2] Though she responded calmly, inside she was seething. The Kentucky native and former maid bitterly resented Fort Devens's relegation of its black, but not white, members of the Women's Army Corps (WAC) to permanent cleaning detail. Orderly duties, the army called it, but it was maid work all the same.

Mary Green took the stand next. In poor health, the single mother of two had more to lose than her codefendants when she agreed to the court-martial and had immediately regretted her decision. The small-town Texan and, like Morrison, a former maid, well understood the fruitlessness of fighting the system that cast colored women as servants. At Fort Devens, she also understood the need to fight it. "Why didn't you go to work after the General ordered you to go?," McCarthy asked her. Green admitted that she thought she was pregnant and therefore could not do the heavy work orderly duties required. Additionally, she told the court, the members of her detachment "had been having trouble about we being colored," and she needed to take a stand. The army's refusal to countenance a racial defense defined McCarthy's conjecture: "your mistreatment was because you were doing work you didn't like?"[3] The trial for which Green and her codefendants had risked so much was twisting their explanations into excuses.

At twenty-three, Alice Young was the oldest of the group, and she took the stand with the confidence of an urbane Washington, D.C., native with experience and opportunities that eluded most African American women in the 1940s. Unlike Morrison and Green, she had left behind a well-paid government job to enlist. Young aspired to be a nurse, and recruiters assured her that her year of nursing college qualified her to train and work as a medical technician. Instead, she too was cleaning floors and running errands because, she surmised, she was African American. To bolster her argument to the skeptical prosecutor, she recounted her hospital commander's announcement that "I do not have colored Wacs as medical technicians. They are here to scrub and wash floors, wash dishes and do all the dirty work." The incriminating statement sent reporters' pencils whirling yet did not deter McCarthy's singular interest in whether or not the enlisted women had disobeyed orders. "You were acquainted," he asked Young, "with the fact that you were in the Army and expected to do your duty in the Army as a soldier, whatever the assignment was?" In fact, the former coed had enlisted in order to fulfill her duty as a soldier, not work as a maid. During increasingly teary testimony, Young tried to explain the relevance of her nurse's training, promises made by army recruiters, and the crippling limitations of permanent orderly detail while the prosecutor insisted that racial discrimination did not exist in the segregated U.S. Army.[4]

McCarthy questioned Johnnie Murphy last. Murphy was not one to mince words and did not plan to do so that day, though her brashness tended to get her into trouble. This was her second court-martial. Whereas the first was over profanity and alcohol in the barracks, she rooted her participation in the strike in the nation's civil rights struggle. The only northerner among the four defendants, Murphy had had enough of the army's outright southern-style segregation practices. When McCarthy asked her if she had told her white female lieutenant, "I would take death before I would go back to work," Murphy affirmed it. By refusing to return to duties she considered discriminatory to black Wacs, she told the court, "I believed that I was doing the right thing."[5]

Morrison, Green, Young, and Murphy risked everything to make visible the discriminatory treatment black Wacs were subjected to at Fort Devens. Nine jurors would determine the price they would pay for that defiance.

* * *

The events that led to the court-martial of the four young African American servicewomen began on March 9, 1945, when fifty-four orderlies of the black WAC Detachment staged a strike in protest of the discriminatory treatment they experienced at Fort Devens in Massachusetts, fortysome miles northwest of Boston. For five months they had labored as cleaning women at one of the post's hospitals while white Wacs in the other hospital worked at a variety of skilled jobs. They complained, though to no avail until the strike. At last the women had found a way to force their officers to react to their concerns, though not in the manner they had hoped. Within days, military authorities had arrested four of their number: Privates Anna Morrison, Mary Green, Alice Young, and Johnnie Murphy. Each had expressed her preference to take a court-martial rather than return to orderly duties.

In an unexpected turn of events, black and white reporters converged on the case, sending dispatches about black Wacs on strike that stirred Americans from around the nation and across racial divides to weigh in. Many white readers denounced the act as mutiny, and others expressed sympathy for "the girls." In contrast, the black press and local activists immediately mobilized support for the defendants, while prominent civil rights leaders and several congressional representatives demanded War Department investigations into the causes of the strike. So swift and unrelenting was the civilian uproar that within three weeks it had compelled the WAC director's attention to the case, the Secretary of War's intervention, and a senior career officer's resignation. The civilian reaction also caused bewilderment among the women's white army officers who wondered how a routine disciplinary hearing for an obvious act of insubordination could have warranted such widespread debate.

The army's perplexity over the surge of interest in a case featuring low-ranking African American servicewomen is understandable. Similar protests by black male troops during World War II were so common that they rarely piqued mainstream interest.[6] Furthermore, the national obsession with the still new phenomenon of female soldiers fixated, outside of African American communities, solely on white Wacs. Then suddenly, four years into the war and three years after the creation of the women's corps, the Fort Devens incident riveted many Americans precisely because it featured black Wacs. Through their decision to take a court-martial, Young, Morrison, Green, and Murphy injected fresh complexities into three of the nation's most hotly contested issues: racial segregation in the military, the role of women in uniform, and the democratic ideals for which nearly all Americans professed that they were fighting the war.

The War Department unwittingly invited such controversies when, in 1942, it enlisted women for the first time in its history and, in an era when "women" typically meant white women, accepted African American women, albeit in segregated units. As leery of altering gender roles as it was racial boundaries, the War Department created the Women's Army Auxiliary Corps (WAAC) as a separate force to assist the all-male regular army rather than be a part of it. Prioritizing gender roles, it designed the WAAC as a temporary measure, promoted its assignments as appropriately feminine, and denied members full military status.[7] Indeed, the army's first female troops were so loosely connected to the regular army that they operated under a confusing tangle of unfamiliar rank classifications and regulations that befuddled even seasoned soldiers.[8] Within a year, the War Department replaced the ambiguous WAAC with the Women's Army Corps (WAC). Though it remained separate from the main force, most of its policies and protocols readily conformed to standard army operations. It was under the WAC designation that Morrison, Young, Murphy, and Green enlisted in 1944. Less than a year later, their detachment's strike and their court-martial put into sharp relief the complexities of the army's racial, sex, and rank divisions.

Over 6,500 black Wacs served during World War II, yet their wartime contributions and experiences remain largely underexplored. Seventy years later, Americans are left with the impression of those in uniform, as the 1982 groundbreaking analysis of African American women's invisibility quipped, "all the women are white, all the blacks are men."[9] Black Wacs accounted for just 4 percent of the WAC, which itself constituted just 2 percent of the entire strength of the U.S. Army, yet their presence and their assertions of their rights as military personnel influenced WAC policies and also helped advance the civil rights movement. Their exploits are not as well-known today as those of black servicemen, perhaps best symbolized by the famed Tuskegee airmen, though these women similarly championed the cause.[10] Of the seventeen most publicized cases involving African American military personnel during 1944 and 1945, two centered on black Wacs.[11] The most famous of these was the Fort Devens strike.

As a case study, the well-documented Fort Devens Wac strike presents a rich microcosm in which to explore the army's personnel policies and the status of African American servicewomen during World War II. Because military policies were rooted in civilian policies and attitudes, the incident, as told through the experiences and the voices of black Wacs, lends insight into the nation's social and economic structure and its effects on this one group of marginalized American citizens. Thus this book probes the unique situation of black Wacs as they navigated, negotiated, resisted, and defied army policies that typically isolated them into menial labor. It examines the War Department's reluctance to upset prewar racial and gender conventions and its insistence that its policies were colorblind and that its protocols were guarantors of standard treatment regardless of race and, to a lesser degree, sex. The Fort Devens strike illustrates how African American Wacs tested the limits of War Department regulations and the army's logistical abilities to segment its troops by race, rank, and gender. As a cause célèbre, the case showcases the wartime civil rights movement as an emboldened force due to the effectiveness of its various arms when they coalesced, as they did over the Fort Devens case, to galvanize national support for the women and reinvigorate the national debate over segregation in the military. Finally, an analysis of the Wac strike adds breadth to the scholarship recognizing the critical role of women in war and African American women in the civil rights movement. The establishment of the WAC during World War II laid before African American women a powerful road by which they could claim their full measure of citizenship. A thorough examination of the Fort Devens Wac strike explores ways in which they negotiated the rough terrain that featured more roadblocks than freeways.

Historical scholarship has recognized World War II as a watershed moment for social change, and the defense industry and the military major catalysts in this effort.[12] During the war years, when the state required the cooperation and willing labor of its citizens, minorities and women targeted military service as a promising venture to assert their patriotism and advance their opportunities. The army, as the nation's largest employer and with its stated mission to secure the world for democracy, seemed a particularly promising platform for subordinate citizens to prod social change.[13] Top army officials adamantly rejected this notion, insisting that "the Army is not a sociological laboratory." Focused on winning the war, they warned that "experiments to meet the wishes and demands of the champions of every race and creed for the solution of their problems are a danger to efficiency, discipline and morale and would result in ultimate defeat."[14] The Fort Devens strike encapsulates the conflicts arising from the army's refusal to examine its racial policies and black Wacs' assertions that these policies, not resistance to them, were the real danger to the army's efficiency, discipline, and morale.

The circumstances that led to the Fort Devens strike were in large part embedded in the long history of African American soldiers and their service in the segregated army. With so few other options open to them, black men attached particular importance to military service as a means to advance their claims of earned citizenship. In contrast, the army discounted their value as soldiers, recruited them to bridge its occasional shortages of white men, and relegated them to menial labor. For centuries, the army treated black men as reserve troops to enlist during a crisis and dismiss following the cessation of hostilities. By World War II, and in the militant shift of the era, civil rights leaders openly rejected such exploitive practices by demanding reform and state concessions in return for African Americans' cooperation.[15] W. E. B. Du Bois, who during World War I had urged African Americans to unite with the nation around the war, declared during World War II that "now is the time not to be silent." The fiery A. Philip Randolph, president of the Brotherhood of Sleeping Car Porters, translated this strategy to a pithy "pressure, more pressure, and still more pressure."[16] The War Department conceded on several points, including an announcement that "Negroes will be utilized on a fair and equitable basis" and, unlike the other services, an agreement to enlist black women into the new women's corps.[17] It refused to budge, however, on the movement's chief demand to racially integrate the army.

Black and white Americans in 1945 typically contextualized the Fort Devens incident in racial terms, yet the strike resulted from the army's segmentation of its troops by sex as well as by race, binaries that black Wacs, as both female and African American, complicated. For instance, the War Department reviewed its racial policies with black soldiers in mind and negotiated gender policies with white Wacs in mind. When it later agreed to enlist African American women, the War Department assumed that these policies sufficiently overlapped to cover black Wacs. They did not. Rather, they often conflicted, thereby excluding black Wacs from the majority of army training programs, skilled assignments, military posts, and consequently rank promotions. Furthermore, under the leadership of its director, Oveta Culp Hobby, the corps regulated the conduct of its female soldiers in comportment with white, middle-class standards. Realizing that many Americans were uncomfortable with the concept of female soldiers, Hobby presented her troops as upstanding models of womanhood whose model behavior fell well within acceptable feminine boundaries. Conflicts arose when Wacs resisted these boundaries—and when they did not fit into them in the first place. Race alone assured an uneasy fit for African American women in uniform.[18]

The story of African American servicewomen therefore adds to the studies of the intersectionality, the theory that societies determine an individual's place and value according to a multiplicity of intersecting identities. As legal scholar Kimberlé Crenshaw, who coined the term in the late twentieth century, has noted, though "people don't experience discrimination . . . solely on the basis of race or solely on the basis of gender," discussions of race and gender tend to be "mutually exclusive." Furthermore, she argues, societies also segment its members based on their economic status, national origin, sexual orientation, and hundreds of other factors, all of which intersect to produce a whole that is greater than its parts. Consequently, policies geared for minorities and those for women inevitably fail to adequately address the unique circumstances of minority women.[19]

The concept of multiple systemic oppression was familiar, if under different names, to previous generations of black women. In 1944, Pauli Murray proposed the term Jane Crow to describe the dual disadvantages African American women suffered due to their twofold subordinated status within the patriarchal and racist society they lived. Her personal experiences illustrate her point: denied entry into the University of North Carolina due to her race and later to Harvard's law program because of her sex, Murray bore an additional blow when her African American male counterparts at Howard University found the latter exemption humorous. Arguably one of the top legal strategists of the last century, Murray had learned by 1944 that while black women struggled for race equality with white women and for gender equality with black men, they did not fully share in the dividends of either campaign. Indeed, they quite often, for reasons not easily defined, faced further marginalization instead. Were they denied jobs, for instance, due to their sex or to their race? Within a year of Murray's coinage of Jane Crow, Morrison, Murphy, Young, and Green, whom the army exempted from all but cleaning jobs, revealed that Jane Crow struggled in the military, too.[20]

Given the historical marginalization of African American women, black Wacs served as flashpoints for debates about race and gender during World War II, a point that the strike and the civilian reaction to it dramatizes. Black Wacs at Fort Devens and elsewhere enlisted in the new women's corps under guarantees of specialized training and equal treatment regardless of race. When the army fell short of these promises, it compelled many of these women to take a stand and assert their rights. Many of those at Fort Devens who participated in the strike grounded their action in the civil rights struggle, as did Morrison when she declared that she would undergo a court-martial to "help my people." The comment strongly resonated with African Americans who rallied around her and her codefendants. Many white Americans, also troubled by segregation or simply uncomfortable sending women to prison, joined them. Other white Americans blamed civil rights leaders for riling up black Wacs over racial discrimination that they did not believe existed. In each case, news of a court-martial featuring African American women in uniform attracted attention and fueled debates over the reasons for and legitimacy of the strike. For the four defendants at the center of the storm, the strike imbued the struggle that black Wacs, at Fort Devens and beyond its gates, faced as African American women.

By insisting on respect as citizens, they defied both military and civilian attitudes that disparaged their character. By insisting on their rights as Wacs, they challenged military policies that restricted their opportunities and relegated them to menial duties.[21]

Certainly, separate but equal laws in the South reinforced the position of African American women as menial laborers, yet so did federal legislation in the North through the guise of colorblind intentions. Both the Social Security Act, which provided unemployment and pension benefits, and the Fair Labor Standards Act, which set a minimum hourly wage and a maximum work-hour week, excluded service workers and agricultural laborers and, therefore, most African Americans. This was especially true of African American women, who were, as Pauli Murray asserted, a "minority within a minority."[22] Nationally, less than 10 percent of African American women benefited from these New Deal provisions, thereby leaving them particularly vulnerable, economically and socially.[23] As these policies conversely improved employment conditions for white men and secured them and their families into middle-class prosperity, they gave credence to a common perception that black women's overall low socioeconomic status was a natural condition, a result of their combined racial and gender deficiencies. Most white Americans remained unaware how state policies privileged them.[24]

African American women's attempts to break from their designated cast as menial laborers persistently encountered roadblocks. Formal segregation in the South forced the majority into domestic service. In search of improved opportunities, millions migrated north, only to find familiar barriers. Factory employers, for instance, generally declined to hire African Americans, women or men, for well-paid industrial jobs. Infuriated, Randolph announced in 1941 a march on Washington in protest. Eager to prevent tens of thousands of African Americans from heeding Randolph's call and converging on the nation's capital, President Franklin D. Roosevelt offered as a concession Executive Order 8802. The order established the Fair Employment Practices Committee (FEPC), which prohibited racially discriminatory hiring practices in defense industries. It had little teeth, however, and factory managers often ignored it. Of the thirty thousand women employed by Detroit's war industries in 1942, for example, fewer than a hundred were African American. Nevertheless, the percentage of black female factory workers quadrupled during the war years, though typically because these women accepted the dangerous, dirty, and grueling work that white women rejected. So pigeonholed into domestic service were black women that it was not uncommon for managers who declined to hire them for factory jobs to offer them instead work as maids for their wives.[25]

The backgrounds and experiences of the four Wacs court-martialed at Fort Devens illustrates the pervasiveness of the limited opportunities for black women in the mid-twentieth century. Born in the 1920s when 90 percent of African Americans lived in the South, three of the four—Green, Morrison, and Young—knew well the region's social and employment stipulations that cast black women as laundresses, agricultural laborers, and domestic servants. Both Green from Texas and Morrison from Kentucky worked as maids before entering the WAC. Seeking anything but service work, the latter migrated North, yet found only maid jobs there, too. Murphy, the only northerner of the four, remained unemployed until her enlistment in the WAC (army records listed her occupation as "homemaker"). Young, raised in a middle-class African American neighborhood in Washington, D.C., managed to escape service work, at least until she arrived at Fort Devens. As a Wac orderly, she, along with two-thirds of her detachment's members, cleaned and ran errands at a post hospital. The Fort Devens Wacs maintained that the army did not give them a chance to prove their abilities and learn new skills, yet in a nation where 70 percent of black employed women worked in service jobs, their situation did not register as scandalous, but as the norm.[26]

Black Wacs resisted subordination during World War II, and they did so by employing strategies that their foremothers had honed over the centuries. Without legal or social protection of their employment, womanhood, or citizenship, African American women had long turned to each other and worked collectively to strengthen their voices and initiatives. Working-class women joined and led strikes and traded advice about employers and working conditions. They and other African American women formed clubs and established women's auxiliaries. Typically dominated by middle-class professionals, these organizations promoted the respectability of black women to nurture and celebrate its members' contributions to society. Working together, African American women organized consumer boycotts, united around the nation's wars, supported their men in uniform, and honed leadership skills that provided much of the backbone of local civil rights efforts. So effective were these clubs that their umbrella organization, the National Association of Colored Women's Clubs (NACWC), established in 1896, stood as the nation's largest and most influential civil rights organization through World War I. Eclipsed in the postwar years by the National Association for the Advancement of Colored People (NAACP), women's clubs and associations remained essential to the movement by continuing to inspire women, as the NACWC's motto urged, to "lift as we climb." The growing militancy of the era, however, brought a shift in emphasis on the lifters' wages, status, and political influence.[27]

During World War II, many African American women recognized the WAC as a new platform to directly assist the war effort, support their communities, and improve their future employment prospects. The most prominent was Mary McLeod Bethune, the renowned educator, former NACWC president, and founder of the National Council of Negro Women (NCNW). A respected leader of the civil rights movement and revered symbol of African American womanhood, she also served in the 1930s and 1940s as director of Negro affairs in the National Youth Administration and, less formally, as a member of President Roosevelt's "Black Cabinet." Bethune employed her various connections and the sheer force of her personality to support the African American women who enlisted in the corps including, in 1945, those who took part in the strike at Fort Devens.[28] The most essential components to ensuring the vitality of this new platform were the 6,500 African American women who took a chance on the segregated army and enlisted in the WAC. Though many gained the useful training and social status they expected, the majority encountered the familiar obstacles that for centuries had impeded the prospects of black women. As had their foremothers, black Wacs across the country resisted subordination, often by working together to strengthen their voice.[29] The Fort Devens strike was the most publicized of these collective efforts.

Through a chronological unfolding of the Fort Devens case, this book details and analyzes both the experiences of black Wacs during World War II as they asserted their rights as uniformed personnel and the army's response as it contested its role as the nation's sociological laboratory. With the backdrop of the Fort Des Moines, Iowa, induction center, where most black Wacs began their military service, chapter 1 considers the long history of African American male soldiers, the first years of the WAC, and the significance of military service to black women as a means to claim full citizenship. Chapter 2 analyzes the military policies that marginalized black Wacs by race, sex, and rank; examines these women's protests over the resulting marginalization; and recognizes their demands as based on their entitlement to standard military protocol. Chapter 3 illustrates how conflicting dynamics between army policies and black enlisted Wacs' expectations erupted in the strike at Fort Devens and led to the arrests of Privates Morrison, Murphy, Green, and Young. Chapter 4 details the court-martial through an analysis of the military justice system, which the army presented as transparent and colorblind, and its effect on female African American defendants. Chapter 5 considers the civilian reaction by probing the wartime influence of the civil rights movement's loose coalition of national and local organizations, prominent leaders, the black press, and ordinary African American citizens and their grassroots efforts. Chapter 6 returns to Fort Devens to investigate how War Department officials, the four court-martialed Wacs, and other military personnel involved in the case sought to extricate themselves from the incident. The conclusion revisits the premise of the U.S. Army as a sociological laboratory to discuss the implications of the Fort Devens incident and, more broadly, the service of African American Wacs during World War II.

For two months during the spring of 1945, the Fort Devens incident transcended racial, gender, and class lines, bringing uncustomary attention to African American women. Then, suddenly, news of the incident vanished from the public domain, and with it recognition of the contributions of black Wacs—if not their mere existence—during World War II. Apart from anecdotal references by scholars, the case has been largely forgotten.[30] The story of the Fort Devens strike illustrates that along with the formidable histories of white and black male soldiers, white pioneers of the WAC, and members of the officer corps stand equally compelling and heroic stories of enlisted black Wacs, who operated under different military policies than other personnel.[31] The following pages explore how Mary Green, Anna Morrison, Johnnie Murphy, and Alice Young challenged the U.S. Army over its discriminatory treatment of African American servicewomen and the profound mark that their protest has left on the history of World War II and the nation's ongoing struggle for social justice.

1

The Army Diversifies

Fort Des Moines

I wanted to prove to myself, maybe the world, that
we would give what we had back to the U.S. as a
confirmation that we were full-fledged citizens.
—Veteran Elaine Bennett, quoted in B. Moore,
  To Serve My Country, To Serve My Race

The four young women who made headlines during World War II were
but school girls when the mechanisms that set the course for their once
improbable journey began falling into place. In 1940, wars were igniting
across Europe and Asia; the U.S. War Department, with watchful eyes on
the unfolding crises, was readying plans to expand its forces; and civil
rights leaders, wary of the nation's call for African American troops only
in emergencies and to serve in segregated units, were leveraging their rising influence to negotiate the treatment of black servicemen. Alice Young,
Mary Green, Johnnie Murphy, and Anna Morrison would have taken little
personal note of such high-level discussions. In their mid- to late teens, they
had futures to forge, and as women, military service was not an option. In
1940, no U.S. military service enlisted women.

Hailing from different regions of the country and various family and economic backgrounds, the four teens represented a diverse cross-sectional slice
of African American women and their circumstances in the mid-twentieth
century.[1] Eighteen-year-old Alice Young was finishing high school in her

hometown of Washington, D.C. Reared in a middle-class family that encouraged educational achievement, she planned to attend college.[2] Farther west,
in Chicago, Johnnie Murphy, though Young's junior by two years, had already
earned her high school diploma and was enrolled in vocational training,
most likely a clerical course. She liked school, she said, perhaps because it
offered a reprieve from an otherwise disjointed childhood. Murphy was born
in Georgia but spent her early childhood in Pennsylvania, first in Pittsburgh
and later in nearby Rankin, a small industrial town. Her father died when
she was six and her mother three years later. Following the loss of her parents, Murphy also lost touch with her siblings after loved ones separated
the children and sent her to live with relatives in Chicago. The changes took
their toll, and Murphy was restless. Apparently eager to strike out on her
own, she graduated at sixteen looking for a fresh start—or perhaps simply
a return to her abruptly curtailed Pennsylvania childhood.[3] Down South
in Richmond, Kentucky, Anna Collins [Morrison] was also eager to move.
Like Murphy, she lost her mother when very young. For a short while, she
lived with her father, although his alcoholism left him "a helpless invalid"
and the family destitute. County services stepped in when she was no more
than six years old and sent her and at least one of her brothers to a farm
in nearby Tates Creek. It was not an ideal childhood, noted Morrison years
later as she recalled the hard work she had to do. By 1940, she had returned
to Richmond, found work as a maid, and, desiring another line of work,
contemplated trying her luck in the North.[4] Out west in Texas, just north
of Houston, Mary Magdaline Amerson (Green) lived in all-black Tamina, a
small town on the outskirts of all-white Conroe. There, according to a longtime resident, "everyone knew their place" and "if you could not remain
in your place, there was a group that would remind you."[5] The daughter of
a minister in his seventies and his wife thirty years his junior, the "quiet,
soft-spoken and genteel girl" was part of a large, close-knit family of twenty-
seven siblings. Young Mary Amerson struggled to balance both school and
romance, and when romance won, she left school after ninth grade, found
employment as a maid, and soon married.[6] By 1940, Green was expecting
her first child. Regardless of regional locations or personal aspirations, as
African American women all four expected their futures to necessitate a
lifetime of paid employment. Most black women in the 1940s—when nearly
70 percent of wage-earning black women worked in the service industry and
overwhelmingly as domestic servants—eventually worked as maids.[7] Given

its poor pay, long hours, and lowly social status, domestic service was less a desired option than a default position in the absence of other opportunities.

Then came the war.

Desperate for additional personnel, the army created its first women's corps in 1942, an event that Young, Murphy, Green, and Morrison could not have foreseen two years earlier. Suddenly, the army flung open hundreds of specialized jobs to women and a year later was offering them the same rank pay and many of the same benefits that white male soldiers earned, a racial and gender parity virtually unknown elsewhere in the United States.[8] Additionally, most Americans traditionally showed respect to members of the armed forces, which African Americans felt would naturally extend to them. By the summer of 1944, all four had enlisted. Each entered the WAC assured of employment opportunities and citizen status that they previously could not have fathomed—not as women, and most certainly not as black women.[9]

U.S. military leaders also could not have predicted the enlistment of women, yet hostilities abroad and understaffed forces at home forced them to expand their ranks beyond their preferred population of white men. As the armed forces' largest service, the army took the lead by acting quickly, decisively, and at times surprisingly. In two stunning reversals of its usual practices, the army began to admit African American men in larger numbers than at any time since the Civil War and, for the first time in its history, enlist women. It took another unprecedented move by enlisting black women. As a result, the nation's largest force would look far different by war's end than it had in 1940 when an all-male and virtually all-white entity. By 1945, 9 percent of the army consisted of black men and 2 percent consisted of women, including, over the course of the war, 6,500 African American women.[10]

Occupying the lower rungs of civil society as both African Americans and women, black Wacs faced challenges distinct from those of other personnel, yet they also gained through their enlistment an important vehicle not available to their civilian counterparts to confront those challenges. Following the tradition of civilian policies, the War Department divided its troops by race, rank (class), and gender. Just as these delineations marginalized African American female civilians, so did they marginalize African American women in the military. Consequently, black recruits who enlisted expecting the army to respect their rights as service personnel encountered instead a lack of training opportunities, specialized jobs, and timely promotions. Conflict was inevitable though black Wacs had two important advantages to call upon in the ensuing contests: World War II army policies that, unlike civilian laws and conventions, clearly documented the entitlement of all military personnel to fair and uniform treatment in accordance with military protocols; and the legacy of their foremother's legacy that they shared with their civilian sisters. Generations of African American women's struggles against labor exploitation and assaults on their character provided this new category of soldiers well-honed strategies to resist discrimination and assert their rights. As the Fort Devens incident illustrates, black Wacs serving during World II would need both of these advantages.

There was never a question that the War Department would open its ranks to African American men during World War II, but rather how many it would accept. Since colonial times, black men had stood reliably as the nation's ready reserve. In crises, the state called on them and they proudly served despite conditions rife with racial exploitation and ridicule. In return, the state relegated them to menial labor in segregated units and discharged them after the urgency subsided. By demeaning their intelligence, leadership skills, and masculinity, the army justified segregating African American troops from its main white force, denying them useful training and regular promotions, and excluding them from combat units where they could distinguish themselves and their race.[11]

Despite these degradations, African Americans championed military service. The army offered a decent salary and the respected uniform to men typically consigned to menial labor and subservient status. Military service also provided a rare platform for black men to claim earned citizenship as defenders of the nation. The military's declared democratic mission lent further appeal to a population yearning for democratic freedoms. During World War I, for instance, when the army once again called on black men to shore up its forces, many civil rights leaders urged African Americans to unite with their fellow Americans in support of the war. They hoped that their solidarity with the nation, best symbolized by their men who served, would encourage white Americans to recognize the disconnect between fighting for democracy overseas while subjugating its own citizens at home.[12] Instead, African Americans suffered in the wake of a postwar upsurge in violence, particularly against veterans who presumably entertained notions that they had earned their rights to equal citizenship.[13]

The experience spurred a militant impatience among African Americans who had tired of the empty rhetoric of a nation united under the banner for liberty and justice for all. Taking little note of the rising sentiment of resistance, the War Department, when needing additional soldiers to meet the challenges of yet another world war, expected African American men to patriotically enlist as they always had.

Civil rights leaders continued to regard military service as a tool to advance their cause, yet by the late 1930s they would not offer their full support without concessions. Representing over 10 percent of the nation's population, they understood the state's need for African Americans in its military—and its factories and farms—and that this yielded them significant wartime bargaining powers.[14] From this emboldened stance, the movement made demands of the state, both its civil and military arms, in exchange for African American support, labor, and troops. Desperate for a reliable labor force and domestic peace, the state at last began to budge, most notably on the civilian front in 1941, when President Franklin D. Roosevelt signed executive order 8802 banning discrimination in defense industry hiring. On the military front, the War Department agreed to a 10 percent quota of black male enlistment (in proportion to the 10 percent representation of African Americans in the population). It commissioned the army's first black general, Benjamin Davis Sr., and approved the appointment of a civilian aide of Negro affairs to advise the Secretary of War on racial matters, a position that Judge William Hastie immediately filled. In a seemingly groundbreaking policy shift, the War Department also announced that "Negroes will be utilized on a fair and equitable basis."[15]

Despite their new wartime clout, black leaders were unable to secure their most important demand, the racial integration of the armed forces. Throughout the 1940s, the War Department stood firm on its position that racial segregation was the only reasonable way to avoid racial problems. Insisting that "the policy of the War Department is not to intermingle colored and white enlisted personnel in the same regimental organization," it concluded that "this policy has been proven satisfactory over a long period of years."[16] African Americans vehemently contested the "satisfactory" aspect, yet military officials countered that, with the nation at war, their priorities could not, and would not, include race relations.

In rare circumstances, the sheer impracticality of segregation in terms of cost and efficiency compelled the army to relax the practice. During World

War I, the army integrated its officer candidate training schools due to so few African Americans it had at last allowed into the program, and during World War II, it directed the integration of recreational facilities on bases. These were not major attitude shifts, however, as noted by the army's refusal to allow black officers to command white troops and the persistence of segregated recreational facilities throughout the war.[17] (In the final year of the war, Fort Devens still maintained separate clubs for its black personnel.)[18] Piecemeal compromises without genuine concessions underscored the War Department's contention that racial issues were not part of its purview. "The immediate task of the army is the efficient completion of our Defense Program," declared a senior War Department spokesperson in November 1941. "Nothing should be permitted to divert us from this task."[19]

To the frustration of African Americans in and out of the service, the War Department consistently prioritized its segregation policies over its racial equality policies. As a result, white officers who ignored the military's racial parity directives rarely suffered consequences while black service personnel who asserted their rights granted under these same directives frequently faced charges. News of disciplinary actions against African Americans in uniform filled the pages of the black press, as did reports of white civilians attacking black military personnel for breeching, purposely or not, color lines.[20] Countless racial incidents during the war years testify to the reluctance of many white Americans to come to terms with African Americans' increasing confidence to assert their rights. Being female offered little protection. In 1944, police officers attacked two black Wacs traveling on a civilian bus after they refused to vacate their seats for white passengers. "Just because you're in the uniform," shouted one of the officers, "you think you're smart. You're still a God-damn nigger down here in the South with us."[21] So rampant was the problem of civilian hostility to black troops that the National Lawyers Guild alerted the Justice and War departments that "civilian violence against the Negro in uniform is a recurrent phenomenon."[22]

Astounded by the hypocrisy, a young black man in 1941 poured out his frustrations in a letter to a newspaper asking if it would be "demanding too much to demand full citizenship rights in exchange for the sacrificing of my life." Succinctly expressing the feelings of African Americans everywhere, James Thompson gave voice to the two-front war that African Americans understood they were fighting, the one against fascism abroad and the other against racial discrimination at home. Drawing on Thompson's protest, the black press—boldly led by *Pittsburgh Courier* editor Percival L. Prattis—launched the "Double V" (Victory) campaign. Anchoring African Americans' demands for full citizenship rights to their patriotic support of the war and its democratic mission, the black press inspired its readers around the world to raise two fingers on both hands in a double-V fashion.[23] The black women who began enlisting the following year soon had cause to consider what might be called a Triple V campaign as African Americans and as African American women.

Unlike their countrymen, neither black nor white American women at the beginning of World War II had definitive historical roots in the military. Wartime armies had traditionally utilized them as nurses and cooks as needed and occasionally as spies and guides.[24] The army's rapid buildup during World War I and the increasingly bureaucratic nature of the modern military opened a new chapter for their service as the army hired them as clerical and communication specialists.[25] The experience demonstrated to military officials that women formed an ideal reserve force to tap in a crisis. Indeed, women's restricted employment options, low salaries, and perceived status as temporary workers (before marriage and children), ensured a ready and affordable workforce that the army could employ when needed and discharge after the urgency subsided.[26] This was the same pattern it had perfected with black soldiers, though with a major difference. The army enlisted men whereas it hired women as civilian employees, who were therefore not entitled to military status or benefits.

Whereas African Americans historically promoted military service for its community, women leaders of the early twentieth century displayed negligible interest in this traditional bastion of masculinity for female citizens. Edith Nourse Rogers, the Republican representative from Massachusetts, proved an exception. In France during World War I, Rogers had personally witnessed the army's neglect of the women it employed. The shabby conditions in which they worked and lived and the army's failure to accord them health care and veterans' benefits committed her to their cause. In 1941, Rogers drafted a bill to create a women's army corps, and she was determined to use it to better equalize women's service to men's. War Department officials, leery of upsetting the military's male culture and society's gender roles, rejected Rogers's call for equitable status. Instead, they defined the role of female personnel as assistants to the main male force. Even under this traditional gender norm, Congress balked at the concept of women soldiers and the threat it posed to accepted social patterns. "Think of the humiliation! What has become of the manhood of America?" heaved one alarmed congressman. Proponents of the new corps stressed the nation's need for women to replace men for combat, the corps' suitably feminine duties, and its slated termination six months after the end of the war. The word *auxiliary* in the title clarified the corps' position as *with* rather than *in* the army. At last Congress relented, allowing for the establishment of the Women's Army Auxiliary Corps (WAAC) on May 15, 1942.[27]

The new corps required a commander, and U.S. Army chief of staff George C. Marshall knew exactly who he wanted in the role: the accomplished Oveta Culp Hobby. Impressed with her extraordinary organizational and leadership skills, Marshall also appreciated Hobby's sensitivity in the matter of maintaining gender conventions. Both understood that the War Department had created the WAAC to temporarily supplement its forces, not alter the traditional domestic and male-helpmate role of women. Hobby's job was to ensure that female recruits readily adapted to the army, an institution marked by masculine independence and leadership, and then return to civil society as feminine homemakers dependent on protective husbands. Hobby would not disappoint.

A Texas native and daughter of a prominent lawyer, Hobby had already carved out successful careers as a journalist, publisher, businesswoman, and government official, the latter as director of the War Department's Women's Interest Section, where she came to Marshall's attention. Hobby was also married (to former Texas governor William Pettus Hobby) and the mother of two young children, thereby seemingly able to reconcile her public duties with the conventional image of female domesticity. Not yet forty, she came of age just as the hard battles for women's suffrage had been won. Successfully negotiating existing gendered conventions to pursue professional positions that enfranchisement had opened, Hobby saw little need to overtly question society's gender roles.[28] Her personal example seemed proof of the possibilities available to other hard-working American women in the modern twentieth century.

Hobby's privileged upbringing and acceptance of the existing social order led her to fashion the corps around her vision of exemplary womanhood, a sorority of sorts of educated white middle-class women from "good" families. Such standards largely discounted the potential of those who did not look the part, in particular her black recruits. Hobby publicly rejected racial discrimination, yet her neglect of this contingent—whom she tended to fault for deficient skills, intelligence, and character—ensured its marginalization.[29]

The renowned activist Mary McLeod Bethune also took an early lead role in the WAAC. Though not officially a part of the corps, she was not without influence in its policies and practices. Bethune helped recruit black women, met monthly with Hobby as a member of the National Civilian Advisor Committee, and worked in front of and behind the scenes to gain fair treatment of black Wacs. According to historian (and World War II WAC veteran) Martha Putney, Bethune was "for all practical purpose the surrogate mother of the black Wacs."[30] By then in her late sixties, Bethune embraced the role. Military service, she believed, offered these women, and by extension their communities, invaluable training, skills, and status.[31]

Born to impoverished former slaves in South Carolina, Bethune became a tireless educator and activist whose actions served to inspire African American women. She established a school in Florida (now Bethune-Cookman University), served as president of the National Association of Colored Women's Clubs (NACWC), founded and chaired the National Council of Negro Women (NCNW), and served on social welfare commissions for three presidents. Bethune was the only female member of President Franklin D. Roosevelt's "Black Cabinet" and friends with First Lady Eleanor Roosevelt.[32] Her primary role was as an advocate for ordinary citizens, particularly black women whose struggles under layers of discrimination she could personally relate to. Her message to young people was to take advantage of every opportunity so when the WAAC opened its door to black women, she urged them through it. Bethune's strategy to work within the system—"We are not going to be agitators," she advised new recruits—had its detractors, yet through her various roles and associations, Bethune did what she could to ensure that these women got a fair shake.[33] She recommended the first officer candidates, frequently visited the Fort Des Moines induction center where the majority of female recruits first served, consulted Hobby about their training and assignments, kept tabs on their treatment, and intervened when necessary.[34] The Wac strike at Fort Devens was one of those necessary moments, and Bethune would take a personal interest in the incident and actively support the four defendants.

The War Department kept Bethune and other supporters of African American servicewomen busy during the war years, in large part because it had not prepared for this unusual category of military personnel. Prior to the establishment of the corps, several congressional representatives attempted to ensure the inclusion of black women and the equality of their treatment by proposing an antidiscrimination amendment in the WAAC bill. The War Department preempted their efforts when it announced that the army would enlist black women on the same basis as black men.[35] In other words, while the War Department offered them equal treatment regardless of race, it also subjected them to segregation. With the debate closed, so were discussions as to the utilization of black Wacs and how these women would, or could, effectively function under policies that separated them from the main (male) army and segregated them from white Wacs. Instead, the army subsumed black female recruits into its categories of either black men or white women, neither of which these women entirely fit. Its failure to recognize the challenges it policies presented for black Wacs—and their commanders—plagued these women's service throughout the war.

These challenges would manifest themselves soon enough, but in 1942, the War Department's inclusion of African Americans in its first women's military corps marked a victory for the civil rights movement. According to recruiting materials, the corps offered servicewomen opportunities to acquire meaningful job skills, demonstrate their abilities, and directly contribute to the war effort. Any one of these possibilities was a rare occurrence for most African American women, so when they came as a packaged deal, many sought to take advantage. Over 6,500 enlisted during World War II, among them Johnnie Murphy, Alice Young, Anna Morrison, and Mary Green. The latter two, like other African American recruits, left behind cleaning jobs in expectation of specialized training, practical experience, and respect as members of the armed forces. Though many encountered instead labor exploitation and ridicule so familiar to generations of black servicemen, they also gained through their enlistment an important platform to resist subjugation, assert their rights, and demonstrate their patriotism. On balance, the civil rights movement had greater initial success with the army on this front than with any of the other services. The navy only accepted black women in 1944, the coast guard in 1945, and the marines not until 1949, four years after the war ended.[36]

African American women joined the corps for a variety of personal, community, and patriotic reasons. Victims of discrimination at home, they wholeheartedly supported the fight against fascism abroad. As one

Waac wrote, "I am deeply conscious of the war against fascism and have dedicated myself to do all possible to bring the day of victory closer." With three brothers in the service, Anna Morrison felt that "whatever I could do to be of help to them, would help everyone." In double-V fashion, new recruits also desired to combat racism at home. Dovey Johnson, a protégé of Bethune, later recalled, "I never felt I was there for me, I was there for my people." Johnson recounted that in making her difficult decision to join the women's corps, she consulted her grandmother, who "thought it was alright for me to go into the WAAC because Mrs. Bethune had something to do with it." Years later, Elaine Bennett explained her reasons for enlisting: "I wanted to prove to myself, maybe the world, that we would give what we had back to the U.S. as a confirmation that we were full-fledged citizens." Mary Green's letters to her family expressed her desire to "carry out the principals of democracy," improve her prospects, and make people back home proud of her. According to her mother, "she was proud to be in the WAC." A desire to contribute to the war effort, help others, and advance their prospects were common attitudes among black Wacs during World War II, as was the optimism they shared as they answered the nation's call to duty.[37]

Despite the WAAC's well-publicized job opportunities and the patriotic appeal of military service, enlisting as a black woman ultimately required a leap of faith that the army would keep its promises to them. Those from the South who were personally familiar with Jim Crow practices could reason that the equal-pay provision at least ceded a racial and gendered equality unimaginable at home. Those from the North did not always fully comprehend the implications of institutionalized segregation. Such was the case of Bernadine Flannagan, who later recalled her shock at the discrimination she encountered in the military: "I was surprised because in New London, Connecticut, where I grew up, everything was integrated." Morrison, a native of segregated Kentucky who enlisted in Ohio, assumed that the army's racial policy would be more akin to the North's than the South's. She later conceded that she probably would not have enlisted had she been living in Kentucky, with its daily reminders of state-legislated segregation.[38]

In fact, African American women did not readily enlist. Comprising just over 10 percent of the female population of the United States, their participation in the corps ranged from between just 3 to 5 percent of all corps personnel during the war. This was in part because the civilian labor shortage improved their access to factory jobs, nurse training programs, and domestic service positions that paid better than the customary subsistence wage. Additionally, many were wary of any institution that practiced segregation, which the appointment of Hobby as WAC director and her support of segregation did little to assuage. Hobby's pledge that the corps would "have the same liberal policy with respect to Negroes that exists in the Army" no doubt troubled those more familiar with the army's treatment of its black soldiers than the privileged white southerner.[39]

Having assumed her post, Hobby attempted to allay concerns among African Americans when she scheduled her first recruiting speech as director at Howard University and delivered a personal appeal to sorority members. Hobby assured the coeds that African American women could help their country by doing important work for the army and afterwards return to society "a more efficient wage-earner, a more skilled worker." The director's interest in Howard University students reflected her three initial concerns regarding race in the corps. First, anxious to meet recruiting goals, she hoped black enlistees would help her meet the numbers the WAAC needed to succeed. Second, she wanted to dispel civil rights leaders' predictions that the corps' segregation policies would dissuade qualified African Americans from enlisting. Most importantly, she needed capable black officers. In contrast to the army, which placed white officers over black men, the women's corps stipulated black female officers for its black female units. Company-level racial incidents among male troops were common in the army, and Hobby wanted to avoid such flare-ups in the WAAC by securing top black candidates to lead her enlisted black troops. At Howard, she described the new corps as "a truly democratic women's Army" and guaranteed her audience that black Wacs would be treated on par with white servicewomen of equal rank.[40] Such claims had already paid off handsomely, at least in regard to the crucial first class that would soon begin training. Hobby met her goal of 440 candidates, including the full 10 percent quota of African Americans that the army allowed.

When Hobby addressed the first graduating class later that year, she aptly summed up the short history of the WAAC: "you do not come into a Corps that has an established tradition."[41] In fact, the corps did not have much of a future, either. Because Congress and the War Department intended to dissolve the WAAC six months after the war, they designed it as a separate force, complete with ranks and regulations that differed from the regular army's. This led to questions as to whether female personnel were accountable to military protocols and disciplinary measures. For instance, could Waacs who failed to report to duty be charged with AWOL, given their vague connections to the army? Congress replaced the WAAC with the Women's Army Corps (WAC) in 1943, thereby partially equalizing benefits, shifting the corps' base of operations to the main force, and bringing Wacs under the jurisdiction of the army's military justice system.[42]

Hobby's determination to retain a say in the disciplinary policies of her troops after the WAAC/WAC conversion indicates the priority she gave to maintaining distinct gender paradigms in the military. The WAAC had operated under a unique code of conduct that mandated high standards of feminine behavior. Clarifying her expectations, Hobby noted, "particularly, we want to emphasize what it means to be a gentlewoman." Apparently, a gentlewoman did not drink, would not be "found all evening in bars even if sober," and did not engage in sexual activity. The WAAC's exacting code of conduct gave its officers grounds to discharge those whose behavior deviated from its desired decorum of femininity. After the conversion, the War Department, preferring a uniform disciplinary standard, refused to formally recognize that code. Hobby and her staff responded by advising court-martial boards, which would not ordinarily discharge male personnel for crude language or behavior, to consider the option for nonconforming Wacs by keeping in mind the interest of the "good" women in their units.[43]

The new corps leaders assumed that they had reason to insist on exacting standards of femininity. After the initial deluge of more volunteers than they could induct, enlistments plummeted from 65,000 in its first year to an average of just 3,000 a month thereafter until the end of the war.[44] The ensuing struggle to meet recruiting goals heightened Hobby's and her officers' already intense attention to the reputation of the WAC. Indeed, they considered safeguarding the reputation of the corps paramount in their bid to attract respectable recruits. Fiercely protective of her troops, Hobby tirelessly fought publicity that reflected negatively on them, made light of their vital role, or adversely affected their morale.[45] The exception was her black troops, for whom Hobby did not demonstrate this same dedication.

Hence, while the WAC claimed to offer opportunities to all recruits, its leaders focused on those who fit the white, middle-class prototype of feminine respectability. Many white women failed to meet these standards, particularly the working poor, suspected lesbians, and those who held unconventional ideas about proper gendered behavior. In general, black Wacs were more likely than white Wacs to fall short—or to be perceived as falling

short—of desired standards of appearance and conformity and therefore
more prone to run afoul of military policies. An African American identity
alone automatically conveyed for many whites a natural lack of feminine
respectability, intellect, and character. Furthermore, since black Wacs of all
backgrounds and classes were likely to encounter, and therefore in some
form resist, army policies that discriminated against them, they appeared
as a whole uncooperative. The WAC leadership had little patience for those
who challenged army policy and, as did the army, considered such personnel
troublemakers, radicals, and even subversives.[46]

Hobby displayed a general unwillingness to work with her African American troops or to incorporate them into the WAC's main functions. She
enforced racial segregation, and, by delegating a black officer for every black
unit, expected each unit to operate largely self-sufficiently and with minimal
attention. As early as mid-1943, in an apparent move to curtail black enlistments, Hobby pulled all five black recruiters from the field over concerns
that they were deterring the potential white recruits she preferred.[47] She
also refused to send black Wacs overseas, fearing that they could then not
be properly monitored.[48] The WAC advertisements, pamphlets, and publicity she approved projected the ideal Wac as a model of femininity through
images almost exclusively of white Wacs. A 1943 recruiting manual, for
instance, carried sixty photos of Wacs, not one of whom was a woman of
color. It even included nineteen pictures of men, all white, yet no black
Wacs.[49] The WAC director's determination to sideline African American
troops took precedence over effectively training and employing them so
that they, too, could replace the soldiers urgently needed for frontline duty.

Black recruits may well have gauged the WAC's disinterest in them on
arrival at Fort Des Moines, Iowa, the only one of the five induction centers
open to them (other than, for six months, Fort Devens).[50] Among the first
was Charity Adams, who recalled that when debarking from her transport,
uniformed personnel loudly announced, "Negroes on one side! White girls
on the other." Having traveled by train from Ohio to Iowa with a congenial,
racially diverse group of new recruits, Adams found the abrupt separation
humiliating. Dovey Johnson more graphically described the painful announcement: "this is like taking a nail and crossing your heart, I mean flesh
bare."[51]

By the time, Green, Morrison, Murphy, and Young arrived at Fort Des
Moines, their predecessors—Adams and Johnson among them—had

fended off some of the most outright discriminatory policies and offensive behavior. They got the "colored" signs removed from mess hall tables, implemented dining "Desegregation Days" on weekends, and held the bar on other forms of blatant racism, including one white male officer's penchant for addressing them as "Darky." Several officer candidates reported the matter to Bethune, only to face the man's threats to charge them with treason. Two of the women, Dovey Johnson and Irma Cayton, knew their rights and did not back down, causing the man to back down instead.[52] The contests continued throughout the war. Indeed, Green, Morrison, Murphy, and Young witnessed a well-publicized case shortly after they arrived at Fort Des Moines. Barred from the post's segregated white WAC band, black musicians formed their own, which their commander closed down in the summer of 1944 on grounds that the post already had a WAC band. Presaging civilian support for the Fort Devens Wacs after their 1945 strike, a coalition of civil rights organizations, national leaders, the black press, and ordinary citizens across the country mounted a national publicity campaign that soon forced Secretary of War Henry Stimson to intervene. In this case, Stimson gave into the demands and approved the black band at Fort Des Moines.[53] As these examples illustrate, black Wacs could urge the army to honor its obligations to them and, when more convincing was needed, reach out to civilian supporters who were keeping a watchful eye on them. This was especially true at Fort Des Moines, where the largest contingent was stationed.

These triumphs at Fort Des Moines were often the result of individuals putting their military careers on the line for the same privileges automatically granted white female service members—and they did not always win. Complaints from white parents that their daughters were, or might be, training, eating, or living next to black women gave cover to the WAC leadership's insistence on maintaining strict segregation. Congressman George H. Mahon of Texas related such a concern to Hobby: "this fine girl along with others is now forced to share the same living quarters, bathroom, facilities, restrooms, and reception rooms with Negroes."[54] Hobby typically responded with assurances that the WAC segregated as much as possible. In a letter to another man equally fretful about any racial mixing among servicewomen, she explained, "I am satisfied that such occurrences as you mention are infrequent, and when they do happen are temporary and practically unavoidable."[55] Even when "practically unavoidable," integration as a solution commonly was pushed off the table. When severe overcrowding in the black Waacs' area prompted the transfer of black cooks and bakers to the white Waacs' cooks and bakers' barracks, a white officer immediately sent them back. Dismissing the women's protests, he scolded them with a reminder that "democracy was respecting the feelings of these white women who did not wish to share the same building with them." According to a subsequent report of the incident, the women "swallowed this pill—trying to get along."[56]

Certainly, these recent inductees tired of the routine assaults on their character and understood the need to deal head-on with discriminatory policies and behavior, yet they knew to choose their battles carefully. There was little point in protesting Hobby's requested transfer of all black male soldiers—though not white male soldiers—from Fort Des Moines within days of the arrival of the first black Wac recruits despite the offensive message it broadcasted about African American morals.[57] They also bore the humiliation of segregated post clubs whose officers ignored the War Department's 1943 directive to integrate them and the draining of the post's swimming pool each week immediately after their single hour to swim.[58] Notions that black women were promiscuous, unclean, and generally inferior to white women were as deeply embedded in WAC policies as they were in the minds of many of its white personnel. According to Martha Putney, her white bunkmate in officer candidate school told her that if her mother knew that she was "sleeping next to a Negro (she didn't say Negro), she'd want her to come home right away."[59] Black Wacs at Fort Des Moines could not fight every battle, and neither could those at Fort Devens and elsewhere when they encountered discrimination.

The most problematic issue for black Wacs during the war, and the one that they were most often prepared to protest, was the lack of training and meaningful army assignments. Black Wacs' occupational expectations were well-grounded in the women's corps mission to free men for combat.[60] Moreover, aggressive advertising and individual recruiters assured volunteers of practical training and experience in over 230 essential military positions, including assignments as hospital technicians, radio operators, photography specialists, and aircraft mechanics.[61] The army instead assigned most black Wacs to work as hospital orderlies and laundresses and in other menial labor roles. In response to persistent protests over the lack of technical training and skilled jobs for black Wacs, officials defended their compliance to the army's equal opportunity directives by noting that "selection for training and duty is based on aptitude and ability."[62] The experiences of black Wacs indicate that selections were more frequently based on prevailing white attitudes regarding the "aptitude and ability" of African American women.

The Army General Classification Test (AGCT) helped validate the consensus among officers that the majority of black Wacs were intellectually incapable of performing the same jobs they assigned white Wacs. Dismal scores on AGCTs placed 66 percent of African American Wacs, compared to 15 percent of whites Wacs, in the lower two of the five grade categories. These statistics fed officers' claims that low scores, not discrimination, blocked black Wacs from skilled assignments. Throughout the war, white officers dismissed black Wacs' complaints that their duties did not give them the opportunity to prove themselves. According to Mattie Treadwell, the official WAC historian and a former WAC staff officer who worked closely with Hobby, the WAC sought ways to employ the women, yet "every possible solution appeared [to African Americans] tinged with discrimination."[63] In a pointed evaluation of Wacs who proved difficult to place (overwhelmingly African American), Treadwell described the women's deficiencies as "mental and not educational."[64]

Evidence to the contrary emerged during the war that army test scores did not fully provide a measure of a military personnel's abilities. For instance, during its rush to train medical personnel, the army occasionally admitted into its medical programs white Wacs who had scored below the desired cut-off point. Nevertheless, even when the army instituted a fast-paced six-week course in place of the usual three-month program, most of these women successfully completed their studies. Additionally, Army Manual M5, *Leadership and the Negro Soldier*, cautioned officers from viewing AGCT scores as IQ tests, assuring them that the results measured "an enlisted man's working level and ability to learn," not a soldier's level of intelligence. Noting that southern states spent on average one-third less on black students than they did on white students, it reminded officers that personnel from poorly funded schools were unlikely to test as well as those from better-financed institutions.[65] Furthermore, anthropologists Ruth Benedict and Gene Welfish found that environmental factors accounted for the bulk of disparities on military tests. Comparing the scores of African Americans in the North to the lower scores of white Americans from generally underfunded schools of the South, they argued that access to a decent education, not race, was key.[66]

Privately, Secretary of War Henry Stimson was having his own doubts about the AGCT's influence on job placements, at least in the case of white male recruits. Low scores, he lamented, also disadvantaged poor white southerners by limiting their access to skilled positions. Confiding in his journal, Stimson acknowledged that the "Army had adopted rigid requirements for literacy mainly to keep down the number of colored troops," and yet this factor was "preventing us from getting some very good illiterate [white] recruits from the southern mountain states."[67] Stimson was convinced that if disadvantaged white soldiers were given the opportunity, they could prove to be major assets to the military. He did not make the same connection in regards to African Americans' test scores and intellectual ability.

Low AGCT scores fed into the familiar images of African American women working as household domestics and laundresses. Many white Americans reasoned that black women's usual position as low-paid menial laborers rested with the natural weakness of their sex and the cultural backwardness of their race. Stereotypes of happy mammies born to such work provided convenient justification. Popular literature, films, and folklore, along with casual conversations among white Americans often ridiculed black women's intellect, mocked their ambitions, and sexualized them as jezebels, or wanton women best kept busy and closely monitored by their employers.[68] Even the magic of Hollywood could not release African American starlets from playing mainly servant roles. The popular actress and crooner Lena Horne fought such typecasting and, consequently, worked very little when on contract with MGM.[69] The general acceptance of most black women's narrow confines and unfavorable labor conditions fueled assumptions that these women were best utilized in menial tasks.[70]

The African American women who enlisted under guarantees of specialized training and jobs encountered a military bureaucracy that took its cues from civilian employment practices. Consequently, officers often viewed black Wacs as best fit for menial labor and quickly tired of their complaints to the contrary. As Colonel Frank McCoskrie, the post commander at Fort Des Moines, grumbled, "the Negro problem is a difficult one at best since both officer and enlisted personnel take every small advantage to press the racial question." According to McCoskrie, the problem wasn't racism, but the ineptitude, laziness, and gullibility of black personnel who, all too impulsively, allowed ringleaders to stir up trouble among otherwise content soldiers.[71] This was a widely held assessment, as pervasive at Fort Des Moines as it was at the War Department in Washington, D.C., and other posts, including Fort Devens in Massachusetts.

The military's marginalization of black women patterned itself on civilian practices and the prejudices that supported them. Whether Jim Crow laws or federal mandates parlayed as colorblind legislation, state policies gave free reign to attitudes that African American women were best suited for menial labor and that engaging them otherwise invited problems. Consequently, factory managers refused to hire them to avoid, they claimed, white female walk-outs known as "hate strikes"; office and store managers cited their white clientele's objections to dealing with black secretaries and clerks; and employment agencies noted that "we cannot put black women in the front office" where they would be seen by white customers.[72] Similarly, no one raised objections when the commander of Fort Devens's Lovell Hospital assigned his black servicewomen to one facility to perform cleaning duties and white Wacs to another to fill a wide variety of administrative, clerical, and medical positions.

African American women had long rejected society's diminution of their labor, intellect, and citizenship and developed strategies to protect themselves. Asserting one of the main advantages they had, their labor, they frequently left unsatisfactory employment, and even their homes, as did millions of southern women who migrated North. Wherever they lived, African American women joined black women's clubs where they freely discussed employment issues, coalesced with others to boycott businesses that refused to hire African Americans, and pushed for labor rights. It was a black woman who first proposed to A. Philip Randolph a mass march on Washington, D.C., the plan that compelled Roosevelt to order war industries to hire African Americans.[73] At Fort Devens, black Wacs would tap into this legacy of collective action to protest labor issues.

A year before Morrison, Green, Murphy, and Young enlisted, the lack of assignments for black Wacs had led to severe overcrowding in the black WAC section at Fort Des Moines. In a bid to relieve the glut, the WAC sent its lone black staff officer, Harriet West, to posts around the country to solicit job assignments for its excess troops. Few commanders expressed interest in black Wacs for specialized roles. On the other hand, the tight labor market and undesirability of menial jobs spurred scattered requests for them as orderlies, laundresses, and KP (Kitchen Police) personnel.[74] Eventually West relented and agreed to release black Wacs for work "in laundries, hospital messes, salvage and reclamation shops, and chemical processing of clothing." Even with these accommodations, requisitions remained low, and overcrowding at Fort Des Moines persisted.[75]

Bethune grew concerned with the disappointing trend in black Wac assignments, and in August 1943 she discussed the matter with Hobby. Bethune noted that the placement of most black Wacs in menial jobs suggested widespread misassignments due to race. Hobby dismissed the assumption, claiming that misassignments occasionally occurred throughout the army regardless of race. Bethune proposed that the director assign more black Wacs to recruiting duty rather than pull back those in the field. This, she argued, would productively employ select officers who in turn could enlist qualified personnel. Hobby rejected the notion, insisting that the former recruiters were needed on posts to deal with the black enlisted women. Bethune volunteered to personally recruit for the WAC. Hobby demurred. There was no need, she said, as black enlistments were on the rise. Bethune inquired about black Wacs' options to train for finance department jobs and other specialized positions. Hobby replied that not all army schools would accept black Wacs and, anticipating Bethune's follow-up comment, added that she could not force them to do so. Could they work as radio operators? Not without requisitions for black Wacs. Could the WAC send black instead of white Wacs for a given job requisition? Not according to army policy. To this and other questions, Hobby gave no ground, instead consistently stating that she was beholden to army dictates.[76] Meanwhile, she was rejecting an army request for black Wacs from the European theater.[77]

As the overcrowding in the black WAC section at Fort Des Moines increased, morale sharply declined. By the spring of 1943, one of its two black WAC companies was over capacity at 208 women when orders came down to make room for another two hundred trainees. By replacing couches and card tables with bunk beds and footlockers, Charity Adams, the commanding officer, managed to convert dayrooms into sleeping quarters. Maintaining the morale of her troops proved more difficult. They understood, explained Adams, that "these conditions existed because post commanders did not want Negro personnel." That summer, Fort Des Moines recorded an excess of nine hundred black Wacs.[78] The cramped conditions had only worsened by the time Morrison, Green, Murphy, and Young arrived a year later.

Weeks before the June 6, 1944, Allied invasion of Normandy, Anna Morrison, Johnnie Murphy, and Alice Young enlisted in the WAC, although the army did not send for them until after D-Day. Delays in activating black Wacs were as common as they were offensive to African Americans, who were well aware of the army's desperate need for military personnel. Whereas the army typically mobilized white Wacs within two weeks, it often delayed activating black Wacs for three to four weeks.[79] If Green's experience is any indication, D-Day temporarily rectified the situation. Having enlisted shortly after the invasion, the small-town Texan arrived at Fort Des Moines just six days later. In any case, by late June, all four were in basic training. Murphy, Green, Young, and Morrison were among the 260 African American women who had enlisted between June and September of 1944, and each arrived with her own story.[80]

In the years since Johnnie Murphy had graduated from high school at sixteen, she spent a year in vocational training in Chicago before moving back to Rankin, Pennsylvania, where she had lived as a child before her parents' deaths. Once back in her hometown, Murphy considered her options. Perhaps she would become a mechanic or work on a farm. Neither plan materialized nor did others. Ambitious yet directionless, and with many possibilities closed to her as an African American woman, Murphy grew increasingly unhappy in the tiny community. The year before her enlistment had been particularly painful. She had no paying job and no close family. Separated from her brothers and sisters after her mother died, Murphy had little memory of her siblings a decade later. She had a boyfriend for a time, but that relationship soon fell apart. Whatever Murphy had hoped to find in Rankin had yet to manifest itself, and, by the spring of 1944, she was ready to move on. She later claimed that she had joined the WAC in order to gain a skill, yet it appears, as an army report later cited, that the young woman mainly saw the WAC as her chance to get away and "find herself."[81] Just as soldiers have always done, Murphy joined the military seeking change and adventure.

Mary Amerson (Green) had been working since she left school in her teens. Jobs as a maid in Galveston and a nursemaid in Houston paid just $7 a week. In 1942, she secured employment as a nurse's aide at the city's Jefferson Davis Hospital, where she took home an additional $3 a week. She needed every cent. Six years earlier, she had married Joseph Green in what turned out to be a brief union. By the time Green entered the military, she had two children to support on her own.[82] Presumably, the WAC's offer of

$50 a month with benefits and the opportunity to learn new skills was attractive to the struggling young mother. Letters from her brother serving in the navy assuring family that he was doing well and advancing in his ratings likely proved a further incentive to enlist. The WAC did not accept women with dependents under the age of fourteen, so Green apparently signed over custody of her children to a trusted relative. Once in uniform, she wrote home that she wanted to "get something out of the Army," and "make her friends proud of her." The positive attitude she expressed in these letters was in keeping with her mother's description of her as an "obedient, docile youngster" with ambitions to "serve others while seeing life at its most exciting angle."[83] No doubt eager to put distance between herself and a failed marriage, Green joined the WAC to earn a steady income to support her children, learn valuable skills, and contribute to the war effort.

Anna Collins (Morrison) had spent much of her impoverished childhood working on a farm outside of Richmond, Kentucky, where the county sent her after her mother died. Close to her brother, who shared her plight, and estranged from her alcoholic father, who had not been able to care for her, Collins had few resources when she entered adulthood. She returned to Richmond, where she earned just $3 a week as a maid. Yearning for employment that did not involve "scrubbing floors and washing dishes," she moved north to improve her prospects, yet in Ohio she could only secure work as a maid. "What else was there?," she rhetorically asked years later recalling the lack of nonservice jobs available to black women in the 1940s. In 1944, WAC recruiting campaigns seemed to have the answer she sought. In addition to helping bring the war to a close so that her two brothers in the service could return home, Morrison enlisted in the WAC because it offered opportunities to learn skills for other types of employment and thus an escape from domestic service.[84]

Alice Young was twenty-three when she enlisted, and she had definite plans for her time in the service. Following her high school graduation in 1941, she enrolled in the Howard University nurse training program at Freedman's Hospital in Washington, D.C. She struggled with her courses, however, and failed two of them. Invited to retake them, Young instead left the program after that first year and from 1943 to 1944 worked full-time as an adding machine operator at the U.S. Treasury Department. Though she earned a decent salary, she still harbored nursing ambitions, so when the WAC called for women to fill its urgent needs for medical technicians, Young made inquiries. A recruiter assured the former nursing student that, with her background, she would be eligible for medical training. Joining the WAC meant trading in her civil service job and its $120 a month paycheck for a military uniform and less than half her former salary, yet it was a bargain Young was willing to make. Expecting to take advantage of the army's medical training programs, she viewed her enlistment as a stepping-stone to a nursing career. It was a reasonable expectation given her education level, nursing experience, and the army's well-publicized shortage of medical personnel.[85]

Morrison, Murphy, Young, and Green each expected advanced training in specialized fields where the army had great need. Recruiters described such opportunities, as did the extensive WAC publicity that showcased an enticing array of assignments in medical, clerical, and mechanical fields. A WAC recruiting pamphlet listed the "239 important Army jobs" that awaited qualified volunteers.[86] Despite the trepidations of committing to the unknowns of military life, Murphy, Green, Morrison, and Young considered the unique opportunities the WAC offered as a means to contribute to the war effort and improve their future employment prospects. Fort Des Moines, they assumed, marked their gateway to exciting new careers and experiences.

Though the enlistments of the four coincided with the heightened personnel needs of D-Day and the Allies' push into Europe, the military had been requesting more white Wacs than were available since the establishment of the corps in May 1942. General Marshall continually stepped up the army's personnel demands, at one point informing Hobby that he needed another 600,000 Wacs. It was an exaggerated figure calculated to stimulate recruitment, yet the War Department's more practical figure of 200,000 was also highly optimistic. (At its peak strength in April 1945, the WAC had fewer than 93,000 Wacs on active duty.)[87] By the spring of 1944, Marshall needed additional Wacs to fill the positions of the men he required for combat duty and to care for the wounded returning from the frontlines. At this critical juncture, the army ramped up its campaign for military medical personnel. At Fort Des Moines, Young in particular, given her nursing ambitions, would have taken note of the numerous solicitations in local newspapers urging women to enlist. They were hard to miss. A full-page advertisement in the *Morning Register* announced that "More Wacs are Needed in Medical Department" and emphasized the army's goal of 50,000 Wacs. Army ads assured women that "any recruit . . . may request assignment as a medical WAC whether or not she has had previous medical experience." Stressing the urgency, it claimed that "those qualified will be sent directly to medical units, while others will receive training in Army schools for medical technicians."[88] On completion of the six-week basic course, Young expected to train for this essential role.

Meanwhile, Fort Des Moines was quickly dispatching white Wacs to posts in the continental United States and overseas. The demand for white Wacs had not come automatically, as many officers initially opposed the idea of female soldiers. A year after the establishment of the corps, Major General Lewis H. Brereton declared that, "fortunately, I've no experience with that particular species [Wacs] and what's more I don't want any of them around here."[89] The severity of troop shortages forced even reluctant commanders to put aside their reservations and request them. Once given the opportunity, Wacs quickly proved their value, and requisitions surged. Nearly all, however, were for white personnel, even after D-Day battles flooded hospitals with injured soldiers and expanded the army's European theater operations overseas. Regardless of how shorthanded commands were throughout the war, requests for black Wacs were rare. While requisitions for white Wacs quickly exceeded the number of women in the corps, black Wacs remained stranded for months at Fort Des Moines.[90]

The steadfastness of the army and WAC to segregate and therefore underutilize its black Wacs in the face of urgent demands abroad indicates the determination of military officials to avoid questioning the nation's racial and gender norms. The consequences were devastating, and not only for black Wacs. Personnel shortages forced the War Department to base its combat strategy around a force of just ninety divisions. With no spare divisions to rotate in, the army had to replenish units with "replacements," typically new recruits fresh from stateside training centers. Lacking the camaraderie and experience developed over months of training with and later fighting alongside the same men, replacements quickly fell in battle. As military historian Peter Mansoor argues, "a greater number of divisions would have enabled American commanders to rotate units more frequently . . . thereby reducing the rate of casualties."[91] In fact, the army had other troops for the purpose—nearly a million black male soldiers, most of whom desired combat duty. Despite extensive losses of white men on the frontlines, army officers refused to hand black men weapons and deploy them into battle.[92]

The army also had at its disposal black Wacs whom it did not efficiently employ and whom Hobby refused to release for overseas duty.[93] As a result, beleaguered white soldiers pushing through Europe and Asia were unable to rotate out for periodic rests, while thousands of African American Wacs, who could have freed for combat duty equal numbers of male technicians, clerks, drivers, and others, were scrubbing floors and pushing food carts.

The backlog of black Wacs at Fort Des Moines demonstrates that neither the WAC nor the army had plans to meaningfully utilize black female troops. As the glut of unassigned black Wacs grew, a memorandum based on WAC reports and staff observations evaluated African American recruits in general as "of such inferior quality, not only in ability, but in character."[94] Disparaging views within the WAC leadership about its own troops could not have inspired the confidence of post commanders on whose requisitions the WAC relied. Some officers took the chance and properly prepared for black Wacs anyway, as did the commander at Camp Atterbury, Indiana. Going beyond the customary orientation program for new troops, he personally greeted the women on their arrival and, atypical for black Wacs, he ensured a variety of military jobs for them at the post's hospital, Wakeman General.[95] Despite the dire personnel shortage, however, many more black Wacs faced delayed transfers and, once on a new post, demoralizing menial assignments.

By the summer of 1944, Murphy, Green, Young, and Morrison had completed the induction training program and were awaiting transfers. By then, successive waves of white Wacs had arrived and then soon after left for advanced training courses and army assignments in the United States and abroad. In contrast, black Wacs remained at Fort Des Moines vying for space with new black recruits. According to Morrison, after her six-week basic course ended in July, she and others did "nothing" except detail and "clean up different classrooms." The WAC did not provide additional training or special classes to equip the women with skills the army needed. Instead, Morrison recalled, "We had lectures on Russia and saw films that we had seen time and time again. I mean it was all the same thing."[96] With other black Wacs who were also awaiting transfers, the four watched an Iowa summer turn into an Iowa fall.

Restlessness set in as the cohort to which Morrison, Green, Murphy and Young belonged pestered their officers for word on their transfers and training. Not until September did their officers have information to share with them. To the delight of the enlisted women, they announced that the army was holding them back until it had enough personnel to train as medical technicians. Young had never been in doubt about it. Indeed, two officers at Fort Des Moines had casually referred to her and another Wac, Private Ruby Pierce, as medical technicians.[97] Excited about the new skills they expected to learn, the group of a hundred servicewomen looked forward to their transfers to begin in earnest their military careers. The wait, however, continued. By mid-October, nearly three months after completing basic training, they were still at the induction center and anxiously awaiting orders to leave.

Many black Wacs later reflected on the advantages they had at Fort Des Moines. The constant stream of African American women flowing onto the base and the far fewer departing ensured overcrowding but also the relative safety in numbers in which to resist discriminatory practices. Additionally, because Fort Des Moines hosted the WAC officer training school, a number of black officer candidates were on hand with enough civilian degrees and military rank to be taken seriously. Finally, as the home of the largest contingent of black Wacs in the army, the induction center attracted the attention of prominent African Americans who continually monitored the women's progress while praising their courage in breaking new ground. Mary McLeod Bethune, NAACP officials, black journalists, and famous entertainers, including the actress and singer Lena Horne and the opera star Marian Anderson, paid visits to Fort Des Moines. There, black Wacs had a chance to be noticed, heard, and appreciated. Once distributed to other post, they left these favorable circumstances behind. Historian Martha Putney, who as a young Wac had also spent time at the induction center, suggested that "more than a few who were at Fort Des Moines would probably agree with the black enlisted woman who said that she found conditions there 'pretty fair' when compared with other camps at which she subsequently was stationed."[98] After their transfer to Fort Devens, Young, Murphy, Morrison, and Green were undoubtedly among them.

The WAC held possibilities for black women that their foremothers could not have imagined, nor could have Morrison, Murphy, Young, and Green four years earlier as teenagers. Once sent to Fort Des Moines, black Wacs soon discovered that securing these opportunities required much of the same fortitude and strategies on which previous generations of African American women had relied. The legacy of these struggles was mired in painful labor exploitation and social marginalization, yet it was also built on proud traditions of black women resisting oppression and asserting their rights as valued members of their communities and of the nation. The army was obviously unaware of this tradition of activism, but then, the history of black women was not well known by many Americans in the 1940s. Black Wacs knew it, though, and they understood its primary lesson: standing together offered them their best chance of success in their continuing battles to fight, in Triple-V fashion, for their rights.

2

Fort Devens

You people have to stay in your place.
—Reprimand from an unnamed white male officer
   to black WAC officer Charity Adams

In late October 1944, Johnnie Murphy, Mary Green, Anna Morrison, and Alice Young received welcome news. After four months at Fort Des Moines, Iowa, their orders arrived at last, directing their transfer to Fort Devens, Massachusetts. Given their assignment at the post's Lovell General Hospital, the servicewomen assumed that the army needed them as medical personnel and clerks and would train them accordingly. They were unaware that the true purpose of their journey was to help relieve the glut of black Wacs in their segregated sector at Fort Des Moines. Army policies and officers' prejudices had led to such severe overcrowding that the situation had become fodder for civil rights leaders who contested the notion that African American recruits were "unassignable."[1] In the fall, the commanding general of the Army Services Forces, Lieutenant General Brehon Burke Somervell, took the matter in hand, and rather than wait for requisitions of black Wacs, he demanded them.[2] Shortly afterward, a hundred black Wacs stationed at Fort Des Moines—Morrison, Green, Young, and Murphy among them—vacated their barracks and boarded trains for Fort Devens, eager to begin their training and fill the military positions for which the army had great need.

Though not apparent to them at first, Young, Green, Murphy, Morrison, and the others in their detachment had left behind the crowded conditions of Fort Des Moines but not the prejudices that had created them. In preparation for their arrival, the women's new officers, Lovell Hospital's commander Colonel Walter Crandall and the WAC detachment's senior officer First Lieutenant Victoria Lawson, focused their efforts on isolating the women rather than incorporating them into the post's regular functions. As the situation gained clarity, members of the new detachment struggled to gain the training and respect due all service personnel, though in new territory and as the lone contingent of black Wacs. Marginalized and ignored, they would soon conclude that gaining the attention of their officers required extreme measures. Though the army had transferred the women to avoid the glare of the black press and the criticism of the civil rights movement over its treatment of black Wacs, it had inadvertently prepared the grounds for a far more damaging storm of controversy.

The events at Fort Devens following the arrival of the black WAC detachment demonstrate how the addition of African American servicewomen tested the army's ability to segment its troops by race and by sex in addition to rank. Though the War Department insisted that racial segregation was a military necessity, the practice had never proved an efficient use of military personnel or resources. As the largest service, however, the army had the critical mass of male soldiers it needed to derive at least some degree of efficiency from the duplication of facilities, programs, and timetables. The further division of its forces by sex during World War II created a women's corps of just 140,000 personnel, which, when segregated, left just 3,000 to 4,000 African American women at any time in yet another separate force.[3] Since each personnel category generally required its own training programs, assignments, barracks, and recreational facilities, the logistics and costs of segmenting troops by both race and sex were staggering.

Transfers of black Wacs to posts therefore were accompanied by a list of demands on receiving commanders' resources, space, and day-to-day operations that other troops did not. Without a doubt, the presence of black soldiers and of white Wacs on a military facility also tested the army's policies that segmented its forces, yet the arrival of black Wacs tended to overwhelm the practical implementation of those same policies. Some commanders properly prepared for these troops and assigned them to essential military jobs; however, far from the spotlight of Fort Des Moines and dealing with units of much reduced numbers, most opted for the expedient solution of sidelining black Wacs rather than incorporating them into their usual operations. By using the army's personnel policies to marginalize black Wacs, commanders in fact created the conditions that often led to these women's low morale, disciplinary problems, and collective protests.

The most publicized of these Wac protests took place at Fort Devens when fifty-four members of the black WAC detachment failed to report to their duty stations. The army would fault the women for violating military protocol. In fact, their collective refusal to obey their officers amounted to, in military parlance, mutiny. An examination of the events leading up to the strike reveals, however, that the detachment's officers also violated military policies by failing to attend to the women's training, duties, promotions, and morale. Colonel Crandall's and Lieutenant Lawson's negligence of their responsibilities to these troops led to a breakdown in unit morale that itself indicated a breakdown in the chain of command. As the circumstances leading up to the Fort Devens strike demonstrate, army policies that separated black Wacs by race and sex created the propensity of both black Wacs and their officers to violate military protocol. The fallout, however, differed for each party, as the army disciplined the former and excused the latter.

In September 1944, the War Department ordered General Sherman Miles, the commander of the First Service Command, to prepare for a detachment of African American Wacs.[4] As Miles considered where to place the servicewomen, four pragmatic considerations undoubtedly cast his attention to Fort Devens, a post just forty miles northwest of his Boston headquarters. First, it had briefly served in 1943 as a WAC induction center that, along with Fort Des Moines, accepted black Wacs. Second, as home to 250 Wacs (all white) at the time, it already had the facilities to accommodate female troops. Third, its two large military hospitals guaranteed a large number of feminine-appropriate duties. Lastly, Fort Devens was a massive post—a prerequisite for placing black Wacs. Meeting army regulations that stipulated these women's physical separation from white women and from black men was most feasible at a post strewn over 10,000 acres with another 235,000 leased acres for field training.[5] All in all, the base offered an ideal site.[6] Having settled on Fort Devens, Miles charged his chief of staff to telephone Lovell Hospital's commanding officer, Colonel Crandall, and direct him to requisition 120 black servicewomen.[7]

Crandall strongly resisted the order. First he claimed that he "didn't have quarters available" for black Wacs. When told to make room by reassigning the same number of white Wacs to other posts, he cited another concern. "There were at the time about ten thousand colored men at the post, and I figured we would have a little headache with social problems." It took several phone calls to convince Crandall that the order would stand. At that point, the veteran career officer declared with patriotic resolve, "we could take as many headaches as necessary because we had to win the war," and proceeded, as ordered, to request the unwanted personnel.[8] Though Crandall did not have leeway on the race, gender, or number of the personnel that the army had suddenly foisted on him, he had control over their job assignments. Preparing for the 120-person unit, Crandall requested three cadre (essential company personnel), ten drivers, and twenty cooks. He filled the remainder of his order with eighty-seven medical aidmen, or orderlies, personnel charged with keeping the hospital clean and the patients fed. Crandall then made plans to segregate his full complement of female troops by assigning all black Wacs to Lovell Hospital South and all white Wacs to Lovell Hospital North. This required removing white Wac orderlies, clerks, and medical technicians from Lovell South. Despite the outflow of these specialized personnel, Crandall did not request black Wacs with the requisite military training to replace them. As a result, white Wacs at Lovell North held a variety of skilled jobs, while all black Wacs assigned to Lovell South worked as orderlies.[9]

Crandall submitted his requisition to the First Service Command's WAC director in Boston, Major Elizabeth W. Stearns. Despite the overload of orderlies and absence of technician and clerks, Stearns approved it without comment and forwarded it to Fort Des Moines. The induction center filled the request for orderlies by sending "basics," a Military Occupation Specialty (MOS) denoting personnel with no special skills beyond basic training to be assigned as commanders saw fit.[10] Per WAC policy, the new detachment also required a black WAC officer. Lawson requested two, and the WAC obliged, sending Second Lieutenant Sophie Gay to serve as the new detachment commander and Second Lieutenant Tenola Stoney as its supply officer.[11]

The black WAC detachment arrived at Fort Devens at the end of October. By then, Crandall had transferred all but a small contingent of white Wacs from Lovell Hospital South to Lovell Hospital North and its newly constructed WAC barracks nearby. Having reached his WAC quota, he marked eighty-eight white Wacs, including thirty-nine orderlies, for reassignment to other posts.[12] Several other white Wacs who Crandall sent to Lovell Hospital North returned to their former wards during the day, though just long enough to train their black replacements. Five months later, just four white Wacs still worked at Lovell Hospital South, retained for the officers' convalescent and the maternity wards. Assigned to these specialty wards located at the far end of the hospital that was close to Lovell North, where they were attached, this small contingent of white Wacs did not interact with black Wacs. "I haven't come in contact with them in working," said ward mistress Private Wanda Blount. Black Wacs noted the same.[13]

The new orderlies quickly settled into their jobs at Lovell South, where they washed dishes, cleaned windows, delivered meals to patients, ran errands for the medical staff, and performed other such chores. Initially accepting these basic tasks as integral to patient care and part of the initiation for new hospital personnel, they diligently attended to their work and waited for the specialized training and assignments they expected. As Young stated at her court-martial, "I didn't mind doing the work as long as it would help me to get where I wanted."[14] Thrilled to be assigned to a hospital where they could help wounded soldiers, the new arrivals demonstrated positive attitudes and performed their duties with few complaints during their first weeks at Fort Devens. "They really cleaned up the place," recalled Technical Sergeant Harold Wicks, the supervisor of enlisted personnel at the hospital.[15] Orderly work was not what the new arrivals had in mind when they enlisted, but given the seeming progression of white Wac orderlies at Fort Devens to other jobs, it was presumably only temporary. Meanwhile, they could enjoy their new home. After all, Fort Devens, situated in a northern state, was not a wholly unsatisfactory location for African American women during World War II.

Established as Camp Devens in 1917, the site was elevated by the War Department to a permanent fort in 1932 due to the efforts of Edith Nourse Rogers, the congresswoman from Massachusetts who later drafted the first WAAC bill. A longtime resident of nearby Lovell, Rogers so successfully encouraged Fort Devens's development that by World War II it was well-positioned to serve as a site for regional operations. In the early 1940s, the post became the central troop processing center for New England and, for six months in 1943, had served as a WAAC induction center.[16] Fort Devens hosted numerous schools, including training centers for cooks, drivers, chaplains, and infantry troops. It also boasted a new airport and a vast hospital complex. Lovell General and New Station Hospitals, in particular, were large, modern facilities that offered care for patients and training for medical personnel, including medical technicians and nurse cadets.[17]

Hundreds of thousands of soldiers passed through Fort Devens's gates during World War II, from new recruits to wounded soldiers, and even five thousand German and Italian prisoners of war. In January 1944, Wacs (all white) returned to Fort Devens to staff its Lovell General and New Station hospitals. In July, the two medical facilities merged in order to manage efficiently the uptick in wounded soldiers flowing in from overseas. Thereafter, they were known, respectively, as Lovell Hospital South and Lovell Hospital North. By the fall of 1944, this once remote camp less than an hour's drive from Boston had grown to a large and bustling base. That October, the arrival of black Wacs rendered Fort Devens yet another distinction as one of the military's most personnel-diversified posts.

The women of the new detachment did not lack for things to do when off-duty. On base, they could use the swimming pools and attend USO movies, dances, and lectures. Fort Devens also sported a skating rink, a bowling alley, tennis courts, and a service club for enlisted black service personnel to meet and socialize (despite War Department orders to integrate recreational facilities, these were to varying degrees segregated).[18] Nearby Boston proved a major draw, and the women could catch a train on its hourly runs to the vibrant metropolitan center. Closer to home, restaurants and movie theaters in Ayer, Shirley, Lovell, Worchester, and other neighboring towns offered welcome respite from military life.[19] Twelve-hour workdays with just one day off a week ensured that the women spent most of their time at the hospital, yet by all accounts they were pleased with their environs and initially adapted well at Fort Devens.

The Wacs' positive attitudes began to unravel when weeks and then months passed without any indication that their duties would change. Unlike nearly all of their white counterparts who worked at more choice assignments at Lovell Hospital North, they seemed permanently exiled to scrubbing floors and running errands. Other inconsistencies were also jarring. White Wacs did not have KP duty, a traditionally unpopular, labor-intensive, and best-avoided GI job. They had pulled KP duty when they had lived in the barracks next to Lovell Hospital South, but not after their transfer to Lovell Hospital North and its new barracks, where their nearest mess hall hired civilians for kitchen work. As a result, the only Wacs whose names appeared on the KP roster were African Americans.[20] Their officers put the matter down to happenstance, yet this situation profoundly upset the members of the black detachment. They did not pull this duty often, so it was less the work that bothered them than the suspected reasons behind being the only Wacs on post assigned to this menial job.

By the end of 1944, and during the darkest days of a bitterly cold Massachusetts winter, the reality of the situation slowly sank in, and it hit the women hard. They had enlisted because of WAC assurances that they would have the same opportunities as white Wacs for advanced training and skilled work. Instead, their jobs stood apart from those of other military personnel. Furthermore, they worked alongside civilian orderlies who had the same duties without the same military restrictions (civilians worked fewer hours and could quit). Black Wac orderlies did not even dress like Wacs. Instead of the smart khaki and drab olive uniforms issued to most white Wacs, they had to don blue smocks that indicated their general housekeeping role.[21] As one woman protested to Lieutenant Lawson, she had not "come into the Army to scrub floors."[22] It was a common grievance among black Wacs, and not only at Fort Devens.

Whether cleaning hospitals, pulling KP duty, or working in laundry rooms, most black Wacs during World War II labored in low-skilled and often physically demanding jobs. At Fort Knox, Kentucky, they were subject to permanent KP duty. At Camp Breckinridge, also in Kentucky, graduates of an army administration school swept warehouse floors. The commander of Camp Rucker, Alabama, assigned the lowest ranking of his requisition to housekeeping in the white nurses' quarters. In a letter to Eleanor Roosevelt, a Wac stationed at Fort Clark, Texas, described the conundrum of patriots stuck in menial duties. She assured the First Lady that the members of her unit were "all very willing though to offer our services for the causes of 'Why we fight,'" but were not given the chance. "The strain under which we work is almost defeating in itself," she explained. "Our ratings are frozen, our file[s] of varied training is limited, our jobs here are limited and our assignments equally so.[23] Menial duties ill-afforded opportunities to acquire advanced skills, gain promotions, and bolster morale. Rather, they fostered resentment.

Alice Young's experiences at Fort Devens illustrate the obstacles black women encountered when they attempted to break out of the pattern of servant work and map out a different career path. After a challenging year of study at nursing school, Young joined the WAC to gain training and practical nursing experience. Given her recruiter's assurances of medical training, Young reasoned that her transfer to Lovell Hospital indicated the army's interest in her nursing skills. Aggressive WAC campaigns seeking female volunteers, especially those with medical experience, substantiated this expectation. Since early 1944, the Army Medical Department, needing to replace the five thousand soldiers lost to overseas infantry units, had been publicizing its urgent need for military personnel. Just two months prior to the Fort Devens strike, the War Department reiterated this urgency by reminding commanders that "it is desired that every effort be made to recruit a maximum number of female technicians for the medical department."[24] Aware of the need, if not the details, Private Young had reason to feel confident that she was the perfect candidate for the job. She had ambitions for a nursing career, experience at a training hospital, and was already a Wac posted at a military hospital.

Young's optimism abruptly ended in December during a brief encounter with Colonel Crandall. When visiting the wards, Crandall noticed Young showing another black Wac how to take a patient's temperature. Without speaking to her directly, he announced to the nurse in charge, and for all present to hear, that the hospital didn't "have colored Wacs as medical technicians." He then added, according to Young, "they are here to scrub and wash floors, wash dishes and do all the dirty work." Crandall recalled his words differently, claiming that he reminded the nurse that taking temperatures "was not their purpose," especially when "the ward work is not done." Whichever version is true, Crandall seems to have realized that he had crossed a racial line. Later that afternoon, he visited Lieutenant Sophie Gay, the black detachment's commander at the time, to apologize for any possible misinterpretations of his remarks. Young, however, had been mortified by his public humiliation of her, the women of her detachment, and her race..In that moment, Crandall had also dashed her plans for the advanced medical training that had spurred her enlistment. It was a bitter lesson. Officers assumed, she later said, that "because we were colored . . . we didn't measure up to their qualifications."[25] Crandall's overall disregard for the black women in his command lends credence to Young's analysis.

A Maine native, Crandall joined the army in 1917 and served for short periods at Fort Sill, Oklahoma, and on a Texas base near San Antonio before a seven-year assignment in Panama. Recollecting his canal zone experiences, he later confided, "of course, the Panama colored race are English subjects and quite different from ours." For the next nine years, Crandall worked with the Army Air Corps in charge of several small dispensaries.

On January 3, 1943, he took over as commanding officer of Lovell General Hospital. A somewhat abrupt and at times sarcastic man, he seemed to some colleagues uninterested in the administrative details involved in the running of large hospitals. To the black Wacs of his command, he seemed equally uninterested in any duties that involved them. As Lieutenant Stoney surmised, "I don't think he cared so much for the ward orderlies."[26]

Crandall's disinterest in the black WAC detachment greatly disadvantaged its members. Military protocol demanded an orientation program, in part to introduce new arrivals to their new chain of command. Indeed, the hospital conducted one a week for its largely transient patient population.[27] Crandall did not likewise ensure an orientation program for the black Wacs, and months later he could not say if anyone on his staff had taken the initiative to do so. (No one had.)[28] Consequently, the members of the new contingent began their assignments with little guidance as to their duties, word about their access to training, or an introduction to their new chain of command.

The hospital administrator, who frequently made the rounds at Lovell Hospital South, made little attempt to meet with the members of his lone black Wac detachment. An investigating officer inquiring into the senior officer's rapport with the servicewomen asked Crandall if he had ever approached "a colored Wac and ask her how she was getting along and how she liked her work." Crandall replied, "no, I don't recall that I did." He did remember unsuccessful attempts to greet them while passing in the corridors, noting that "rarely did any of them salute and usually they turned their faces another way and gave me no opportunity to pass the time of the day with them."[29] Whether by their own direct observation or through hearsay, the women sensed the veteran officer's dislike of them, a perception Crandall did little to hide from them or others. After seeing black Wacs carry meals to the patients, he reportedly told one white ward nurse, "Don't let those niggers serve that food." Crandall flatly denied the accusation.[30]

By Christmas, tensions were clearly on edge at Fort Devens. Black Wacs working at the hospital were openly expressing concerns that Crandall considered them incompetent, unintelligent, and unfit for work beyond keeping the wards clean and running errands for others. The colonel remained above the fray, either unaware or uninterested in the growing dissatisfaction of his only black female unit. Dining in the mess hall with his officers, including Stoney, he occasionally remarked that "it was black bean soup because the black Wacs cooked it" (to which Stoney responded, "I wouldn't want to comment on that, Colonel").[31]

Crandall's reaction to his new recruits and his racial comments were somewhat clumsier than those of others in similar positions, yet his reservations over having black women in his command were widely shared with other officers. This was in part because hosting black Wacs *did* pose problems for post commanders. Under military policies, their combined race and gender presented a cumbersome list of additional planning and organizing requirements, often for a relative handful of women. The difficulty of finding segregated accommodations and appropriate assignments for black Wacs gave commanders little reason to welcome them, as did concerns over their presumed loose morals.

Doubts about African Americans' moral character ran deep among the white officer corps and up to its highest levels. When ordered to requisition the detachment of black Wacs, Crandall protested that black men and women on the same base could lead to what he euphemistically called "social problems." Director Hobby apparently agreed with the sentiment. During a 1944 telephone conversation with President Roosevelt's civilian race relations coordinator, Jonathan Daniels, she proudly described how she kept eight black female officers from mixing with men at Fort Oglethorpe, Georgia. By ensuring the reassignment of its male black officers to other posts, only black enlisted soldiers remained. Since the army then and now prohibits socializing between officers and enlisted personnel, these women had no officially condoned male companions on base. Hobby then reminded Daniels that while officers' clubs frequently hosted both men and women, they were open to the opposite sex by invitation only. Hobby was confident that, given the mixed-race taboo, white male officers would not risk inviting black female officers to their club. In this way, Hobby had managed to distance the women from all nonwork relationships with servicemen at Fort Oglethorpe, black and white. Clearly impressed, Daniels praised her clever machinations: "no wonder they made you colonel."[32]

Hobby's concerns over the propriety of black Wacs proved the women's greatest obstacle to serving overseas. The European theater of operations had as early as 1943 requested black Wacs. Hobby squelched the plan because of her reluctance to see the women "scattered in uncontrolled field units near male Negro troops." In contrast, she transferred white Wacs abroad once she had secured hazard benefits for them. She would not send black

Wacs overseas until January 1945, when, after intensive lobbying by civil rights leaders, she relented and allowed the 6888th Central Postal Directory Battalion to sail to Europe.[33]

Presumptions of African American women's loose morals also complicated housing issues. Indeed, Crandall attempted to fend off General Miles's order to requisition black Wacs by arguing that he did not have anywhere to house them. Commanders had to secure barracks for black Wacs that were separate from white Wacs and distant from black soldiers. They might also have to address the concerns of the local communities who occasionally assumed a say in racial matters. Satisfying all of these criteria and concerns could prove a logistical nightmare for officers, as the case at Gardiner Hospital in Illinois illustrates.

In April 1945, a committee of Hyde Park residents living near Chicago's Gardiner Hospital expressed deep reservations over the impending arrival of black Wacs. After failing to halt the transfer, they protested to the post commander that the barracks being built for the new unit were so close to the white bathing beach that the black Wacs on base might be tempted to swim there. They also worried that black women would "attract Negro men," whose presence, they feared, could lead to incidents of racial violence. The citizen committee argued for the construction of a separate Wac barracks farther north than noted in the army's plan so that it would be nearer the black community—and as far as possible from the white community. The army kept its original plan, yet its design reflected a highly precautionary formula. The black WAC barracks were to be located "800 feet from the nearest apartment building; bounded on the rear by a series of railroad tracks . . . enclosed within a strong fence; entrance will be through a gate which will be continually guarded."[34]

The combined effects of these multiple segregation requirements that physically isolated black Wacs impeded the women's opportunities to secure fulfilling job assignments, thereby weakening their morale. WAC units, white and black, accepted just about any conditions in good spirits so long as its members felt meaningfully employed. White Wacs in Europe, for instance, recalled the period after D-Day, when they trudged behind combat troops in the same grueling conditions (though in the relative security of the rear), as the "happiest" of their military careers. Likewise, morale among members of the all black 6888th Postal Battalion serving in Europe was at its height during its most challenging and busy periods.[35] Wherever servicewomen had the opportunity to prove their value to the war effort, they earned respect and promotions. Menial assignments, on the other hand, provided little chance of job satisfaction, acknowledgment by superior officers, or promotions. Instead, they nearly guaranteed low morale and its offshoot, disciplinary problems. To be sure, many white Wacs also felt that the army did not effectively use their skills. They did not experience, however, the same wholesale relegation of their units to low-skilled, routine assignments as did black Wacs and were therefore less prone to challenge their officers or resist military policy.

Some white officers took it upon themselves to abide by the spirit of the army's updated racial and gender policies. The commander of Fort Huachuca, Arizona, gave his contingent of black Wacs the "red-carpet" treatment and assigned them to a variety of positions. These women worked as medical technicians, office personnel, drivers, telephone operators, and library clerks. The commander of Walla Walla Air Base, Washington, assigned black Wacs to technical and skilled jobs in the post's photo lab, hospital, and various offices, where he soon evaluated them as "fast becoming an invaluable aid to the officers and departments throughout the base command."[36] Similar comments greeted other detachments of Wacs, regardless of race, wherever they were responsibly employed. However, the majority of commanders failed to responsibly employ black Wacs.

Juggling housing issues, local civilian concerns, and job assignments were hurdles that commanders could expect on the transfer of black Wacs to their posts, yet instead of connecting these problems to military policies, they tended to view the women as the problem. Days before the strike, Colonel Whitehurst of the Surgeon General's Office phoned Captain Sisson at Fort Devens in a bid to transfer more black Wacs to the base. When Sisson told him that he did not need any more black Wacs and to send them elsewhere, Whitehurst replied, "I don't have any idea where to move them." He then expressed his frustrations with black Wacs, if not black women in general: "they're one of those things like the poor—they are always with us."[37] The general unfamiliarity of white officers with African American women afforded narrow grounds for them to develop respect for black Wacs or an interest in their service as military personnel.

In lieu of administrative support in regard to employing black Wacs (and in the absence of disciplinary measures against those who practiced sex and race discrimination), commanders depended on their personal experiences to navigate the lines between separate and equal treatment among its various categories of troops. Unfortunately, formal and informal segregation practices throughout the nation meant that few officers would have encountered African American women other than those who worked as charwomen, maids, laundresses, and agricultural laborers. Consequently, most white officers' personal experiences with African Americans were extremely limited. After the court-martial, Crandall admitted, "I have very little to do with the colored people in this country, and I realize that I don't understand their psychology."[38]

If Crandall felt that in his position he had no need to try to understand black Wacs, he was not alone. At Fort Devens, he and Lieutenant Lawson, the post's chief WAC commander, were operating after all according to policy by ensuring the segregation of their female troops. Furthermore, Lawson requested two black officers rather than the requisite one for the detachment. In consultation with Crandall and two other officers, she claimed that she thought it best to make the black WAC unit "as much an individual organization as we could," assuming that "they [black Wacs] would prefer that."[39] Lawson made a point of letting black officers manage their troops on their own while she attended to white Wacs.

The commander, Lieutenant Sophie Gay, and supply officer, Lieutenant Tenola Stoney, of the black WAC detachment were the link between the enlisted women and the post command. In this position, they, like other black officers during World War II, walked a fine line. On one hand, they were responsible to their superiors and their agendas, and on the other, they had a duty to their troops and their morale. Contradictory separate but equal policies thwarted honest efforts to perform both tasks. Shiny bars on crisp uniforms offered little protection against white suspicions that African American officers were inherently unqualified for their roles and inept as leaders. Female or male, they had all of the responsibilities of their commissions though few of the benefits and almost no respect befitting their rank. During World War I, white officers had barred their black counterparts from officer clubs, filed reports on their perceived weaknesses and uppity behavior, and labeled them as "good" as long as they "stayed in their place."[40] Little had changed during World War II. After accepting a white male officer's invitation to the Fort Des Moines officer club, Captain Charity Adams received a reprimand from her superior officer for her supposed arrogance. "Don't let being an officer go to your head," he warned her. "You are still colored and I want you to remember that." He then informed her that he was from South Carolina, her state of birth. "Why, your folks might have been slaves to my people right in South Carolina, and here you are acting like you are the same as white folks." Before giving Adams permission to leave, he warned her, "you people have to stay in your place."[41] Despite the stepped-up rhetoric of equality during World War II, post policies and racist attitudes often blocked black officers from officer clubs, assumed their incompetence, and labeled those who confronted their officers over troop grievances as uncooperative.[42] The usual one or two black Wac officers on posts suffered additional isolation. They did not have others to confide in or, given the lack of recreational facilities for them, to informally socialize.[43] At Fort Devens, Gay and Stoney managed their roles by consulting each other, dealing with problems internally, and occasionally mentioning them to Lawson.

Spending most of her time at Lovell Hospital North, where the white Wacs worked, Lawson remained at best aloof to the concerns of the black enlisted Wacs in her command. Her lack of knowledge of their conditions and morale, therefore, was by design. Lawson explained that she had requisitioned two black officers because she "felt that the girls would be freer to come and present their problems to colored Wac officers than they would to a white officer." In fact, leaving the detachment to these two officers allowed her to disengage from these troops' training, treatment, and morale. An investigator later asked the lieutenant about her knowledge of the black Wacs' grievances at Lovell Hospital South. Lawson responded that Lieutenant Gay had spoken to her about the objections, but that she had not taken them seriously. "Well, frankly, there are the normal complaints that they don't like to do scrubbing, but when those things were reported—well, I really can't say that complaints that they didn't like to scrub came to my ears."[44] Given the dramatic events in the month leading up to the strike, Lawson should have been well aware of the women's situation and how desperate they were to gain their officers' attention in order to air their grievances. That she was so unaware indicates the dysfunctional chain of command through which the black Wacs had attempted to work prior to the strike.

The situation at Fort Devens, already rife with turmoil that winter, came to a head after a series of events that began just five weeks before the strike action. The first occurred on February 2, 1945, when detachment commander Lieutenant Gay received an honorable discharge (most likely for health reasons given her recent convalescence at Lovell Hospital North). In her early thirties, Gay had been popular among her troops and had managed to maintain their morale as the months of orderly work dragged on. After her departure, command of the detachment fell to the twenty-five-year-old supply officer, Lieutenant Stoney. As the only remaining black Wac officer at Fort Devens and new to a position she had not expected, Stoney struggled to maintain a balance between her duties as an army officer and her role as an advocate for her enlisted women. The grievances among her troops continued after Gay's departure, and Stoney attempted to field them on her own.

Stoney was deluged with complaints, and not only from her troops. The enlisted personnel supervisor at the hospital, Sergeant Harold Wicks, funneled reports of the women's tardiness and behavior to her, as did occasionally the nurses on the wards. Stoney also heard from Captain Russell Elliott, an African American company commander and military police officer stationed at Fort Devens, after six members of her detachment appealed to him for his help. One told him that a medical officer called her dumb and lashed out, "why the hell didn't they get all of these damn black Wacs out of here?" Elliott advised Stoney to look into this serious allegation, but to his surprise, she told him that she did not believe the story. Handling on her own the numerous protests of discrimination, a situation that she could not reverse, had overwhelmed the beleaguered young officer, so she turned to a seemingly less controversial issue. Confiding in Elliott, she revealed that she was busy ferreting out homosexuality among her troops. Meanwhile, criticism of the orderlies continued to reach her desk. Once the Wacs' supervisors informed Stoney of the situation, they left all disciplinary matters in her hands.[45]

It was a tough spot for a young black lieutenant anxious to please and averse to making waves. A more confident officer might have taken the chance to air her detachment's grievances, as did Lieutenant Margaret Barnes at Camp Breckinridge, Kentucky, the year before. She and her company commander, Captain Myrtle Anderson, frequently brought their troops' grievances about orderly and laundry duties to the attention of their superior officer. The post commander's failure to respond led the enlisted women to threaten mutiny, whereupon he ordered their "arrest in quarters." This prompted Barnes to go over his head and, through her connections at Fort

Des Moines, drew into the matter a white general. His intervention immediately improved her troops' assignments, yet the risks Barnes took for this favorable outcome were so great that she had not informed Anderson of her plan should it have backfired.[46] More often than not, standing up for enlisted black Wacs backfired. At Camp Rucker, Alabama, a commander similarly protested the relegation of her black troops to menial duties until the morning that her commander angrily bellowed "you have no detachment!" and disbanded her unit on the spot.[47] Pulled in two directions and on her own at Fort Devens, Stoney played it safe. She continued the weekly meetings that Gay had instituted with enlisted personnel, assured the orderlies that their work was important and appreciated, and on rare occasions brought up her troops' grievances to Lawson, but she remained reluctant to take matters to the next level in her chain of command, Colonel Crandall.

Only after the strike did the First Service Command's chief officers realize the extent of the confusion within the detachment's command structure that had so confounded black Wacs' attempts to work through their officers. Stoney later testified that she assumed that Lawson was her next level of command. Lawson countered that though she was in charge of all Wacs at Fort Devens, she gave Stoney free reign as commander of the black detachment to take issues directly to Crandall. In any case, Lawson's claim that she "had no idea that there was anything brewing at all . . . until just before the strike—before the mutiny" is curious. In her position, she had a responsibility to check in with all members of her detachment. Had she attended the weekly meetings of her African American troops, she would have been treated to a barrage of their concerns. Had she made the rounds at Lovell Hospital South, she would have heard their objections—"hundreds" of them, according to Wicks—which they regularly related while on duty.[48] Instead, Lawson engaged with the black detachment only after situations had turned into problems that required her attention.

One such occasion evolved in early February, when Private Harriet Warfield, Private Inez Baham, and Technical Corporal Thelma Allen (T/5) arrived at Lovell Hospital South. All three held surgical technician classifications and expected to work in this capacity. Unaware that their orders listed them as aidmen, they were astonished when Lawson and Stoney assigned them to orderly detail. The three balked at performing duties below their technical ratings and insisted that they would rather take a court-martial. It was a drastic move, but then so was their sudden reclassification as orderlies.

As the three took in their predicament, they witnessed the deteriorating situation of which they were now a part. A month later, conditions had only worsened, causing Warfield to lay out her observations in two letters, one to her aunt in Philadelphia, Mary Smith, and the other to her member of Congress, William T. Granahan (D-PA). Together, these letters give insight into Warfield's experiences before and after her transfer to Fort Devens and to the crumbling morale of the Wacs in her new detachment.[49]

Enlisting in March 1943, Warfield earned some hometown fame as one of the first black Wac recruits from Philadelphia. Until Fort Devens, she had enjoyed her army experiences, first at Fort Des Moines and then at Fort Oglethorpe, Georgia, and was proud of her army training and exemplary record. While awaiting assignment as a surgical technician, she learned that Colonel Hobby had approved the transfer of black Wacs to Europe and that she was one of the eight hundred selected to serve in the unit, the 6888th Postal Battalion. Warfield was looking forward to the assignment, a great honor since the battalion was the first (and only) black Wac unit that Hobby agreed to send overseas. Warfield, however, would not be aboard the ship. When the army noticed her qualifications, it held her back, claiming a domestic shortage of hospital technicians. Likewise, Baham and Allen, who were also surgical technicians, found that their MOS exempted them from overseas duty with the 6888th Postal Battalion. Disappointed yet aware of the army's need for their medical training stateside, the three arrived at Fort Devens prepared to work in their authorized capacity. They would not, however, work as orderlies, and they rejected any downgrading of their assignment classification.[50]

Unlike the other Wacs in her new detachment, when Warfield arrived she had the advantage of knowing up front that, as a black Wac at Fort Devens, her services would be confined to orderly detail. Also unlike the others, Warfield had the confidence of a veteran with two years' experience in the WAC, a solid military record, and army training as a surgical technician. After her first day of duty at Fort Devens, Warfield joined Allen and Baham in a collective refusal to work as orderlies.

Stoney spoke to the new transfers about complying with military orders, but they remained firm. Warfield explained that she would work as an orderly if overseas, but not stateside because the army had held her back from the 6888th Postal Battalion due to its shortage of hospital technicians. Stoney apprised Lawson of the situation, whereupon Lawson retorted that the servicewomen's action constituted mutiny. Rather than bringing the three up on charges, Stoney suggested putting them in for a transfer. In the meantime, she said that she would keep them busy with chores around the barracks. Crandall agreed to the plan and on February 14 reported the three "surplus in skill."[51] With the transfers logged, Stoney, along with Warfield, Baham, and Allen, most likely assumed that the situation would be temporary and soon forgotten. Instead, the work stoppage undoubtedly factored heavily into the detachment's orderly strike a few weeks later.

By mid-February 1945, the situation was fast deteriorating on several fronts. Nearing their fifth month of orderly work, the women of the black WAC Detachment were having few qualms about questioning their confinement to cleaning duties. They communicated their dissatisfaction regularly to their detachment commander, ward men, and officers at Lovell Hospital South, and they sought outside help—all to no avail. Meanwhile, the three new arrivals were conducting their own strike. Morale among the black Wac orderlies plummeted, yet the women's officers did not take notice, or rather they did not take action. "I sensed trouble . . . when I first came here," admitted one colonel, "and I hedged around it, to tell the truth, because I did not want to get in it."[52] Rejecting the army's attempts to disparage their intelligence, abilities, and character, the women attempted to work through their chain of command, of which they had only a rudimentary sense, to gain their superiors' attention to their grievances and opportunities to prove themselves. Stranded on the periphery of base functions where normal military protocol did not extend, Morrison, Young, Green, Murphy, and other orderlies considered their options to advance their goals. Others were ready to give up.

Private Beulah Sims was the first. On February 14, 1945, she attempted suicide. Days before, the authorities had charged her for being AWOL and confined her to quarters. Sims instead headed to the nearby town of Ayer, where that evening she overdosed on atropine sulfate. Regaining consciousness a day and a half later, Sims told psychiatrists at Mason General Hospital in Long Island, New York, about her frustrations at Fort Devens. In their evaluation, the psychiatrists cited Sims's orderly assignment as a possible contributing factor, noting that she was "surprised and disillusioned at having menial duties to perform in the Army instead of specialized work."[53]

After Sims's suicide attempt, Stoney continued to advise her troops to stay strong and on task, offered assurances of the value of their work, and mentioned their grievances to Lieutenant Lawson. She did not, however, take decisive action by enlisting Lawson's assistance or calling Crandall's attention to a situation that was rapidly escalating beyond her control. While other members of her detachment were sinking into despair, as had Sims, the best Stoney could manage during her first month as detachment officer was a single meek remark to Crandall that "the girls were kind of disgusted about their assignments on the wards but I was trying to make them feel it was a big job even though it was just scrubbing."[54]

Between Stoney's vague remarks to Crandall and Lawson's disinterest in the detachment, the concerns of the black Wacs at Fort Devens festered unattended for nearly five months. Even Sims's suicide attempt did not move them, Crandall, or anyone at Fort Devens or the First Command Headquarters in Boston to look into the issues of its only black Wac detachment. (Stoney spoke privately to Sims afterward, though neither she nor Lawson sought to investigate the matter or console their troops after the troubling event.)[55] Meanwhile, the three surgical technicians were still performing odd jobs around the barracks and awaiting transfers that never came. A month after her arrival, Warfield had seen enough. It was then that she wrote to her aunt about the combustible situation at Fort Devens. Upset by the news, Smith visited her NAACP branch in Philadelphia, her niece's letter in hand.

The next day, Wednesday, March 7, sixteen black Wacs took advantage of the army's annual inspection tour of the hospital to air their grievances to members of the visiting team. Lieutenant Colonel Henry C. Ransom and Major George H. Miller accorded each an interview and wrote down their concerns. Private Anna Morrison objected to the fact that "they had to do KP (kitchen police) duty though white Wacs did not." Several spoke of the discrimination they encountered at Fort Devens, particularly at the post exchange (PX). Private Dorothy Petty described an episode when a white clerk told her that she was out of a particular item, only to produce it for a white Wac when she requested the same thing. Private Esther Watts wanted to "know why they can't get ratings [for promotions], the white detachment gets ratings."[56]

Most of the grievances centered on the women's orderly assignments. Privates Alice Young and Ruby Pierce claimed that their recruiters and some officers at both Fort Des Moines and Fort Devens indicated that they qualified as medical technicians and would receive training for this specialty.

Several sought transfers to other areas for improved assignments. Morrison wanted to move to the motor transport course, Private Verna Jones to physical therapy training, and Private Lillian M. Wallace to "medical technical school as promised before enlistment." All viewed their current duties as in line with servant work. Furthermore, they protested, they were doing the same cleaning jobs and running the same errands that civilians had been hired to do and for longer hours and less money—Wacs earned $50 a month and civilian orderlies approximately $40 a week. Furthermore, some of their civilian counterparts ordered them around and left work for them when their shifts ended, a charge Stoney later acknowledged, noting "the Wacs were doing the work and the civilians were getting the pay."[57] A distraught Private Lucille Edmonds, in what was likely a last desperate effort to turn things around, encapsulated the women's objections, which Ransom and Miller recorded: "She wants to learn things, is tired of being pushed around. Help in the PX do not want to wait on them. The white Wacs do not do KP. She has to work too hard."[58] With so many complaints from the hospital's black Wacs (the only other from an enlisted black man), Ransom and Miller planned to investigate. They were unaware that in less than forty-eight hours, the situation that the Wacs described would explode.

The next day, March 8, tensions between the Wacs and civilians at Lovell Hospital South erupted in a fight, giving rise to yet another layer of segregation at Fort Devens. That morning Germaine Morissett, a civilian orderly, claimed that Private Ora Mae Bell had tried to choke her and then beaten her once she had fallen to the floor. Bell countered that Morissett had shoved and then slapped her. The scuffle quickly caught the attention of a male soldier, who notified Lawson.[59] Resorting to the usual solution of separating black troops from others when racial issues surfaced, Lawson prepared a plan whereby the enlisted women would work on certain wards and the hired civilians on others. This, she assumed, would eliminate "the opportunity . . . to quibble about the amount of work assigned to them." Announcing the plan fell to Stoney, who ordered all orderlies not on duty to gather in the squad room for a 7 p.m. mandatory meeting.[60] The meeting would not go well.

Crowding in the squad room in Barracks No. 2 that evening, the women learned of the plan and immediately pounced on it. The civilians, they argued, had been hired to scrub floors and were being well paid to do so. They, on the other hand, had joined the army to train and work in military assignments such as the ones that white Wacs performed at Lovell Hospital North. Moreover, they had learned that officers were organizing a training program for civilian orderlies. Morrison was appalled, assuming that the army was giving their civilian counterparts, but not them, the chance "to learn how to go out of the ward." Green, who had just begun a three-day pass when called back for the meeting, stood up and spoke for the majority when she told Stoney that "we wouldn't like the alteration one bit." Without the civilians, she explained, black Wacs would not be able to take their two-hour afternoon break, thereby forcing them to stay on the wards for the full twelve-hour shift.[61] The women shot back that separating civilians from black Wacs did not deal with their grievances but instead ignored them. Clearly, the orderlies recognized that the root of their problems was not the civilians but their officers who failed to provide opportunities for other assignments.

When investigators later looked into the differences between black and white duties, they learned that prior to the arrival of the black detachment to Fort Devens, a large number of white Wacs had worked at Fort Lovell Hospital South as orderlies.[62] They also learned that these servicewomen had access to medical training, though Lawson insisted that "it was rather hard to conduct any [regular] program" because the nursing staff continually changed.[63] Fragmented and inferior as Lawson described the training, it was more than black orderlies received. This led to black Wac perceptions that the army at least made an effort to prepare white women for technical jobs and then move them to more satisfactory positions when possible. This possibility arose for white orderlies when black Wacs arrived at Fort Devens to replace them. Moreover, black Wacs rarely encountered white Wacs performing orderly duties. In fact, there were not many to encounter anywhere at Fort Devens. In March 1945, just 15 of the 180 white Wacs worked as orderlies, compared to 75 of the 100 black Wacs (see table 1).[64]

Investigators looking into the causes of the strike asked Crandall why he had not requested black technicians in addition to orderlies so as to create a more equitable distribution of personnel. Crandall responded that he did not need technicians, just orderlies. They then asked why he reported so many white orderlies as surplus if he was experiencing a shortage of them. His response was the same, that he needed more orderlies. No matter how investigators framed the question, Crandall did not veer from his initial reply. Apparently, it had not occurred to him to retain some white

Table 1. Comparison of White Wac and Black Wac Assignments, March 9, 1945

Enlisted Wac duties	Basics	Mess personnel	Motor transport	Other technical duties	Medical orderlies (or ward masters— white wacs only)	Hospital technicians	Clerical	Cadre
White Wacs		8%	12%	6%	12%	19%	40%	3%
Black Wacs	4%	11%	6%		75%			4%

Source: Summary, 5, WDI.

orderlies or to request black technicians. Nevertheless, when asked if racial discrimination existed in job assignments at Lovell Hospital, Crandall replied that it did not. Despite his assurances, a racial balance was clearly missing.[65]

The women present at the March 8 meeting with Stoney did not have these statistics, but they were keenly aware of the difference race made in job assignments under Crandall's administration. Therefore, instead of allaying their frustrations, Stoney's description of the new policy to separate black Wacs and civilians galvanized many of them into taking action. A furious Anna Morrison warned that "if we don't try to get something better now, we never will get it," and broached the idea of a strike. Some of the orderlies, including Morrison, said that Stoney had cautioned them at the meeting to "not plan anything in front of her."[66] Either way, the strike option was already on the table due to the ongoing work stoppage of the three surgical technicians, Warfield, Baham, and Allen.

The formal meeting lasted just over half an hour, during which time Stoney urged the women to work the way they had when they first arrived. Since working hard had not gotten them very far, this advice did not go over well with her troops. As Morrison later explained, "it looked like not only the people over in the hospital were against us, but our own company commander."[67]

Afterward, most of the women dispersed. Private Ola Jackson and a few others took in a movie that evening and some went ice-skating, though the majority either retired to their bunk areas or gathered to talk about the meeting. In Barracks No. 1, the women discussed the situation yet seemed resigned to it. Even as rumors of a strike surfaced, they settled down for the night, assuming they would be at their wards, as usual, by 7 a.m. A much more rancorous discussion erupted in Barracks No. 2, where Morrison and Murphy, who bunked in Barracks No. 1, had stayed after the meeting. Later, Green would say that she had no inkling of a strike action because after the meeting she left Fort Devens to resume her pass, although other accounts place her in the thick of the discussions prior to her departure. There she would have heard Anna Morrison angrily propose some sort of direct action. They had been "working like dogs," Morrison argued, and yet their commanders ignored their grievances. Alice Young and others directed their outrage at Stoney, whom they blamed for not going to bat for them. While some of the women felt that Stoney had done all that she could for them, all agreed that there was little likelihood that their former supply officer and current commander would take up their cause. As the hour grew late, the contingent in Barracks No. 2, who had been making the rounds and talking to orderlies on both floors, concluded that black Wacs at Fort Devens would not get attention for their grievances without demanding it and settled on a work stoppage. As had their foremothers, they determined that a collective action offered them their best chance of success.[68] Since most of the other Wacs had left the dayroom immediately after the meeting, those remaining had little opportunity to gain consensus that evening. A strike remained a possibility, however, and in that state had a chance to incubate overnight. The morning of March 9 would begin with much excitement—and trepidation—as to whether the detachment members would collectively commit to a strike action.

After the 6 a.m. reveille, as most of the women in Barracks No. 1 donned their blue smocks, GI'd their areas, and went to breakfast, those in Barracks No. 2 engaged in a hot debate over what to do. By 6:45 a.m. some had dressed, though others, including Morrison who was determined to go through with the strike, were still in their nightwear. In this early hour, Morrison and a few others in both barracks tried their hand at cajoling, persuading, and even threatening others to go along with the action. Private Lula M. Johnson testified that some of the women (she claimed she could not remember who) warned her, "it's all right if you go; you will see what we will do to you." Morrison later brushed off the alleged threat as a joke, claiming that even Johnson had a good laugh because she had not been serious about going to work.[69]

Nonetheless, other Wacs from the detachment reported similar warnings, especially by Morrison. In Barracks No. 1, Morrison and three others spotted Private Ruth B. Waller getting dressed for work. "I may not like a thing," Waller later explained, "but what use is there standing up and arguing about it?" The four felt differently and suggested, in no uncertain terms, that Waller change her morning plans. "They were very convincing," she admitted, particularly Morrison, who "told me she was going to whip the hell out of me."[70] Waller insisted that she did not "pay any attention" to any threats, yet others likely did succumb to them. Only four Wacs reported to work that day, including Waller and her friend Private Thelma Thomas. Aware of the hostility that these women would likely face on return to the barracks that evening, Lawson summoned them after their shift and asked if they wanted to spend the night at Lovell Hospital North. They accepted the offer.[71]

The other orderlies stayed in their rooms, many waiting to see what would pan out. Private Tommie May Cartwright later confided, "I wasn't sympathizing with them . . . but I stayed there." According to Private Lorraine Overton, when she awakened to find the barracks still full, she quipped, "you all strike while I sleep," pulled her blanket over her head, and did not get up for another hour. During their court-martial, Young and Morrison testified that they also did not know if a strike would take place that morning. While true, the two were among the dozen doing their best to bring it about. This included Overton, who apparently got less sleep that morning than she claimed. Some of her bunkmates recalled her rallying and even threatening members of the detachment to join the strike.[72]

Most of the women, though recognizing the seriousness of participating in a strike, had reached a point where they were ready to protest their treatment in hopes of improving it. "It may be wrong," admitted Private Amanda McCord, "but I think we all want to do as much as we can to better ourselves." Explaining why she joined the strike, she added, "I didn't want a dishonorable discharge to take back home to my family, but I felt that [because of the strike] someone would listen to us at least a little bit."[73] That morning, a few individuals led the charge for a strike while a handful rejected it. The majority, though initially unsure, ultimately needed little coaxing to join the action. "We might have gone at it wrong," said Private Mary Johnson, "but the thing we were fighting for was justice and rights. We want to live like other people."[74]

The decision to strike invited risks that these women, who had enlisted to demonstrate their patriotism and contribute to the war effort, were reluctant to take. Furthermore, they understood that the consequences could be severe. At the same time, they recognized the importance of standing united to protest the discriminatory treatment of African American women. "I knew that in time of war the soldier wasn't supposed to strike. And I knew that it was a serious offense," affirmed Private Willie Mae Miller. She did not go to work that morning, she said, because she was unwilling to let down the women in her detachment. Others recognized that those who took part in the strike would be protesting on behalf of all black Wacs in their detachment. "No, I didn't go to work," said Ola Jackson, "because it was a matter of cooperation, that if all the girls refused to go to work, then it was up to me to stay." Others voiced similar solidarity. Though Private Anna Kelly noted that the strike was not her idea, she explained that "by my being their color, why[,] I stayed, too."[75]

The collective nature of the strike emboldened many, though some took part by default. Fears over the reaction of their officers should they strike and concerns about letting down the others in their unit by reporting to work contributed to the haphazard manner in which the action evolved that morning. "We were really afraid to strike," admitted Johnson. Miller's reason for joining the strike was typical. "It seems nobody was going [to work], and quite naturally, I wasn't going if nobody else wasn't going." By biding their time to see how events would play out, their absences were noticed before all had made a conscious leap to activism. Lewis, for example, expected Stoney to call a meeting and discuss the situation, and "then we would all go back to work." Like others, she later said that she "didn't have any intention of not going [to work] at all." When the opportunity to protest presented itself, however, Lewis required little encouragement to be part of it. Neither did Private Jessie Gaines, who joined the strike because she "was just fed up." Though expressed in different ways, being "fed up" registered highly among the orderlies who participated in the strike.[76] As Morrison, Young, Murphy, and Green later explained, they could not continue as they had. This sentiment had already proven a profoundly tragic factor in Beulah Sims's attempted suicide—as it would in three others in the days following the strike.

On Friday at 7 a.m., the reporting time of orderlies at their wards, nearly all of the black Wacs orderlies assigned to Lovell Hospital South remained in their barracks. Shortly afterward, calls began flooding the detachment's phone line in Barracks No. 2. In the nearby supply room, the supply sergeant, T/4 Clotha Walker, was taking the weekly linen inventory when she began hearing repetitive trills of the phone down the hall. Curious, she walked the short distance to the orderly room, where she saw the acting First Sergeant Area Bates handling a succession of calls and, as Walker later described the scene, murmuring between calls that "this one hadn't reported to work and that one hadn't reported to work." Walker looked at Bates and asked, "are all the kids going on strike today?" Bates replied, "I don't know." Before the supply sergeant had asked the question, however, she knew they had.[77] Nearly all of the black Wacs on duty that Friday morning failed to report to their duty stations. It was March 9, 1945, and the Fort Devens strike had begun.

3

The Strike

If it will help my people by me taking a court-martial, I would be willing to take it.

— Anna Morrison testimony, *U.S. v. Young*

On March 9, 1945, fifty-four members of the Fort Devens black WAC Detachment filed into the dayroom of Barracks No. 2. At 9 a.m. on a Friday, most were scheduled for duty and should have been at their stations at Lovell Hospital South, so by presenting themselves in the dayroom, they affirmed their participation in the strike action. All who took part would have been aware, if to varying degrees, of the risks they were taking. Collective actions by African American service personnel were common during World War II, as were the severe consequences so extensively covered in the black press. One particularly well-reported incident took place in June 1943 when Wacs at Camp Breckinridge, Kentucky, organized a work stoppage to protest their cleaning and laundry room detail. The army ushered six of them out of the corps during the WAAC to WAC conversion.[1] Given the vastly larger numbers of black men in the military, disciplinary actions against black servicemen were far more numerous than those of Wacs' and the punishments harsher. For instance, the navy discharged fourteen Seabees serving in the West Indies after the men, at their officer's invitation, discussed with him concerns over their treatment. At Mabry Field, Florida, in 1944, five black soldiers refused to work until they could air their grievances of racial discrimination. That May, a court-martial board sentenced them to prison terms ranging from thirteen to fifteen years. Two months later, an explosion at Port Chicago, California, killed more than three hundred black Navy stevedores loading ammunition. After surviving members refused to work under the same unsafe conditions, the navy court-martialed fifty, sentencing them to fifteen years in military prison.[2] These and other trials, diligently covered by the black press, carried the unmistakable message that no service would accept racial discrimination as a cause for insubordination.[3] Nevertheless, on March 10, 1945, in an attempt to alert their officers to the discrimination they experienced, over fifty African American Wacs stationed at Fort Devens, Massachusetts, took part in a joint action of insubordination.

On learning of the strike, the women's officers immediately turned their attention to the detachment and took action. First Lieutenant Victoria Lawson telephoned First Lieutenant Tenola Stoney, and the two called a 9 a.m. meeting for all on-duty orderlies not already on their wards. They then apprised Colonel Walter Crandall, who agreed to attend the meeting and address the orderlies. Lawson opened the session, warned the women that their action was unlawful under military law, and introduced Crandall. Among those at the meeting were Privates Anna Morrison and Alice Young. Mary Green, who was on a pass, arrived late to the meeting.[4] Also present were T/5 Thelma Allen and Private Inez Baham, two of the three surgical technicians who for nearly a month had refused to work as orderlies. Two other Wacs who soon proved pivotal to the Fort Devens incident did not attend the morning meeting with Crandall. Johnnie Murphy was recovering at Lovell Hospital North from the flu, and Harriet Warfield, the third surgical technician, was in Boston on a three-day pass.

This was Crandall's first meeting with the detachment since the women's arrival at Fort Devens five months earlier and his first inquiry into its personnel's conditions and concerns. For many of the women, this was also their first encounter with the hospital administrator, and they were unlikely to be inclined to warmly welcome him. They had heard of his alleged comments that black orderlies were, as Young had recalled Crandall announcing, to do the "dirty work, and here to scrub floors and walls."[5] Though during the meeting the Wacs did not mention Beulah Sims's recent suicide attempt, their commander's failure to look into the matter undoubtedly troubled many.

Despite the tension in the room, the meeting that morning opened with civility. Crandall stood up, faced the women, and calmly noted the seriousness of their action. In the army, he explained, military personnel had no right to strike and doing so constituted a mutiny that would invoke severe consequences. He then expressed his interest in their complaints and invited them to voice their concerns. The women began describing their low-skilled job assignments, the belligerence of some civilian coworkers, and their impression that their hard work was not appreciated. For his part, Crandall agreed that they should not have to scrub floors and wash windows and promised to look into these issues. When they asked about training programs, however, he replied with his own question: "who is going to clean up the hospital?" The complaints kept coming. For Crandall, it was a lot to take in, yet he continued accepting comments and attempted to respond to each.[6]

As Crandall took questions, his troops were gaining confidence in their act of resistance. Within just two hours of the official 7 a.m. commencement of their strike, they had the attention of their officers, including the commander of Lovell General Hospital, and they were listening to their grievances. Before long, complaints filled the room, often from the same fifteen to twenty people. Five months of pent-up frustration broke open in the dayroom that morning and propelled the meeting into a second hour, though with an increasing intensity marked by a rapid deterioration of military protocol. Tempers flared as some of the Wacs connected their grievances to the historical exploitation of black women and their labor. Those present described a disturbing scene of "swearing, cursing, and stamping of feet." According to Lawson's observations of the mounting mayhem, "in almost every instance the girls who complained said they would not go back to slavery, and a number stated they would take death or a kind of court-martial or dependency discharge or anything to get out of Lovell."[7]

Tensions climaxed over an inadvertent remark Crandall made in response to a question Young asked. The private, who had already spoken several times, stood up to once again recall the day when Crandall had openly admonished her for taking a patient's temperature. This time she added that after the incident she walked to the motor pool to speak to the transportation officer about training as a driver. The officer told her that "colored Wacs" were ineligible and that in any case, a transfer would require the permission of her commanding officer.[8] From Young's perspective, the meeting with Crandall gave her the opportunity to request her commanding officer's permission to transfer to the motor pool. Understandably confused,

Crandall replied, "you just told me a little while ago that they wouldn't take any black Wacs at the Motor Transportation School."[9]

As Crandall awaited clarification, his troops suddenly stiffened in their seats. Momentarily stunned by his use of the term *black Wacs*, the women sat speechless until, in the sharp silence, ten or so of them indignantly stood up and walked out. At this point, the dayroom erupted in shouting and cursing. Crandall, uncertain of what he had said to warrant this jolt of disapproval, was startled by the fierceness of the women's anger. The problem was that, after five months, he knew very little about this category of troops in his command and had not built even a trace of goodwill among them. His limited experience with African American women left him completely unaware of the resentment his phrasing (acceptable at the time of this writing and used throughout this book) would cause.

In the 1940s, the informality of the term *black*, particularly by someone of Crandall's demonstrated racial attitudes, came across as exceedingly derogatory. Explaining the women's anger decades later, Morrison noted that at the time it was like saying "nigger." While "Negro" and "Colored" were generally acceptable, "nigger" and "boy" were not. Whites knew these commonly used terms and their general connotations, though segregation left many insensitive to the offensive nature of those that lay between. African Americans, attuned to the dominant white culture in which they lived, recognized this and often let less respectable forms of address pass despite the personal sting. Martha Putney, for instance, recalled a white Wac in her officer candidate program refer to African Americans in the diminutive "you kids." Putney "let her go on because I knew she was southern and probably that was the best adjustment she could make by using the word 'kids' instead of 'niggers.'"[10] On the morning of March 9, the Wac orderlies at Fort Devens were not so readily inclined to excuse their commanding officer for a similar slip, no matter how unintentional.

Crandall had not meant to offend and was genuinely surprised by the furor his phrasing had sparked. Reports differ as to what happened next, though all describe an explosive atmosphere that rapidly descended into chaos. Some of the women cried and others cursed. Private Willie Mae Miller fainted and had to be helped to her barracks. Crandall attempted to approach Young, who, according to Lawson, was too "hysterical" to listen to him, and he backed away.[11] More women began leaving the dayroom despite the absence of a dismissal. As the room began to empty, Crandall called them back. Some complied. Most didn't. Attending to military protocol, Crandall officially closed the meeting before taking leave with Lawson and Stoney following close behind. As the three departed the room, the few Wac orderlies who had remained until dismissed stood at attention as their officers passed.[12]

Outside the barracks, it was another matter. Twenty or so of the Wacs angrily advanced toward Crandall, several calling him "old mother fucker," "God damn son-of-a-bitch," and "old-gray-haired bastard," among other profane characterizations.[13] From the sideline, the supply sergeant Clotha Walker watched in astonishment and worry. "I hope they don't hit him," she thought. Stoney intervened and ordered the women to their quarters. Across the yard, Young stood in front of Lawson shouting "Push me! Push me!" until her friends managed to pull her away.[14] Others seethed when they saw Private Ruby Pierce politely conversing with Crandall. Pierce later told investigators that she had merely spoken to him about a transfer, though the rumor that morning was that she had instead apologized to him for the unit's behavior. Either way, a conversation with Crandall was not a popular act, and Pierce would pay for it—on her return to the barracks, a large group of Wacs pounced on her.[15] Meanwhile, Sergeant Bates noticed Private Grant Gilliland meandering away from the area in a disoriented stupor and set out to retrieve her. Gently guided by Bates back to the barracks, the private anguished over the situation and confided that "she couldn't live through it, and it had upset her terribly." Gilliland's nerves were frayed more than most (she similarly wandered around twice more that afternoon), yet others were also terribly upset over the meeting, their jobs, the screaming, and the cursing. Several reported seeing Lawson and Stoney on the verge of tears. Walker couldn't hold back hers. As Stoney ordered her troops to their barracks, she noticed passersby stopping to watch and listen. "We were putting on a good show for them," the lieutenant told investigators. Walker felt the same, later lamenting that "it was pitiful that day."[16]

It was also a day of an extraordinary breakdown of military discipline, and Crandall, completely unprepared for the anarchy and verbal assaults, did not know what to make of it. Had the troops been black soldiers, without a doubt he would have called MPs (military police) to the scene and had the men arrested and court-martialed, most likely for mutiny. With far less cause, other commanders in the various services had successfully prosecuted black troops on this charge. Had the men been white, he may have also summoned the MPs, though likely bringing on himself a serious investigation into his handling of his troops. The officer corps did not take the breakdown of military discipline lightly, and Crandall knew it was an officer's duty to take necessary action to restore order. Ordinarily, this would have prompted him or his junior officers to order "a-ten-hut!," the familiar command that compelled troops to stand immediately at attention in complete silence and stiff alertness. Crandall, who had not treated his black Wacs as ordinary troops and apparently did not regard them as such, did not bother with the order. Instead, he seems to have resigned himself to a temporary loss of command of the women. Apparently eager to escape the melee for calmer quarters, he retreated to his office. At this point, Crandall may well have begun to calculate his culpability in the strike. He would take his next steps with extreme caution.

The tumultuous meeting led to a buzz of activity at Fort Devens that at last focused on the post's black enlisted Wacs. Crandall telephoned the WAC staff director of the First Service Command in Boston, Major Elizabeth Stearns, who in turn alerted General Sherman B. Miles, the commanding officer of the First Service Command. Miles ordered Stearns to leave immediately for Fort Devens to assess the situation. Stearns arrived that evening and sent word to the Wacs, by then confined to their barracks, that she would hear their grievances in the orderly room. Approximately thirty trekked down to see her.[17] Stearns listened, reminded them of the seriousness of their action, but said little else. Afterward, she phoned Miles to report on the situation.[18]

Miles was prepared. In addition to Stearns, the general had dispatched another emissary to Fort Devens, Colonel Lawrence B. Wyant. Though white, Wyant had gained a reputation as "a deep student of racial relations and a sincere friend of the Negro people," and for this reason Miles had appointed him as the command's morale officer.[19] Learning of the situation, Wyant called on Captain John Hurd, an African American officer on duty at a nearby post, and enlisted him for "a mission," that he did not divulge until they arrived at Fort Devens.[20] Given his duties as an American Army Education officer, Hurd assumed Wyant had called on him to organize a training program. Instead, Wyant seemed to desire his presence, as an African American officer, when speaking with the women. An accident delayed the men's arrival until after 11 p.m., so they did not meet with the Wacs until the next morning. By then, the strike had moved into its second day.

Shortly after 10 a.m. on Saturday, March 10, Stoney escorted Wyant and Hurd to her detachment's barracks and introduced them to the Wacs on strike. The two male officers charged with ending the action brought General Miles's personal guarantee that he would order an investigation of their grievances—though only after the Wacs returned to duty. Despite Miles's orders not to take or discuss complaints, Wyant and Hurd briefly allowed the women to have their say. As Hurd described the scene, the women were emotional, causing Wyant to advise them to calm down and "look at the whole thing as good soldiers," yet they were also "very courteous," as they took turns to speak. After hearing the Wacs' objections to the lack of training and respect they received at Fort Devens, the two officers repeated Crandall's and Stearns's warnings of grave disciplinary consequences should they continue their strike. As Stoney recalled, Wyant counseled the women that "everyone couldn't do exactly what they wanted to, that some would have to do the little jobs, that all the jobs counted."[21] The Wacs listened, but they did not return to work.

The women's determination to continue the strike perplexed Miles. He had generously offered to look into the detachment's concerns and arranged for its members to meet with three officers he judged best able to relate to them: Stearns, a woman; Hurd, an African American; and Wyant, a noted "friend of the Negro people."[22] These officers' respective gender and racial connections to the personnel on strike seemed to Miles his best chance of bringing the women around. In fact, the three had less in common with the Wacs than Miles had presumed and were thus unable to grasp the women's unique circumstances. If the orderlies had been white Wacs, they would have had access to a variety of jobs, as did the white Wacs at Fort Devens. Had they been black male soldiers, they may have had other assignment possibilities, including at the motor pool, which at Fort Devens trained both black soldiers and white women as drivers. Instead, their dual identities persistently excluded them from the army's regular operations, training programs, and, until two months before the strike, overseas duty. While Stearns may have related well to white Wacs and Wyant to black male soldiers, both were at a loss to understand the servicewomen's unique circumstances and thus their motivations. As an African American, Hurd may have been more sympathetic to the women's plight than Stearns and Wyant, yet the former Tuskegee ROTC instructor had learned how to succeed in the army. Quickly deducing his role in the mission, he stood with Wyant and urged the women to obey orders and return to their duty stations.[23]

Thus, rank presented an additional divide between the three officer envoys and the enlisted women on strike. Commissioned officers represented the upper echelon of military personnel. As privates, the black orderlies occupied the lowest level of the rank structure. In itself, the hierarchal segmentation of personnel was not an entirely disagreeable one for these women or the vast majority of American military personnel. Rather, its assurances of merit-based upward mobility was a major draw of military service. In reality, the multiple intersecting axes of enlisted black women's subordinate identities excluded the majority from advanced assignments in which to earn promotions. Stearns, as a women, and Hurd, as an African American, most certainly faced hurdles in the military, yet as officers they seemed proof that hardworking Americans, regardless of their sex or race, could rise through the ranks. As illustrated at Fort Devens, a system deemed wholly merit-based led to assumptions that those who failed to advance in their assignments and through the ranks had reached their full potential.

Stearns used her officer status to set the terms for her encounter with the enlisted women. She would meet with them one to five at a time in the orderly room. Annoyed by these stipulations, a group of Wacs gathered in the dayroom and, through Sergeant Bates, informed Stearns that "we're waiting for her over here." The major ignored the message.[24] Given Crandall's disastrous morning meeting in the dayroom, where he had been greatly outnumbered, Stearns had reason to consider her terms a sensible approach, though an unlikely way to end the strike. Nevertheless, expecting Stearns to come to them was an audacious move among the Wacs and a further sign of a breakdown of military discipline at Fort Devens. This breakdown, however, was not all one-sided.

Crandall and Stearns may have been aghast by the enlisted Wacs' display of disrespect to them and for their rank, yet these officers had also violated army policies by neglecting these troops. As members of the armed services, black Wacs were entitled to consideration for training, assignments, and promotions.[25] Instead, when Crandall and Stearns prepared for the new troops' arrival, they considered little more than how to isolate the detachment from base operations through separate housing and work assignments. Crandall put in a requisition that was heavy on menial labor, and Stearns approved it without query. Neither arranged for an orientation program that would have explained the Wacs' assignments, discussed post rules, and defined the post's chain of command. "They were just picked up, so to speak, and dumped on the wards," recalled Stoney.[26] Five months after they arrived, most of the Wacs remained unclear of their opportunities, expressed low morale, and claimed to have never heard of Stearns, the highest-ranking Wac in their chain of command, until she summoned those wishing to lodge complaints. In violation of their military responsibilities as officers, these and other officers had not demonstrated interest in the welfare of their black female troops nor shown them respect as service personnel.

Determined to reverse these circumstances, the Fort Devens black orderlies launched a strike. On day two of their action, the strategy seemed to be meeting its preliminary goals. Their officers were paying attention to them, meeting with them, asking about their grievances, and offering to look into these matters. On the other hand, none of the six officers they had seen in the last two days had yet to satisfactorily address their core issues of training and assignments. With growing resolve, the Wacs stood together and continued the strike.

Though Miles's headquarters was located in Boston, he learned of Wyant's and Hurd's failure to break the strike while sitting in Crandall's office, just blocks away from the black WAC detachment area. Earlier that morning, he had pushed aside other business, gathered his staff, and driven the forty miles from Boston to Fort Devens. On arrival, he conferred with Wyant and Hurd before they met with the Wacs, instructing them to keep his presence on base quiet. Miles wanted to give the men the opportunity to end the strike on their own yet was prepared—on-site and accompanied by his legal team—to handle the mutiny himself if necessary.[27]

Later, army investigators asked Miles why he, the command's chief officer, responded in person to the actions of fifty low-ranking enlisted personnel. Miles replied that "the order of a Lieutenant is just as good as the order of a General, but the prestige is different, and I was dealing with a rather ignorant and rather misguided group of women."[28] He was also concerned with the threat that a collective action of insubordination could pose to a command and was unwilling to let it get out of hand. Consequently, when Miles received word from Hurd and Wyant that the Wacs planned to continue their strike, he took command of the situation and ordered the women to assemble in their dayroom. Miles had tried working through his officers, but with the strike well into its second day, he felt he had no choice but to intervene. The time had come for him to personally order the Wacs to work.

At noon, Miles addressed the Wacs on strike. In his no-nonsense manner that brooked no discussion, he reminded them that as military personnel they were duty-bound to obey the orders of their superiors. Refusing to work was not an option in the army but an offense punishable by court-martial. After repeating earlier guarantees to investigate the complaints of those who returned to duty, he introduced his inspector general, Lieutenant Colonel Sumner W. Elton, and invited the women to register their grievances with him. As an added incentive, Miles offered to drop all charges of prosecutable misconduct thus far accumulated, making it clear that "very few members of the Army are given the consideration that I am giving you today." Next he introduced his judge advocate, Colonel Edward W. Putney, who he said would immediately begin court-martial proceedings against those who did not return to their wards. "Refusal of duty cannot be tolerated in any Army," he warned. Miles then directed Putney to read aloud the 64th Article of War detailing the charge of disobeying a commanding officer.[29]

While addressing the women, Miles did not label the strike a "mutiny," though he considered it nothing less. Only practical necessity deterred him from threatening the women with article 66, which pertained to this most serious charge. Miles purposely avoided invoking the term *mutiny* because he considered mutinies contagious. With 3,700 African American soldiers stationed at Fort Devens, he had no desire to inadvertently spark similar actions. Miles was also concerned with the negative effects that news of a WAC mutiny could have on recruitment. As he later explained to investigators—ironically given the main reason for the strike—"We were in the midst of a drive to recruit Wacs for hospitals, and here was an open mutiny among Wacs in a hospital."[30] For these reasons, Miles, who could have justifiably invoked Article 66, opted for the lesser charge of Article 64, a catchall indictment that covered a wide range of crimes, from willful disobedience of a superior to violence against an officer. The maximum punishment for Articles 64 and 66 was the same: "death."[31] In the Fort Devens case, however, this extreme punishment was never discussed during the court-martial proceedings.

Miles clarified the Wacs' situation to avoid any misunderstandings and then, after directing his secretary to write down his precise wording, issued a direct order: "You will immediately fall in ranks in front of this building and be marched to your posts of duty, and you will continue thereafter to do your duty. Fall out and fall in front of this building."[32] Without a word, the women stood up and filed out of the dayroom. Their compliance lasted only until they had exited the building. Too frightened to disobey yet too invested in the strike to abandon it, they stood despondent, uncertain as to what to do. Stoney ordered them to fall in (formation). No one did. The lieutenant then asked the women to fall in. Still no one moved. Finally, one of the older women said, "Please, let's not do this to her. Look, she's trembling, almost crying." The others turned to Stoney, who appeared on the verge of tears. "She didn't do anything to us," added the woman. As the lone black female officer at Fort Devens after Gay's departure, Stoney was in a difficult position, and her troops understood that. At this point, they fell in and marched to their jobs. Green, Morrison, and Young were among them. "We did it for her," Morrison said.[33]

Back in the dayroom, T/5 Thelma Allen and Private Inez Baham remained seated, seemingly in direct violation of Miles's order. Unbeknownst to General Miles, the two surgical technicians, who had been conducting their own strike along with Private Warfield (still on her weekend pass) for nearly a month, did not have wards to go to. Miles ordered the two taken into custody, at which point Lawson explained that they did not work at the hospital. Unimpressed with the reason why, he repeated his order. As the day progressed, three others—Privates Morrison, Green, and Young—would join Allen and Baham. The following Monday, Murphy's arrest would bring the number of Wacs facing court-martial to six. Of this group, only Morrison, Green, Young, and Murphy would stand trial. Their circumstances following the March 10 meeting with Miles therefore deserve attention.

Wholly distraught, Private Morrison marched with the others to Lovell Hospital South and reported to her ward shortly after 1 p.m. Without uttering a word, she sat down by the window, looked out, and cried. When her ward master, Sergeant John Froias, asked her what was wrong, she shot back, "don't speak to me, none of you!" Her friend Private Alberta Doss, who had arrived just five minutes earlier, put her arm around Morrison and suggested that they both go out for some air. Gently leading her out of the ward, Doss told her, as Morrison recalled, that Froias had released them for the day—a point the prosecutor would contest at her court-martial.

By then, Morrison had caught sight of the chaplain's office. Once seated there with the chaplain, Morrison attempted to explain the situation and her desperation with it yet, by her own account, fell into "hysterics" instead and cried that she couldn't go on. At her trial, she described the depths of her emotions that day as feeling that "I could just lay down and die." Inconsolable, she returned to her ward and asked Doss to walk with her to see another friend before leaving. Doss told her she planned to stay, so Morrison set off on her own. Unsure what she was going to do, though feeling that "anything would be better than to be put back on the wards," Morrison began walking back to the barracks.[34]

Like Morrison, Green had misgivings about returning to work, and she showed it. She walked to her ward, as Miles directed, but did not enter it nor attend to her task. Her ward master, Sergeant Rhoyd Heath, asked her if she was on duty. Green said she was only to spend the next half hour standing outside of the ward talking to a patient. With growing frustration, Heath told her that if she was going to work, she had to come into the ward. Green refused, informing him that she was not going to work. Exasperated, her ward master ordered her to "go on back to your company and report to your First Sergeant or your Company Commander." During the exchange in the corridor, Sergeant Area Bates appeared and, after some words with both parties, ordered Green to the detachment barracks before scurrying off to check on the other Wacs. Green was in no hurry to comply. On her way out, she stopped to talk to another patient before joining the trail of other black Wacs, including Morrison, who were making their way to their barracks.[35]

Young also reluctantly obeyed Miles's order and, like Morrison, Green, and many of the other Wacs, reported to her duty station visibly upset. As she tried to work, a woman, perhaps a civilian orderly, noticed her distress and advised her not to feel bad. Young replied, "well, there's nothing I can do," only to add "I can't help from feeling bad about it though." A phone call to the ward dispatched her on an errand to the kitchen. There, she encountered an enlisted soldier in charge of another ward who, finding humor in the situation, tried to prod her into talking about the strike. Young instead snapped, "that's our business and not to be discussed in the ward here."[36]

Young endeavored to plow through the day and even advised others to do the same. She coaxed her coworker, Private Mary Driver, out of leaving, even volunteering to assume her duties so that she could take it easy for the day. When Driver persisted, Young advised her to ask their ward master, Private First Class Gene Beale, for the day off. "Gene is willing," she assured her, "and he won't make you stay here." As Young predicted, Beale excused Driver for the day. Private Lucille Edmonds, who worked on another ward, also spoke to Young about her misgivings over returning to work. Recognizing Edmonds's fragile state, Young talked her out of continuing the strike and escorted her to her work area. On their way, the two ran into Sergeant Harold Wicks, the supervisor of Lovell Hospital South's enlisted personnel. According to Young, Wicks said that he thought the black Wacs were getting "a dirty deal" and regretted that he could do nothing about it. Young admitted that she was having as hard a time with the situation as the others and that she wasn't sure she could go on, either. Wicks remembered the chat differently, telling investigators that Young had said it would take "gunfire" to get her to go back.[37]

The Wacs' mood was downcast and tense that afternoon. By obeying Miles's order, the women had abandoned the strike with nothing changed and little better in the offing. Miles's big carrot, a guarantee of an investigation, provided little comfort. They could not be sure of army promises. Young later described the disillusionment of the orderlies at the hospital that afternoon. "The majority of the girls were walking around, bewildered," she said. "They wanted to stay there, and didn't want to stay there." As she made her way back to her ward, Young was leaning toward the latter. Nearing her station, she called over to Beale and announced, "Gene, I am leaving. I will take a court-martial."[38]

At her trial, Young explained that even then she was not sure what to do. After Miles's order, she had returned to work "with the intention of staying, but was confused" and needed to get away and think. Mainly, she said, "I wanted to go back to the barracks and get some rest because I was so upset." Young recollected that after announcing her departure to Beale, she had heard him respond "OK" before she exited the hospital.[39] Whether this signaled the ward man's acknowledgment of her departure or his permission for her to leave her duty station would prove a point of contention during the trial.

An hour after Stoney had marched her detachment to the hospital, Morrison, Green, and Young joined the stream of approximately thirty others flowing from their wards and down the road toward their barracks. In pairs and in small groups, with some lagging far behind, they grimly proceeded to their barracks, whereupon most dispersed into the dayroom and their bunk areas. Morrison and, according to most reports, Green headed to the orderly room, where Stoney sat at her desk filling out paperwork (the court-martial charges for Adams and Baham). Lawson stood nearby. Neither enlisted Wac spoke, so that when Young arrived shortly afterward, the attention turned to her. Young declared, "Lt. Stoney, I'm reporting back from my ward, and I feel like I'd rather take a court-martial than go back under present conditions, unless the conditions are changed." Stoney asked Young, "Do you?," and Young confirmed that she did. "What about you, Pvt. Morrison?" Morrison replied in the affirmative. According to Young, Stoney repeated the question to Green, who nodded in agreement. At this point, Lawson intervened. She ordered Young to announce in both barracks that all those who intended to take a court-martial rather than return to work were to report immediately to the dayroom.[40]

Young completed her task and joined six or so other members of her detachment in the dayroom, where Lawson was taking each aside individually to ask her intentions.[41] Lawson spoke first with Morrison. Conflicted and wrought with anxiety, Morrison told Lawson that she had tried to return to work, but that she could not do it again. "I don't think I can go on," she told her. "Put my name down for a court-martial." Lawson wrote down her name and serial number and told her to pack her bags. She spoke to Young next and added her name. According to Lawson, Green also told her that she preferred a court-martial to returning to work, at which point Lawson asked for her name and serial number. Afterward, the women dispersed. Shattered, Morrison headed outside, where she collapsed in tears while Green and Young, equally despondent, walked to their quarters to prepare for their confinement.[42]

Young welcomed the retreat to her bunk area, where she could think through her decision. As she later recalled, "I only wanted to have things half-straightened out and I would go back to work." Both she and Green broke down in tears as they packed their bags. Soon after, Private Alberta Doss appeared and advised them to rescind their statements, insisting that it wasn't worth a court-martial. By this time, the two privates agreed, although Young was certain that Lawson would not drop names once she had recorded them. Considering how little time had elapsed, Doss reasoned that Lawson would and convinced her friends to chance it.[43]

The two Wacs found Lawson in the dayroom. Young spoke first. She assured the lieutenant that she had changed her mind and would return to work. Lawson told her it was too late, but Young persisted: "isn't there any way you can stop this?" Though Young was adamant that she "didn't want a court-martial, that I would go back to work," there was, according to Lawson, no turning back. At this point, Green informed her officer that she might be pregnant. That was why, she insisted, that she did not feel she could do the heavy work her duties required. At her court-martial, Green offered a second reason for not working that day: "we had been having trouble about we being colored and I didn't feel right going back on the ward with the same girls I had been working with and get the same treatment." During the March 10 exchange with Lawson, however, she cited only her health issues. She, too, asked Lawson if she could avoid the court-martial by returning to work. Lawson would not budge.[44] Within the hour, MPs arrived to drive Green, Young, and Morrison to the confinement quarters at Lovell Hospital North.

Murphy's situation differed from her codefendants in three important ways. First, she had a previous conviction for disrespecting an officer (Stoney), whereas the others had unblemished records. Second, she had been convalescing from a bout with the flu at Lovell Hospital North on March 9 and the morning of March 10, so she had not taken part in the initial strike nor been present when Miles issued his direct order. Third, whereas the others faced charges for disobeying Miles's order, Murphy had disobeyed Lawson. After her release that afternoon, Murphy walked back to her barracks, where she saw Morrison crying outside. Morrison told her about the strike, which Murphy was eager to join. She immediately sought out Lawson and told her to put her name on the list. Declaring her position in no uncertain terms, Murphy added, "I would take death before I would go back to work."[45]

Lawson decided to overlook Murphy's comment and give the private the weekend to reconsider. Technically, Murphy could not be on strike because she was not on duty that day. She was on duty Sunday and did not report to her ward. On Monday, Murphy presented herself before Lawson and repeated her refusal to work. Once again, Lawson cautioned her, "Private Murphy, you don't realize what you are doing," to which Murphy retorted, "I think I do." Lawson then formally ordered the private to her duty station, and Murphy formally refused, again stating that she would prefer death.[46] At this point, Lawson had no choice but to put the private on report. Thus, while prosecutors charged Morrison, Green, and Young with disobeying General Miles, they charged Murphy with disobeying Lieutenant Lawson.

On Sunday, the day before Murphy's arrest, Lawson visited the Wacs she had placed in confinement. The women were held in separate rooms at Lovell Hospital North, so as Lawson made the rounds, she met with each individually. Curiously, she asked Morrison, Green, and Young whether, if given the chance to reverse their decision, they would return to their duty stations. Green and Young said they would. Morrison asked if this was a possibility, and Lawson said it was not. At this point, Morrison answered, "well, if it will help my people by me taking a court-martial, I would be willing to take it."[47]

On Monday, March 13, the army officially charged Morrison, Green, Young, Murphy, Allen, and Baham with disobeying a commanding officer. By then, the NAACP was already aware of their situation. Warfield's letter, which her aunt had taken to her local NAACP office, had prompted the national office to contact its Boston branch president, Julian Steele, to look into the matter.[48] As Miles's go-to man for issues regarding black troops in the area, Steele had already met with the general, whose connection he allegedly highly valued. Though obliged to offer the six defendants assistance, Steele publicly concurred with Miles's narrow reading of the case, that it was a matter of disobedience, not discrimination.

On March 16, Steele issued a statement for the NAACP's Boston branch members that, due to interest in the incident, was widely reported in the newspapers. Prefacing his remarks by asserting the NAACP's complete rejection of segregation, he faulted the "misguided" defendants for refusing to return to work, thereby potentially blemishing the "splendid record which colored Wacs have made in this war." Furthermore, he commended General Miles for his "understanding and forbearance" and insisted that racism was not involved in the Fort Devens case. Suspecting otherwise, local African Americans fiercely criticized Steele for his willful ignorance of "Army Jim Crow" at Fort Devens. "These women did not strike for idle reasons," retorted the leader of the New England Congress for Equal Opportunity, John S. R. Bourne. Without mentioning his name, the *Boston Chronicle* castigated Steele and other cosigners of the statement as the Wacs' "would-be champions," who dismissed the reasons for the strike.[49]

Meanwhile, Julian D. Rainey, the chair of the Boston branch's legal committee, had agreed to represent the Wacs. On March 17, just three days before the trial, Rainey conferred with the six defendants for the first time and afterward met with Miles to discuss the case. He asked Miles to drop the charges against the surgical technicians on the grounds of documented misassignment. The army, he contended, had trained them to work as specialists, not as orderlies. In addition, they were awaiting transfers, and had been for a month. For this reason, Rainey argued, when Miles ordered Allen and Baham to their duty stations, they had nowhere to go but the barracks, where they had been doing odd jobs. Miles remained unconvinced by these arguments yet preferring to "avoid any semblance of persecution," he grudgingly agreed to dismiss the charges against Allen and Baham.[50]

That same day, Miles approved the transfer of the surgical technicians, including Warfield. Though Warfield had been on pass through the strike, her earlier refusal to work as an orderly marked her as sympathetic to the strikers' cause if not an inspiration for their action. Indeed, she told Stoney on her return to Fort Devens that she had discussed the situation with her family, and they supported her decision to take a court-martial rather than work as an orderly. Allen and Baham had earlier told Stoney the same. As the trial date grew near, Miles did not want any of these women at Fort Devens. Intent on "get[ting] them out as fast as possible because I thought they were a bad influence," he promptly arranged to transfer all three.[51]

At this point, Miles must have felt that he had given the case more personal attention and afforded the women far greater leniency than he would have for male troops. He had accorded them a chance to return to work without blemish to their records, offered to look into the grievances of those who complied, and dropped the charges against the two technicians. He also ordered his command's assistant inspector general, William J. White, to conduct a thorough investigation of the situation and to uncover the reasons for the strike. A highly accomplished man with a distinguished record of service, the sixty-three-year-old major general had been as fair as army policies and his personal understanding of race and gender issues allowed.[52] Once the women rejected his entreaties, however, Miles was adamant that they stand trial. Though confident that the court-martial would demonstrate the Wacs' deliberate violation of orders rather than racial discrimination, he was determined that this would not be his call. Once the proceedings were underway, Miles stepped back to allow military justice to take its due course. Murphy, Young, Green, and Morrison would have their day in court.

The swearing-in of Oveta Culp Hobby as WAAC director in 1942, with Chief of Staff General George Marshall looking on. National Archives (208-PU-94A-4)

Black Wacs drill under the command of Captain Charity Adams at Fort Des Moines, Iowa. National Archives (111-SC-238651)

Mary McLeod Bethune, surrogate mother of black Wacs, and her protégé Dovey Johnson. National Civilian Advisory Committee inspection tour of the First WAC Training Center, Fort Des Moines. National Archives (208-PU-10E-2)

Mary McLeod Bethune, First Lady Eleanor Roosevelt, and others. May 1943. National Archives (162-PBA-10-F-5612)

Waac mechanics Ruth Wade and Lucille Mayo, Fort Huachuca, Arizona, 1942.
National Archives (111-SC-162466)

Private Annie Hawking, Halloran General Hospital, Staten Island, N.Y., 1943.
Courtesy U.S. Women's Army Museum, Fort Lee, Va. (B138)

Recruiters Lieutenants
Harriet West (on left) and
Irma Cayton (on right).
National Archives (111-
SC-144958)

Alice Young left a well-paid job
at the U.S. Treasury Department
to enlist in the WAC. Courtesy
Stacie Porter

Anna Collins (Morrison) at Fort Des Moines, Iowa. Courtesy Juanih Campbell

Tuskegee airmen training for military missions. Selfridge Field, Michigan, 1943. National Archives (208-VM-1-5-684)

Anna Morrison.
Courtesy Juanih
Campbell

Anna Morrison at Ft. Devens, undated.
Courtesy Juanih Campbell

Advertising campaign photo depicting the WAC's ideal image of a female soldier, 1944. National Archives (RG 165, series 56, box 175, file 320.2)

PVT. ANNA MORRISON
(Richmond, Ky.) PVT. ALICE YOUNG
(Washington, D. C.) PVT. MARY GREEN
(Conroe, Tex.) PVT. JOHNNIE MURPHY
(Rankin, Pa.)

The court-martial of the women in military uniform became
a media sensation in the black press. Courtesy *New Pittsburgh
Courier*, Pittsburgh Courier archives

Opened to the public
by General Miles, the
court-martial took
place in a makeshift
courtroom in the Fort
Devens headquarters
building. Courtesy, Fort
Devens Museum, Fort
Devens, Mass.

THEY DID NOT DIE IN VAIN

Editorial cartoon by Oliver Harrington, *People's Voice*, April 4,
1945. Courtesy Helma Harrington

Thurgood Marshall, lead attorney of the NAACP's Legal Defense Fund. National Archives (58-10173)

Brigadier General Sherman Miles, at his desk at the War Department, December 1941. National Archives (208-PU-136 DDD-4)

Official WAC historian
Mattie Treadwell. Courtesy
U.S. Army Women's Museum,
Fort Lee, Va. (B182)

Though women also served, the Tuskegee airmen remain the face of the struggle
of the African Americans during World War II. Lt. Lee Rayford, 99th Fighter
Squadron. National Archives (208-NP-6-EE-1)

Commanding officer Charity Adams inspects the 6888th Postal Battalion, February 15, 1945. National Archives (111-SC-200791)

Recognition of the African American women who served during World War II has been slow and uneven, yet the women themselves have expressed pride for their time in uniform and the legacy they left for those who followed. T/Sgt. Tommye Berry at Camp Shanks, Orangeburg, N.Y., Transportation Corps staging area of the New York Port of Embarkation, April 16, 1945. National Archives (208-PU-10D-7)

4

Trial and Verdict

This girl said, "I will take death." Think of the poor
immature girl who says that. They were confused,
gentlemen.
—Julian Rainey, closing statement, *U.S. v. Young*

In the weeks following the arrests of the four Wacs and later after their
court-martial, family, friends, and even strangers rallied to the women's defense. Alice Young's parents sent their support in a telegram: "Dear Daughter, have heard the news. Sorry it had to happen yet we glory in your spirit
and are with you one hundred percent." That same day her sister Julia
sent another: "Chin up. The Youngs are gathering. Help is on the way."[1] For
African Americans, courts-martial did not necessarily imply misbehavior
and could in fact signify valor. Mary Green's father, the Reverend Joseph
Amerson, indicated as much when he told reporters that "he would rather
Mary face trial for insubordination than some question arise against her
integrity."[2] In a biblical quotation-filled letter, a well-wisher from Boston
applauded Anna Morrison for her courage and asked that "God bless you
for the stand you have taken."[3] Johnnie Murphy's friend was less formal
but just as adamant in her praise. "I hear you're in confinement! Good girl,
so am I."[4] The widespread support no doubt provided welcomed solace for
the four defendants while confined at Fort Devens.

On March 19, 1945, just nine days after the strike had collapsed, Privates Anna Morrison, Mary Green, Alice Young, and Johnnie Murphy stood

before a court-martial board accused of disobeying a superior officer. All entered pleas of "not guilty." Thus commenced one of the most highly publicized military trials of World War II. Though not the first disciplinary hearing of Wacs, it was the most open and well-documented of all Wac courts-martial. This was due both to the publicity surrounding the case and to General Sherman Miles, commander of the First Service Command, who intended to showcase, through the Wacs' trial, the impartially of the military's justice system regardless of a defendant's race, gender, or rank. The defendants' testimonies and the trial's proceedings reveal instead a justice system that reinforced the privileges of male soldiers, white personnel, and commissioned officers while discrediting the characters of the enlisted black Wacs on trial. Less than a year before, Howard University law student Pauli Murray had constructed her Jane Crow theory to make sense of the dual subordination of African American women in civil society. Given the proceedings, which the feminist and civil rights scholar undoubtedly followed, she may well have considered a GI Jane parallel.

The Fort Devens court-martial of black Wacs would be no ordinary trial. To begin with, the defendants were servicewomen, an unheard of possibility just three years before. They were also African American women, thereby ensuring a novel public platform for the contentious issue of segregation. Female military personnel on trial galvanized the black press and roused white interest that together elevated the court-martial to a public event of note. Miles, determined to demonstrate the army's colorblind impartiality in the high-profile case, took the rare step of opening the court-martial—usually a closed affair—to the press and public. He also included among the ten members of the court hearing the case two black men and three white women. Wacs in the docket proved so inescapably extraordinary that the prosecutor found it necessary to remind the jury to consider the female defendants as they would male soldiers. (He then proceeded to refer to them as "Miss" rather than their military title of "Private," emphasizing their gender over their military identity.) The defendants' gender also led to a most unconventional defense strategy for military personnel. Instead of focusing on the Wacs' strength as soldiers, their attorney would argue that his clients, as women, were not in full control of their emotions and actions. Racial issues would dominate the discourse of the trial, yet the defendants' gender set the tone and undergirded the arguments throughout the proceedings.

The precautions the army took to demonstrate its impartiality reveal instead how firmly yet imperceptibly the military's judicial system prioritized rank and marginalized black women, thereby preserving the status quo. For instance, Miles attempted to assemble a diverse panel to hear the case, yet, as was military policy, all board members were officers. This standard procedure ensured that officers, though not low-ranking privates, were heard by a jury of their peers. Furthermore, fewer than half of the members hearing the case were either black or female, and none was both black and female. The court also permitted arguments based on popular, yet demeaning stereotypes of black women that would significantly undercut the defendants' testimony and their value to the service. Miles was confident that judicial military protocols assured each defendant a fair and impartial hearing, unaware that these same protocols also undermined African American servicewomen's chances for a fair and impartial verdict.

At the same time, the protocols of a military trial rendered Morrison, Young, Murphy, and Green important rights in the proceedings that black women could not necessarily expect in civil trials. (Indeed, having their day in court was a rarity for African American women in the 1940s.)[5] They could, and did, request the removal of a member of the court, a white Wac officer, whom they considered prejudicial to their case. Perhaps less helpful to their defense though certainly on the advice of their attorney, they waived two of the five days the army granted defendants to prepare their case. Most importantly, the four exercised their right to take the stand to describe the treatment and racial inequities that had fueled their actions. This was crucial because their testimonies offered a perspective distinct from those of both the prosecutor and the defense attorney. For example, while all three parties honed in on the role of racial discrimination in the case, defense counsel focused on the "perception" of racism, the prosecutor insisted on the "absence" of racism at Fort Devens, while the defendants highlighted the "evidence" of racism. Likewise, the women forthrightly asserted their competence by resisting the frequent attempts by the prosecuting and defense lawyers—albeit for opposite reasons—to undermine their abilities. Young, Morrison, Green, and Murphy spoke confidently, forcefully at times, and—as various documentation of the case bears out—honestly in an effort to accurately report their circumstances and explain their motivations.

By 10 a.m. on the morning of the trial, spectators and journalists had crowded into a small room, converted that day to a courtroom, in the Fort

Devens post headquarters building. Captain George H. Schwartz, the presiding "law member," or military judge, took his seat with the nine other officers hearing the case. Major Leon E. McCarthy and his assistant formed the prosecution team. The army-appointed lawyer for the defense also appeared. The women declined his assistance, however, having accepted instead the NAACP's offer of a local civilian attorney and chair of the Boston chapter's legal committee, Julian D. Rainey.

At fifty-seven, Rainey was a prominent African American resident of Boston who had practiced law in Massachusetts for twenty-six years. He was also a veteran, a point he made known early in the proceedings. Rainy had enlisted during World War I, earned his commission, served on the front lines, and worked as a judge advocate.[6] His approach and his comments throughout the trial, particularly those regarding the psychological toll of racism, suggests sustained battle scars from his time in the service. As a black officer during the Great War, he had been among the nation's most promising young African American men who enlisted to prove their manhood and sought commissions to demonstrate the abilities of their race. The men's military superiors responded by targeting their leadership and intellect for relentless ridicule.[7] The experience may explain Rainey's apparent determination to emphasize his fraternity with the male officers of the court, including the prosecutor whom he frequently addressed as "brother."

The public court-martial of black personnel afforded Rainey the opportunity, unavailable to him nearly thirty years earlier, to lay open the scourge of racism in the military, and he would do so with passion and confidence. Indeed, Rainey was an exacting opponent for the prosecution and an intense interrogator of those on the stand—all service personnel who, except for the black Wacs, were unaccustomed to taking direction from an African American. Possibly a courtroom packed with journalists recording the testimony obliged the white enlisted men and the officers Rainey questioned to respond courteously and to respectfully address him as "sir." It may also have been the defense attorney's force of personality that he brought to bear on an indictment he most certainly took personally.

Rainey came prepared with two strategies. The first was a long shot, and he knew it. He began by calling his clients' WAC officers, Lieutenants Victoria Lawson and Tenola Stoney, to testify and then the ward masters involved in the case, Sergeants John Froias, Rhoyd Heath, and Harold

Wicks. He also referred to a written statement that Private First Class Gene Beale had submitted before leaving on furlough. Rainey spent the morning questioning each about the events of March 10 and weaving their responses into his clients' pretrial statements. Then suddenly, after just half a day of testimony, Rainey made his move. Addressing the law member, he called for the dismissal of all charges against Morrison, Young, and Green. (His motion did not include Murphy, whose circumstances on March 10 significantly differed from those of her codefendants.)

Calling for a dismissal of the charges was an audacious move, yet Rainey stood his ground as he invoked the confusion during the day of his clients' arrest and called into question the hands-off nature of the women's ward masters and company commanders. He reminded the court that Morrison and Young claimed that they had left their posts under assumptions that they had been properly released, whereas their ward masters testified that they had not given their permission. Meeting head-on the confusion over the matter, Rainey contended that these men bore some responsibility. On March 10, he argued, they had the opportunity and the duty to clearly state their expectations but did not. To Froias, who stood just ten feet from Morrison when Private Alberta Doss had slowly led her despondent friend from his ward, Rainey asked, "Did you say anything when they went off duty?"

"No, sir."

Rainey repeated the question. "You didn't say anything at all?"

Froias repeated his answer. "No, sir."[8]

Rainey turned next to the written testimony from the absent ward man Gene Beale, whom Young said she had informed that she was leaving. He had responded, "OK," she contended, which she took as permission to go. In his statement, Beale refuted Young's claim. His inconveniently timed furlough precluded Rainey from questioning his statement or asking his response to Young's insistence that "if he had stopped me I would not have gone."[9]

Likewise, Rainey sought to demonstrate that Green vacated the premises only after her ward master, Rhoyd Heath, had told her to leave. On the stand, Heath disclosed that "She didn't tell me she was leaving. I sent her off." He did so, he clarified, only after Green said that she would not work that day. Rainey probed further, zeroing in on Heath's responsibilities as Green's supervisor. "Did you ask her to do anything? You didn't ask her to do any duties at all?" Heath replied, "not that I remember."[10] With this admission, Rainey reminded the court that Green had been standing at the door for half an hour, and yet at no point did her ward man direct her to carry out specific duties.

Calling Lawson to the stand, Rainy noted that within an hour of Green and Young turning themselves in for a court-martial, they had told Lawson that they would return to work and asked her to drop their names from her list. Given the high emotions of the day and the defendants' desire to comply with Miles's order, he questioned the lieutenant's reasons for submitting their names for a court-martial, and hence, her commitment to her troops and their welfare.

Rainey next addressed the board members to discuss the wording of General Miles's order to the women to return to work. He contended that Morrison, Young, and Green had, in fact, obeyed the command to the letter. The general had stated that the Wacs were to fall out (leave the dayroom), fall in (into a formation outside the dayroom), and march to their posts. Rainey insisted that the three had followed through on each of these commands, but that the last part of Miles's order, to "continue to do your duty thereafter," was problematic. Rainey argued that it was too loosely phrased as to identify the exact duties, place of those duties, or timeframe for them to be performed. So broad was the wording, he insisted, that it constituted an unlawful order. For instance, he explained, "thereafter" was an "indefinite" term with no conceivable boundaries and therefore impossible to follow to the letter. Given the seriousness of the charges, Rainey remonstrated that "if there is anything which would require definiteness, it is a specification in courts-martial proceedings."[11]

Of course, there were many holes in Rainey's proposal, beginning with his clients' announcements on March 10 that they would take a court-martial rather than return to work. Not surprisingly, the prosecutor categorically opposed Rainey's motion to dismiss the case. "Now it is true," McCarthy allowed, "that if an order of that nature . . . was given to a person who was not acquainted with military terms, who were told to, 'fall out, fall in front of the building,' [it] might do some hideous things if they attempted to do that." For service members who had completed basic training, this was not an issue. Referring to the defendants, McCarthy added, "they knew what their duties were," and they knew where and how long they were to perform them.[12] The law member denied the motion to dismiss the charges, a ruling that could not have surprised Rainey, who had come prepared with a second, and much more complicated, defense strategy. By the time he introduced it, he already had laid the groundwork of confusion it required.

Rainey understood the racial provocations behind the Fort Devens strike, yet a frontal attack of the army's racist policies was not viable. So vigilantly did the army defend segregation as a fair and equitable policy that it did not entertain racial discrimination as a defense in disciplinary cases. Had Rainey pursued this course, no matter how eloquently and convincingly, he would have lost the case. Therefore, despite the civil rights attorney's extensive expertise in the matter, through legal training and personal experience, he had no choice but to seek another angle to free his clients. Wisely cautious to avoid overtly criticizing the army's segregation policy, Rainey settled on a strategy that narrowly sidestepped racial discrimination as a defense. He would base the case instead on the women's "perception of discrimination."

Rainey proposed that the women's perception of racism, which he carefully framed as a potential misperception, caused his clients to feel confused about their situation. He sketched this "over-all picture" as one dotted with inconsistencies, as the women saw it, that eventually psychologically overwhelmed them: they had enlisted to fight racism abroad, only to feel its sting in the military; they were eager to fill the gap of the army's highly publicized WAC technician shortage, only to be put to work as unskilled laborers; they were Wacs, but they were not given WAC responsibilities. The effect on these women, Rainey reasoned, was nothing short of traumatic confusion.[13]

Throughout the trial, Rainey referred to perceptions of discrimination in order to avoid placing direct blame on the army's segregation policies. This did not preclude him from probing the culpability of individual officers and ward men at Fort Devens in the willful neglect of his clients. On the contrary, questioning their leadership provided practical cover for Rainey to expose the flaws of segregation by drawing attention to the inequities his clients suffered and thus the reasons for the strike. As Rainey periodically reminded the court, his case rested not on whether discrimination led the women to disobey their officers, but on how their perceptions of inequitable treatment had sparked a form of temporary insanity: "If they have violated any Article of War, it was due to the mind of a monomaniac, a mind that was confused, a mind confused by something they couldn't understand because of differentiation made between members of the armed forces because of color, which had driven them to excitement which amounted to monomania and they didn't know what they were doing."[14]

The prosecution flatly denied that discrimination, much less any perceptions of discrimination, had anything to do with the case. Instead, McCarthy's arguments centered exclusively on the defendants' willful decision to disobey General Miles's March 10 orders. While noting that Morrison, Young, and Green had returned to their post that day, McCarthy drew on the ward masters' testimony to contest the notion that the three had secured permission to leave their place of duty. Furthermore, he rejected the possibility of extenuating circumstances of race. The army had a responsibility to place service personnel where their skills were most needed, and at Fort Devens, this apparently meant assigning the majority of the black WAC detachment personnel to orderly duty. McCarthy showed little sympathy for excuses of racism and complaints over assigned duties, menial or not.[15]

Underlying the prosecution's arguments was the notion that the women in the black WAC detachment were not mistreated by the army but had been misled by race agitators. Rather than question the role of segregation in the consistent tide of race-related disruptions in the military, McCarthy targeted those whom he assumed brewed discontent among otherwise satisfied personnel. At Fort Devens, he suspected that Morrison best fit this role and accused her of being the ringleader. "Isn't it true, Miss Morrison, that you told defense counsel that these things bothered you for some time[?]" He then asked, "You were one of the ringleaders in getting them upset about their jobs?" Morrison knew that that she had a hand in encouraging the strike action, but she was also certain that she had not caused her peers' resentment against their menial jobs and the neglect of their officers. Responding to McCarthy's accusation, she replied, "I would not say I was a ringleader."[16]

Lost in the debate over the defendants' perceptions of their situation and their understanding of Miles's order were the Wacs' clearly defined reasons for their actions. These extended beyond their assignments to the overall job disparities between white and black Wacs. "I saw the white Wacs and what they were doing and what we were doing," testified Murphy, noting that "it seemed like they had a difference between them because of the race."[17] Likewise, Young insisted that the white Wac orderlies "do practically nothing, sir. They sit with patients, they read stories to them, help them write letters home, or their own people. The work they do is altogether different."[18] McCarthy made much of the long-handled brooms the army supplied to perform their duties and the relatively minimal effort he assumed, incorrectly, they required. Though relevant details to the prosecutor, the niceties of service work in the army simply had no bearing on the women's decision to strike. The four defendants listened and answered his questions on the matter, but they never addressed these facets themselves, focusing instead on the training they had been promised and the discrimination they faced. Throughout the trial, the prosecution rejected their grievances while the defense connected their actions to a confused state of mind. All the while, the defendants asserted, when given the opportunity, that racial discrimination had sparked the strike.

Rainey partially accommodated his clients' desire to air their grievances in order to draw out the discriminatory practices endemic to segregation. His questions, however, emphasized the women's psychological health rather than their personal experiences. By frequently inquiring into how they "felt" about their treatment, he hoped to elicit evidence of clouded reasoning into which he could then integrate his perceptions-of-discrimination defense. For instance, during his cross-examination of Young, he asked her to describe her encounter with the hospital's commanding officer, Colonel Walter Crandall, on the day he spotted her taking a patient's temperature. Young recounted that Crandall had announced in the ward, "I do not have colored [Wacs] as medical technicians. They are here to scrub and wash floors, wash dishes and do all the dirty work."

> RAINEY: Now, did this have any effect on your mental makeup?
> YOUNG: It affected me because I had been working, doing everything that [the nurse] asked.
> RAINEY: I don't mean that. How did you feel afterwards, mentally?
> YOUNG: I felt very bad about it.[19]

This line of questioning enabled Rainey to probe the significance of race in the circumstances that led up to the strike without directly accusing the army of racial discrimination. In this case, it also gave Young the opportunity to add that though "white Wacs were going to medical technician's school," she had realized after her encounter with Crandall that, as an African American, she would not.[20] Similarly, by Rainey asking Green, "How did you feel mentally? Or, what were you thinking?" in regards to her treatment at Fort Devens, he provided her the opportunity to reply "Sir, I felt that all the whites got better treatment and didn't have to do the dirty work that we did on our ward."[21]

McCarthy challenged the defendants' contentions of preferential army treatment of white Wacs over black Wacs and suggested they were based on hearsay rather than facts. Murphy refused to give in on this point with a firm retort: "I never go by what is told me." McCarthy then asked her if she had any concrete evidence to back up her suspicions. Murphy had a list of them. She testified that she had on occasion witnessed white Wacs in the ward offices sitting around. She said she saw them frequently socializing. She said she had never seen them "working like we did—I mean, scrubbing." McCarthy cast doubt on her expertise on the matter through a series of questions that asked her how many white orderlies she had observed, for how long, and how often. Ultimately, Murphy could supply few specifics. She admitted that she had seen only a few white orderlies and had used these observations as a basis for assuming the preferential treatment of white Wacs. "I went by what I thought," she told the court. By the time McCarthy asked her, "You don't know what work they do, do you?" Murphy could only nod, "No, sir." McCarthy then brought her back full circle to his original question. Once again, he asked her, "You had no evidence upon which to base this?" Despite her previous responses, Murphy would not concede his larger point. "I would not say it thay way," she answered.[22]

Murphy's remark obviously confounded McCarthy. Just moments before, he had demonstrated the limits of her personal knowledge of white Wac duties and had even coaxed her admission that she did not know what white orderlies did. Despite this, Murphy maintained that she had evidence of racial discrimination. It was not a contradiction. Instead, Murphy was referencing a different paradigm than the prosecutor. Whereas McCarthy was comparing the duties of white and black orderlies, Murphy was comparing the assignments of all white and black Wacs stationed at Fort Devens. While she may not have seen every white Wac on duty, she had seen enough to get an idea of the disparity between white and black assignments. Her memories were also recent. While her detachment was on strike, she was convalescing at Lovell Hospital North where hundreds of white Wacs worked a variety of jobs, and just a handful as orderlies. Shortly after this round of questioning, a somewhat flustered Murphy tried to explain: "Our members are orderlies . . . the white Wacs, there are so many and the different things they are doing." Since McCarthy did not see it this way, he found Murphy's testimony confusing. In an attempt to get a handle on it, he summed up her observations. "Is it fair for me to make this statement. . . . You felt the colored Wacs were being mistreated because there were comparatively few colored Wacs on the post compared with the white Wacs, and the jobs the colored Wacs had were fewer, whereas the white Wacs filled a large number of different types of jobs. Is that correct?"[23]

McCarthy intended to show a correlation between the large numbers of white Wacs and hence the large number of white Wac assignments and, in contrast, the fewer numbers of black Wacs and their fewer options. He had expected that these seemingly reasonable parallels would refute Murphy's contention that the army deliberately limited black Wacs' opportunities. Instead, McCarthy's summary pinpointed the precise problem as Murphy and her codefendants saw it: whites Wacs served in a greater number of assignments than black Wacs did. From this perspective, Murphy affirmed McCarthy's summary. "Yes, sir," she said.[24]

Later in the trial, Lawson's testimony corroborated the drastic racial imbalance of WAC jobs at Fort Devens. The army dispersed white Wacs to over twenty-five different hospital assignments, mostly in the desirable positions of clerical specialists and medical technicians. In contrast, it confined black Wacs to just four assignments: orderlies (over 60 percent) and a sprinkling of cadre, cooks, and drivers. As a result, all of the black Wacs assigned to the hospital worked as orderlies, whereas just 8 percent of white Wacs at Lovell North did. As noted, McCarthy justified the additional number of jobs for white Wacs by their larger numbers. However, Lawson's statistics revealed that though the number of white Wacs was double that of black Wacs, the former worked more than five times as many different kinds of assignments than did black Wacs.[25] Murphy could not have known this precise data when McCarthy questioned her claims of racial inequity between Wacs at the two base hospitals, nor did she need it to make her assessment. So great was the contrast between black and white Wac assignments that discrimination was, to her and the others in her detachment, readily detectable.

McCarthy's line of questioning confirmed that the prosecutor considered the gross disparities between white and black assignments at Fort Devens a consequence of different skill levels between the two categories of servicewomen. To substantiate his suspicions, he asked Murphy if she felt qualified to perform the same duties that the white Wacs did in the laboratory and at the information desk. "I would not say so," she answered, thus seemingly validating McCarthy's point that Wacs at Fort Devens worked the jobs that best fit their abilities.[26] Rainey soon gave Murphy the opportunity to explain that she did not feel qualified for technical jobs because she had not been trained for them. Nevertheless, McCarthy's questions and conclusions demonstrate the ease with which army officers were willing to attribute even the most obvious job disparities to perceptions of natural race-based abilities.[27]

McCarthy's direct examination of Young offered the prosecutor an ideal opportunity to press home his point that the army assigned personnel to job assignments appropriate to their skills. Of the four defendants, Young had the most years of formal education, including a year of nurses training at Howard University, and thus a stronger case than her codefendants to expect assignment as a medical technician. On the stand, she explained that she had enlisted to train and work in this capacity. With her education on the table, McCarthy referred to Young's academic record to question her qualifications for the position. He announced to the court that the private with nursing ambitions had failing marks in a chemistry and a psychology class and suggested that Howard had asked her to leave school. Young refuted the charge, claiming that Howard "did ask me to continue on and take my chemistry over again." The prosecutor then tested her medical knowledge.

> MCCARTHY: What is the difference between systolic and diastolic pressure, do you know?
> YOUNG: Not now, sir. I am quite confused. I couldn't directly come out and tell you.
> MCCARTHY: I don't want to confuse you. You testified a few minutes ago that you took blood pressure at the Lovell General Hospital.
> YOUNG: Yes, I did.
> MCCARTHY: You don't know the difference between systolic and diastolic pressure, do you, Miss Young?

Rainey objected to the line of inquiry, interjecting that Young "might be able to read systolic and diastolic and not know the difference between them." The court overruled him and allowed Young to answer the question. At that point, McCarthy volunteered, "I won't press it." He didn't need to. By then, he had seriously compromised Young's credibility to perform as a competent medical technician.[28]

McCarthy characterized the four defendants as women with unrealistic goals. If discrepancies existed between black and white Wac jobs, he argued, they were due to a deficiency of abilities, not discrimination in the army. Wacs, he asserted, enlisted to serve where their abilities best suited army needs. Since the army had assigned the majority of black Wacs at Fort Devens to serve as orderlies, it followed that the majority were best suited for this labor.[29] Though unstated, parallels between orderly work and black women's customary role as domestics were profoundly evident.

The prosecutor's focus on job suitability (and the white conception of black women's suitability for menial labor) compelled Rainey to keep in check references to domestic labor. For instance, when McCarthy asked Young, "Did you ever do menial work before you came in the Army?," Rainey objected before she had a chance to answer. He then rephrased the question to establish that Young had worked in an office before enlisting.[30] No doubt in another attempt to counteract the popular imagery of black women as cleaning women, Rainey called to the stand Private Alberta Doss, the only witness for the defense, and asked if she had "ever been a maid." Doss replied, "only at home."[31]

The image of black women as maids lingered over the trial, thereby allowing McCarthy to link the defendants' refusal to do the work the army expected of them and which they clearly could do to personal character flaws, including a poor work ethic. Doss's testimony in this regard highlights a fundamental difference in the way the defendants and the prosecutor viewed complying with orders given the hierarchal segmentations of U.S. society. For McCarthy, following orders and doing one's job well was a matter of personal responsibility. For Doss and the defendants, following orders under discriminatory conditions required some swallowing of one's self-respect.

> MCCARTHY: (referring to Doss's orderly duties) You didn't get down on your knees and scrub the floor?
> DOSS: No, sir.
> MCCARTHY: You considered scrubbing floors with a long-handled broom beneath you[r] dignity. Is that correct?
> DOSS: That is beneath my dignity.

McCarthy then asked her if she "emptied the garbage" as part of her duties at Lovell Hospital.

DOSS: I did.

MCCARTHY: That was not anything unusual to you, was it, emptying garbage?

DOSS: I done it for a reason at home. I did it because I didn't like the idea of living in filth.

MCCARTHY: (in regards to pushing food carts) You felt that was beneath your dignity?

DOSS: Not exactly beneath my dignity. I couldn't take it out on the patients.

MCCARTHY: What else did you consider beneath your dignity? Washing windows?

DOSS: Washing windows. Sir, I didn't think we went in the Army, when I joined the Army that I joined the Army to wash windows. I could have stayed at home and been a maid.[32]

Cross-examining Doss, Rainey asked what job she had envisioned doing as a Wac. Doss replied recreational hostess and listed her experience working with her former high school sports and drama teams. McCarthy then asked if her recruiter had told her she "would be assigned duties in the Army that you were best fitted for, or that the Army thought you were best fitted for?" Doss replied the latter, prompting Rainey to sharply paraphrase the question: "Have you ever been told you were best fitted, by anybody, for menial service?" The prosecutor objected to Rainey's revision, and the law member agreed.[33] By suggesting that the army discriminated against African American women by assuming they were best fit for menial labor, Rainey had overstepped his boundaries.

The defense attorney had to carefully maneuver around directly implicating the army in racist practices. It was not easy, and he sometimes slipped. For instance, after asking Young to list her duties, which included cleaning wards, washing dishes, cooking, and serving food, Rainey asked if she felt "that work . . . was assigned to you because you were one of the colored Wacs?" The prosecution objected, and the law member sustained the objection on the grounds that it was leading. The message was clear: Rainey could not veer far from his perception-of-discrimination strategy. This plan, however, created a contoured defense that tried the patience of the law member, the other board members, and above all, the prosecutor. By the end of the first day, McCarthy was begging the court and Rainey to know the reason for Doss's testimony. Rainey explained that since Doss was present when Miles issued the order, she could explain the circumstances that "cause[d] these girls to become temporarily insane" the day they disobeyed the general's order.[34]

McCarthy protested. Doss was not a defendant, so her testimony was irrelevant. Furthermore, he explained, "My objection is that anything that happened two or three days before this happened is not material."[35] Rainey countered that the perceptions of racial job disparities were central to the case. To avoid wading into the prohibited territory of institutionalized racial discrimination, he emphasized the anxious state of mind that these perceived disparities had caused his clients.

Rainey sought every available angle to demonstrate how his clients' insubordination evolved from mental instability. The disparity they felt, he argued, led to great frustration, confusion, and the feeling that the army was discriminating against them. Ultimately this resulted in "the temporary condition of irresponsibility." After all, he reminded the court, "at all times, a person must be sane in order to commit a crime in the Army." He urged the court, therefore, to understand that on March 10, when Miles ordered the WAC detachment to duty, his clients "were temporarily deranged. That is, bordering on temporary insanity and so confused that they didn't know what they were doing."[36]

Debunking his clients' legitimate grievances by declaring the women delusional and unable to cope with reality assisted Rainey's attempt to bring the defendants' accounts of discrimination into the public record, yet it also played on the stereotypes of black women that had slotted Murphy, Morrison, Green, and Young into orderly assignments. Many white Americans in the 1940s required little convincing that the defendants were, as African Americans, unintelligent, and as women, childlike and emotional. As an African American himself, Rainey understood and most certainly experienced the indignities of white presumptions of the frailty of the black mind. Nevertheless, during the trial, he sought to exploit this presumption to his, if not the defendants', advantage. Modern readers may note his purposeful irony in describing his clients' "confusion" upon joining the army to fight racism abroad, only to feel discriminated against at home. With this statement, Rainey brought before the court an incredible paradox of the war that African Americans captured in their oft-repeated question, "what are we fighting for?"[37] Similar irony, however, failed to appear in Rainey's comments regarding the defendants' gender. Referring to Morrison's alleged hysteria, a term frequently used at the time to describe women's bouts of crying, Rainey remarked, "we know the sensibility of the female structure, their physical makeup, their sensibility, very delicate, and subject to emotions where man may contain himself."[38]

One might wonder if the defendants had pondered whether their esteemed attorney could have defended them with less insult to their intelligence. Certainly, Rainey's strategy, one that depended on presenting ample evidence of his clients' confused state of mind, provided the four a number of opportunities to describe their treatment at Fort Devens. Nevertheless, his portrayal of them as confused and mentally unbalanced undermined their observations of inequities and their credibility as capable servicewomen. Years later, Morrison expressed her opinion that Rainey took the case to fulfill an obligation to the NAACP. He was "not really interested in us," she said. "We all felt that way."[39]

Rainey's psychological defense signified an important addition to the NAACP's arsenal of legal strategies that would prove increasingly viable by the next decade. In the landmark *Brown v. the Board of Education of Topeka* case, Thurgood Marshall employed a similar argument to demonstrate the deeply negative psychological effects of segregation on African American children. As a veteran, Rainey well understood the debilitating effects of racism on black soldiers' opportunities, discipline, and morale. Through his defense strategy of perceptions of discrimination, he had hoped to convey the extent of this impact to the officers judging the case and to the press covering it.[40] Unfortunately, having learned about the case just a week prior to the trial (and advising his clients to waive the additional two days authorized), he had little time to adequately prepare himself or the defendants on the finer points of a psychological defense strategy.

Evidently, Rainey assumed that a defense strategy based on a lack of maturity and intellect required some distancing from his low-ranking, female clients. "We gentlemen," he would later advise the court, "we must by a measure of our indulgence or plane of our indulgence have to look down to their level, their background, to the way they were thinking, before we can do justice."[41] At times, Rainey appeared more interested in emphasizing his socioeconomic and gender connections with the "gentlemen" of the court than in aligning himself with the female defendants, despite their shared racial identity.

When discussing the race as a whole, Rainey spoke of a unified struggle, declaring that "it is a tough thing to be in this country a colored person."

When discussing his female clients, he described them and their actions as "confused" and "misguided." Referring to Young and her failed attempts to gain nursing experience, he gestured, "note this is a most pathetic case."[42] As racially conscious as the local NAACP attorney was, he demonstrated little sensitivity of his clients' gender or class. Furthermore, Rainey's inclination to address McCarthy as "brother" throughout the trial took a chance that those judging the case would find the address too informal if not, for those not used to considering black men in a fraternal way, outright irritating.[43]

Without a doubt, Rainey hoped to free the women, yet he also appeared intent on using the well-publicized trial to encourage white Americans' understanding of the demoralizing intricacies of segregation in the military. "Many things are involved," he told the court, "not only as to the merits of the particular case, but as to our social order."[44] The social order certainly consisted of a racial hierarchy, but also a gender hierarchy. In fact, Rainey invoked both realities, though to very different ends. While vehemently decrying racism, he advanced a patriarchal perspective of women's weaknesses. This strategy gained Rainey valuable opportunities to stress the racially discriminatory practices at Fort Devens, yet it also gave short-shrift to his clients' capacity as women to appropriately manage the situation. When the Law Member inquired into Morrison's ability to reason between right and wrong, Rainey assured him, "She is a normal intelligent person, but with the circumstances of part of this over-all picture of circumstances had induced a state of mind which she was unable or incapable of differentiating between right and wrong as the Army lays it out."[45]

Rainey's reliance on a state-of-confusion defense often put the defendants in a tough spot while on the stand. This was the case when McCarthy, who ironically gave the Wacs more credit for knowing what they were doing than their lawyer, asked Morrison if she understood General Miles's order to report to work or face a court-martial. Given Rainey's assertions of her and her codefendants' confused states of mind that day, Morrison remained silent. Morrison knew that Miles had clearly delivered the order and that she had fully understood it, yet was not sure how to respond given her attorney's stance. Three times McCarthy asked her the same question, and three times she said nothing in return. At last, Rainey interceded and insisted that McCarthy break down the question into fragments. The prosecutor obliged, and through a series of abbreviated inquiries, he asked Morrison if she understood the order to fall out, the order to fall out in front of the building, the order to fall into formation, and finally the order to march to her ward. Morrison haltingly answered yes to all, only to pause once more when McCarthy repeated the question in full. Again she fell silent until the law member urged her to respond. At that point, she wasted no time conceding that "I understood him."[46]

Rainey questioned the defendants to assess their mental states on March 10 in hopes of substantiating that the four were experiencing "temporary insanity" when Miles issued his order. Morrison, Young, Green, and Murphy readily related incidents in which they felt deeply frustrated—though not to the extent of a "monomaniac." Rainey's dogged efforts to manipulate his clients' testimonies diverted the women from explaining their actions to confessing confusion. Once again, Morrison is on the stand.

> RAINEY: How was your brain functioning? Were you confused, or what was your state of mind?
> MORRISON: The only way I can explain is to tell you this—If I had had time to think it over I know now that I would not have told Lieutenant Lawson what I did.
> RAINEY: I am not talking about that. Did your head feel normal?
> MORRISON: Yes, sir.
> RAINEY: No, did your brain—
> MCCARTHY: She said, "Yes."
> RAINEY: Maybe she don't know what normal means.
> . . .
> RAINEY: Did your head feel as clear as it usually felt, that day?
> MORRISON: Yes, sir.
> RAINEY: Do you understand me?
> MCCARTHY: (Once again stepping in) She said, "Yes."
> . . .
> RAINEY: Did you understand my questions when I asked you if your head felt clear and you could think as well on that day, as you usually felt?
> MORRISON: I felt that day that I wanted to scream and scream, and I did.
> RAINEY: (At last, getting the response he sought) You just felt hysterical.[47]

The prosecutor's questions occasionally elicited more relevant testimony than Rainey's investigations into the defendants' mental states. It was during McCarthy's examination that Green detailed her frustrations over the different duties of white and black Wacs. When questioning Young on her statement that she "couldn't go on," the prosecutor gave her the opportunity to explain that she meant that she could not continue under the same conditions, which she then summarized.[48] Similarly, McCarthy had asked Morrison to explain her startling declaration to Lawson that "I have been to work, but I don't think I can go on. Put my name down for court-martial." McCarthy's questions, therefore, also revealed important insight into the women's condition and their motivations behind the strike.[49]

To varying degrees, the theme of a higher cause ran through the defendants' testimony. Protecting and asserting their rights as African Americans and as African American Wacs had propelled Morrison, Young, and Green to participate in the initial strike and Murphy to join once she learned about it. Seeing their struggle as part of larger struggles explains why the four had refused to work even when they knew they would face a court-martial as a result. No one voiced this theme of a higher cause as stridently as Murphy when she boldly declared that she would "take death before I would go back to work."[50] Clearly, Murphy interpreted her actions in the larger context of the civil rights movement.

Rainey understood the desire to challenge racism and was doing his best to use the court-martial and the publicity it attracted to expose racial discrimination in the military. Less apparent is whether he understood that his clients' commitment to the civil rights movement was at least equal to his own. His characterization of them as confused, "temporarily deranged," and inclined toward displays of a monomania suggests that he did not. Certainly, his creatively-packaged defense strategy, necessitated by the military's disregard of racism as a defense, allowed some discussion of the racial discrimination his clients suffered. At the same time, it also presented his clients as weak-minded and susceptible to outlandish notions of imagined victimization. Portraying Green, Morrison, Murphy, and Young as competent servicewomen consciously acting on behalf of other black Wacs would have severely damaged his argument. If Rainey's defense was a total ruse, and he was in fact aware of his clients' self-sacrifice, he did not let on.

On the other hand, the prosecution's questions leave little doubt that McCarthy was oblivious to the possibility that the defendants had acted for the greater good. On the second day of the trial, he challenged the logic behind Morrison's declaration that she would strike if it would help her people. McCarthy wondered aloud why she was involving others, noting that "your people had not done anything." Dismissing a collective purpose behind her work stoppage, he concluded, "you were only looking out for yourself on that day, weren't you?" Increasingly exasperated, Morrison managed to hold her anger in check. "Exactly not my own self," she replied. Before the prosecutor moved on to his next point, he saw fit to remind the private that she, not her people, had disobeyed the order.[51]

Citizens in the same country, yet with experiences worlds apart, McCarthy and Morrison were speaking at cross-purposes that day. As a white male officer, McCarthy did not have to fight for his basic rights and apparently found it inconceivable that other Americans did. During the trial, he expressed his certitude that army policies ensured fair treatment of all troops. For Morrison and other enlisted black Wacs, however, these same policies rarely stretched far enough to similarly include them, putting them in a position of having to fight for and defend the same rights that McCarthy took for granted. Morrison's powerful statement attests to her understanding that she was not alone in her plight, and to the strength she drew from the civil rights movement's stance against injustice and the inspiration she gained from the many acts of collective and individual resistance measures that fueled it. Morrison, in her unconfused mind, was indeed striking "for her people."

The trial extended into a second day to accommodate the extensive testimony among the key persons involved. It might have required a third had Colonel Crandall been in court. Instead, he was reportedly on a thirty-day leave. The timing of his departure naturally aroused suspicion but was not entirely unwelcomed by the NAACP, whose acting secretary, Roy Wilkins, had requested the colonel's transfer.[52] Without Crandall, the law members and observers would rely heavily on the testimonies of the defendants' two other officers, Lieutenants Lawson and Stoney.

Lawson was an especially significant party in the case of Murphy, who had been convalescing at Lovell Hospital North during the strike. Released shortly after Miles had departed Fort Devens, Murphy insisted that the Wac officer put her name down for a court-martial. Lawson denied her request on the grounds that Murphy was not on duty so could not be on strike. Once Murphy had her assignment, she again reported to the white lieutenant and refused to work. Unlike the others who were charged with disobeying Miles, Murphy was charged with disobeying Lawson.

As commander of all Wacs at Fort Devens, Lawson was privy to essential information to the case. In response to Rainey's inquiries, she revealed that, between the two hospitals, 40 percent of white Wacs were clerical staff, while no black Wacs held this position. Broadening the scope to include the cadre who worked in the barracks, just 6 percent of the entire black Wac detachment served in this capacity. Despite the vast disparities in assignment by race, the prosecution asked Lawson if she had "observed any discrimination between the duties assigned to colored Wacs and white Wacs in the same MOS (Military Occupation Specialty)." Lawson replied that she had not, and recalled her own weeklong convalescence at Lovell Hospital North, where she had seen that white Wacs also "scrubbed, cleaned, mopped up, and washed dishes." Under further questioning, Lawson acknowledged that just 15 of the 173 white Wacs worked as orderlies, proportionally just 8 percent compared to 60 percent of black Wacs.[53] Neither she nor McCarthy felt that these numbers reflected discriminatory assignments.

The court also summoned the detachment's commander, Lieutenant Stoney. Her testimony was additionally crucial because she was, like the defendants, an African American Wac. Consequently, observers could reasonably assume that if racism existed at Fort Devens, she would be aware of it. On the stand, however, Stoney indicated that her primary allegiance was to her superior officers. When McCarthy asked her, "Have you ever observed any difference in the duties that the white Wac orderlies have in the hospital and those duties that the colored orderlies have?" Stoney responded, "I have not, sir." The defense asked her how she knew what white Wacs did in comparison with her own troops. Stoney explained that in December, she had regularly visited Lieutenant Sophie Gay, the officer she had recently replaced, during her convalescence at Lovell Hospital North. While there, she saw white Wacs cleaning the wards and working in the kitchen, thereby offering personal evidence that white and black orderlies did similar work. Likewise, she affirmed the prosecution's position that her troops did not qualify for the same technician and clerical assignments that white Wacs did.[54]

Rainey challenged each point of Stoney's testimony. According to the defendants, he said, members of the detachment had brought numerous complaints before her. Stoney retorted that while her troops had occasionally noted their dissatisfaction with their jobs, they had not tied their complaints to the duties of white Wacs.[55] She recalled one exception, KP, which black but not white Wacs performed at Fort Devens. Stoney said that she had only learned of this grievance during the March 8 meeting with the orderlies, the day before the strike, and therefore had no time beforehand to take it up with Lawson.[56] Young disagreed, insisting that members of her detachment had first complained to Stoney about KP duty as early as November.[57] Rainey also grilled Stoney over a lack of responsiveness to her subordinates' concerns about their duties. She countered that she was in charge only of assignments, not the classifications that determined those assignments.

Stoney was partially correct. Crandall's requisition of black Wacs primarily for orderly duties sent her notice of her superior officer's intentions and her limited authority over her troop's assignments. The reclassification of the three surgical technicians to work as orderlies certainly corroborated this assessment. Without leeway in this regard, Stoney's working knowledge of her authority over assignments paled in comparison with that of Lawson's. As an officer, Lawson assured Rainey, she had the right to submit requests for changes through a Classification Board. She then summarized the qualifications needed for technical assignments.[58] Working with white Wacs, Lawson was familiar with the process. Working with black Wacs, Stoney, and her predecessor, Lieutenant Sophie Gay, were not.

Rainey plied Stoney with questions to ascertain why she had not attempted to address her troops' grievances, as was her duty as the women's detachment commander, a role she assumed a month before the strike. Stoney also had a duty to uphold army orders. She handled these often conflicting expectations by keeping her emotions in check. It was not an easy task, yet one she stoically accepted. Yes, she too had found Crandall's use of the term "black Wac" disturbing. "I got mad," she testified, "and then I got all right." Yes, she had also been deeply embarrassed by her own troops' crying and cursing during the March 9 meeting with Crandall, yet she declined to castigate the enlisted Wacs, noting only that "I felt they could have handled their emotions a little better than that."[59] Pressed between her two allegiances, Stoney played it safe by smoothing over rather than addressing problems and avoiding rather than confronting conflicts. In response to Rainey's questions, she sidestepped these reasons and cited instead the limitations of both her authority and her troops' abilities. When this was not possible, the new detachment commander, neither confident nor comfortable in her leadership role and without a single other black Wac officer on post to consult, aligned her dual responsibilities according to one overriding constant: Crandall's intention that the majority of her detachment members work as orderlies. Stoney may have wanted to address her troops' concerns, though within this limited framework, she resorted to offering encouragement instead.

On the afternoon of the second day of the court-martial, closing statements began. Defense Attorney Rainey reiterated the defendants' perceptions of discrimination that, as he phrased it, "their immature minds" had fostered. In an effort to officially distance his comments (calibrated to subtly invite criticism of segregation) from a formal condemnation of the practice, Rainey insisted that "I am not saying this is true, but they felt they were persecuted, and this persecution complex was driving them on." They were like "misguided children," away from home for the first time and not knowing enough about the intricacies of race relations or military policy. Pointing to Murphy, he lamented, "This girl said, 'I will take death.' Think of the poor immature girl who says that. They were confused, gentlemen."[60]

Rainey explained Murphy and the defendants' state of mind by adroitly inserting many of the arguments against a segregated army. "America, of course, is the only country in the world that segregates soldiers because of color." It was therefore confusing to the women, he argued, to read that black and white troops from England and Canada worked side by side while U.S. troops did not. Rainey added that it was not "you gentlemen's responsibility, not the army's responsibility, but probably the responsibility of a democracy which is somewhat defective." It was the "over-all" picture of enlisting to join the fight against discrimination abroad while being segregated at home that was problematic for the women. "They read the papers and these things are preying on their minds." His clients' feelings, therefore, "whether they are justified or not," were real to them.[61]

Unable to directly link his clients' perceived confusion to racial discrimination in the army, Rainey emphasized the defendants' role in their confused state. "It can be compared to the situation of a rat that has been caught, and it is fighting, popping back, as you hit it, in this terrible position from which there is no escape." It was an apt comparison to describe the trap that segregation created for African Americans and one to which Rainey obviously could relate. Rats, however, also represent small brains, and whether intentionally or not, Rainey exploited this characteristic when he attributed his clients' confusion to their female thought processes. "It is, gentlemen, intellectual development." Shortly after, he proposed, "They were confused, gentlemen. Their minds were not the minds of normal persons. They had what we call a persecution complex." Rainey appealed to the officers of the court to "look down to their level, their background, to the way they were thinking" as they evaluated the defendants and their actions.[62]

When McCarthy rose to offer his closing statement, he summarily discounted the defense's allusions to institutional racism, perceived or real. Stoney's testimony, he asserted, verified that discrimination was not at issue in this case. The defendants were not misassigned or ill-treated. Indeed, he had asked all five of the Wacs who testified, including Doss, about their duties, and heard no complaints that they were too "arduous." The women worked as orderlies, not because they were black, but because their skills were best suited for this task. The army was not racist, he insisted, and no doubt for the benefit of the black press reporters in the room, offered assurance of the army's open attitude toward African Americans: "Just because people are colored from an accident of birth . . . we hold nothing against them." Listing several noteworthy achievements of the race, he added that "we appreciate the fact that some of them, some of their race are the best scholars, orators, lawyers and so forth of our time." Having acknowledged the race issue, he put it aside with a reminder that the court-martial had not been convened to discuss the finer points of army policy but to learn whether the four defendants had knowingly and willfully disobeyed a direct order from their commanding officers. "The issue is as simple and direct as that," he said.[63]

McCarthy then turned to the issue of the defendants' gender and implored the jury to resist a lenient verdict "because they were women and so forth." The defendants were enlisted soldiers who had failed to perform their duties.[64] In a searing indictment of the Wacs for having left their posts, the prosecutor delivered an unsparing chastisement: "These people are members of the armed forces who didn't care for their job, because it was beneath their dignity to carry garbage or do that sort of work. They didn't want to do their job because they didn't like it. We can't run an Army that way. There are lots of things I have to do that I don't like and that you have to do that you don't like, but we do them the best we can, even though we may grumble, and take *a chance of getting something else*" (emphasis added).[65]

With this final statement, the prosecutor had inadvertently hit on the exact motivation behind the strike. The women had risked a court-martial precisely because they had no "chance of getting something else." So at odds were McCarthy's experiences from that of the defendants that he compared the reasons for the strike to common workplace grumbling and condensed their grievances to a simple "They were not satisfied with their jobs. Isn't that just too bad."[66] McCarthy seemed oblivious to the fact that the Wacs' refusal to work had required tremendous courage wrought over months of broken promises. By challenging the army, all four had put their freedom and their futures on the line, hardly the outcome they had expected when enlisting. Except for Murphy, all had spotless military records that they had hoped would translate into skilled army jobs, satisfying civilian careers, and an escape from menial labor. Only after months of unaddressed grievances that threatened these goals did Morrison, Young, Murphy, and Green risk a court-martial. McCarthy was oblivious to the fact that when African American women took the "chance of getting something else," it often required that they *not* follow army policy.

In the late afternoon of March 20, after two days of testimony, the court members adjourned to deliberate the case. Rainey left immediately after the trial for his Boston home, seemingly pleased with his performance. The law member, after all, had given him wide berth to pursue his arguments, and he had taken advantage of the opportunity to expose the debilitating effects of segregation. As he departed Fort Devens, he told reporters that he felt the trial had been fair.

An hour and ten minutes later, the members of the court returned their verdict. In a secret ballot, two-thirds of them found the four women guilty of disobeying their commanding officers. The sentence followed, and it stunned those in the courtroom. For their act of insubordination, each defendant received one year of confinement with hard labor, loss of pay, and a dishonorable discharge. Once in the corridor, Morrison "broke down completely" and had to be carried to a waiting vehicle. From his home, Rainey retracted his earlier statement and declared that "what they did was not their fault, but the result of a defective democracy which rendered them incapable of knowing what they were doing."[67]

Rainey's assessment was only half right. The four defendants had knowingly disobeyed their officers' orders by refusing to work, and on this premise, the army indicted and convicted them. On the other hand, a defective democracy had induced the women to strike, and a defective military court of law had reduced their noble reasons to strike to a poor work ethic. Ultimately, the army tried the women less for failing to report for duty than for drawing a line at the discriminatory treatment they would accept. Within the restricted parameters of the military's justice system, such grounds for insubordination were not permitted, and so they were ignored. Testimony such as Murphy's statement, "I believed that I was doing the right thing. To better the way we were treated," was irrelevant to the proceedings.[68] Reflecting the defective democracy that the army was fighting to safeguard, the court overlooked this and similar remarks.

Consequently, the trial ended in a guilty verdict, as did virtually all courts-martial of African American service personnel before and during World War II.[69] As the Fort Devens court-martial illustrates, the era's military judicial system essentially guaranteed this outcome by dismissing racism as a defense. Unable to argue racial discrimination in cases in which it applied, defense lawyers were forced to seek alternative explanations for their clients' actions. Not surprisingly, fabricated justifications in lieu of the unencumbered truth ensured arguments built on flawed foundations. Awkward justifications also necessitated a convoluted defense. Rainey tiptoed around the actual cause of his clients' actions by submitting that, though racial discrimination may not have existed at the Lovell hospitals, the women perceived that it did, though they may not have, in fact, been experiencing it at all. McCarthy occasionally noted his forbearance of defense counsel's tangled and often preposterous arguments, and he had cause. McCarthy also had the privilege of being able to lay bare his position as he saw it. Rainey did not. In racially charged cases during World War II, defense lawyers did not have the luxury of presenting the full truth in their arguments.

It is doubtful that McCarthy or anyone else present that day would ever hear a case argued in quite the same manner—or would have that day had Rainey been defending black male defendants. Americans viewed servicemen as representing the epitome of manhood, an idealized prototype of strength, courage, and self-control. Lawyers presenting male clients as weak, confused, and prone to hysterics would have delegitimized them as competent soldiers, thereby playing into the hands of those who had long derided the notion of black men in uniform. Female soldiers of any race were not held to the same standards of strength and courage—defined as masculinity in the military—that the army so honored. Deliberately separating them into a corps of their own, the army attempted to preserve conventional gendered distinctions by celebrating Wacs' femininity and their role as assistants to its main forces of men. Despite the focus on race during the trial, the Fort Devens trial indicates how the patriarchal army (as represented by McCarthy) and patriarchal society (as represented by Rainey) defined Wacs as women first and as soldiers second.

The Fort Devens court-martial of black Wacs reflected the entrenched subjugation of African American women in U.S. society in the 1940s, a pattern that the army's system of justice both tapped into and reinforced. To be sure, the trial in some ways broke from those patterns. It boasted a relatively diverse panel of officers, granted Rainey unusual leeway to expound on controversial theories, and allowed the defendants to compare their treatment to white Wacs. Draped in the standard protocols, the trial seemingly enshrined impartiality through uniform military procedures. When the verdict came down, observers could assume that it was free of bias.

Yet, these same features may also be seen as showpieces of a well-choreographed trial designed to assure civilians of the inherent fairness of military justice despite the usual outcome. The army provided the stage (a small, crowded courtroom unsuitable for a lengthy trial), the script (restricting a racial defense and evidently briefing Stoney), and the cast of supporting characters (perhaps the most gendered and racially diverse of the war, yet all beholden to the military hierarchy that controlled the proceedings). Under these circumstances, McCarthy could project black Wacs as best suited for unskilled labor and count on Lawson's and Stoney's agreement of the point. The constraints under which Rainey operated encouraged a defense based on exploiting patriarchal perceptions of women's weaknesses. Indeed, Rainey indulged the male dominance of the courtroom by consistently referring to the officers hearing the case as "men" and "gentlemen" despite the presence of two women on the board. The setting wholly reinforced race, gender, and class hierarchies. Testimonies exhibited the superior status of white Wacs (in the person of Lawson) over black Wacs (Stoney and her troops), and of the all-white and male ward men over the all-black and female orderlies. The members of the court —all officers—ran the proceedings and stood in judgement of the enlisted defendants. With the veneer of blind justice intended to evoke fairness and equality, the trial operated under the same normative patterns that traditionally subordinated African American women, both civilians and military personnel, to the bottom of the state's social hierarchy.

Black women's social subjugation was also apparent in the language used during the trial. McCarthy addressed the defendants as "Miss" rather than "Private." Though quick to recognize their responsibilities as Wacs, he seemed reluctant to accord them the respect of their military status. He and others consistently referred to the enlisted women, all in their twenties, as "girls." U.S. women in the 1940s by and large accepted the reference, unperturbed by its diminutive connotation, yet at the court-martial, "girls" was used to refer to the enlisted women, though not to their female officers. Several testimonies described the defendants' crying as "hysteria," a term denoting an uncontrollable emotional outburst, typically by women. Referring to the ward men as "ward masters" during a trial of black women no doubt conjured connections to slavery. The ease and regularity in which "girl," "hysteria," and "ward master" (instead of "ward men") were used during the trial inconspicuously reinforced cultural stereotypes of black women as immature, emotional, and suited for menial laborer.

As the defendants asserted their rights and described the discrimination they experienced, both attorneys reframed the women's explanations as either delusional self-aggrandizement or as utter confusion, though for different purposes. McCarthy sought to portray the Wacs as subversive and lazy and as stubbornly claiming capabilities beyond their reach. Rainey tried to convince the court that they were mentally immature, emotional, and incapable of making proper sense of their situation. Both men sought to divest the women of their agency to think logically for themselves by exploiting the presumed weaknesses of their female sex. Despite the pronounced focus on race during the trial, the case was firmly rooted in the era's prevailing gendered paradigms.

After the court announced the guilty verdicts and sentence, military police escorted the visibly distressed Wacs from the courtroom. The women may not have been surprised by Lawson's testimony, but they might have expected more support from their defense attorney and their detachment commander. Instead, the latter two had failed them, Rainey as an African American and Stoney as an African American woman. The four also may have felt betrayed by their ward men, with whom they had worked and in some cases were developing friendships. In the end, however, it would not have mattered if Rainey had presented his clients as exemplary servicewomen, if Stoney had backed her troops' claims of discrimination, or if Wicks had testified in court, as Young claimed he had said in private, that black Wacs were getting "a dirty deal." Regardless, the army would have convicted the four. The case was too well-grounded in the prevailing perceptions of race for another outcome. (The first successful use of race as a defense in a military court of law occurred in 1971.)[70] Furthermore, the protocol of courts-martial—which denied the defendants a jury of their peers and permitted demeaning images of black women to stand as evidence—reinforced the status quo. The Wacs were contesting these parameters on multiple levels of race, gender, and class, and for this reason, they could not have won.

5
The Civilian Reaction

[The trial was] NOT a Massachusetts case, [but rather] a showdown between the United States Army's jim-crow, Anti-Negro element and the American Democracy this country is seeking to bring to the world.
—Marty Richardson, *Boston Chronicle*

Following the March 20, 1945, court-martial and conviction of the four Wacs, the army transferred Anna Morrison, Johnnie Murphy, Alice Young, and Mary Green from Lovell Hospital North's wards to the security section of the facility, where bars on the windows provided a harsh reminder of their new status. There they bided their time awaiting the appeal, utterly devastated by the guilty verdict. "If things don't . . . change soon," Young wrote to a friend, "I think I'll just finish things up my way by ending it all in a long, long sleep and tell them I'll see them in heaven on Judgment Day and finish my Courts-martial in Hell."[1] Morrison admitted years later that after the verdict she "had a hate for the whole world." Like the others, she resented the army reneging on its promises, the prosecutor dismissing their concerns, and their defense lawyer's seeming disinterest in their case. Several days after the trial, each received a trial transcript, a weighty document an inch and a half thick. They promptly discarded their copies into the nearest trash receptacles.[2] Held incommunicado and surrounded by officers who opposed their actions and censored their mail, the distraught women had no way of knowing how strongly their strike was resonating among African Americans and with the domestic aims of their Double V campaign.

By opting for the court-martial, four Wac privates had carved out an opportunity to air their grievances in a military court and, due to the emboldened civil rights movement of the war years, in the court of public opinion, too. The civilian reaction to their conviction was swift. "All of Boston is rife with speculation this week as to the pros and cons of the . . . strike," proclaimed Leotha Hackshaw, a *Pittsburgh Courier* reporter who had attended the trial. "Because the strike of the Negro Wacs is the first of its kind," she added, "the case has aroused unusual interest in this city—especially among the Negro residents."[3] In fact, the case was of keen interest to blacks and to whites in Boston and beyond. After the guilty verdict and the stunning sentence, Marty Richardson, editor of the *Boston Chronicle*, predicted that "the Fort Devens Wac case may well become one of the leading court-martial cases of this war." Since the first day of the strike, the case had rapidly gained national attention and stoked readers' passions across racial and gender lines. A hopeful Richardson effused that the trial was "NOT a Massachusetts case" but rather "a showdown between the United States Army's jim-crow, Anti-Negro elements and the American Democracy this country is seeking to bring to the world."[4] Green, Morrison, Young, and Murphy had taken part in the strike to call attention to grievances of discrimination—and so they had.

A court-martial featuring female defendants was bound to attract local interest during the first years of the WAC, yet the Fort Devens case quickly turned into a cause célèbre that attracted the attention of many of the nation's most prominent persons. The remarkable speed at which the strike gained traction attests to the substantial capacity of the wartime civil rights movement's main components—its organizations and leaders, both national and local; the black press; and ordinary African American citizens—to join forces, work in sync, and effectively make their case to the nation. Converging on the strike by female personnel, each of these battle-worn mainstays of the movement vigorously challenged the army over its treatment of black Wacs at Fort Devens and galvanized action on the women's behalf. Collectively, this loose coalition forced the army to address African American concerns about the case, first through the commander of the First Service Command, General Sherman Miles, who had hoped that the verdict would end public interest in the four Wacs, and ultimately by Henry L. Stimson, the Secretary of War and thus the final arbitrator in the case.

Civil rights organizations stood as a solid pillar of the coalition in support of the Fort Devens Wacs, though none more well-known during the war years than the NAACP. It was, in fact, well-positioned to take charge of the case having received, four days before the strike, Private Harriet Warfield's letter warning that trouble was brewing at Fort Devens. Moreover, as the largest and most renowned civil rights organization in the country, the NAACP held a prominence that gave its leaders access to the highest levels of government. Additionally, it had created in 1940 its Legal Defense Fund (LDF) to contest racial discrimination in the courts. The NAACP's stalwart pursuit of justice on the national stage instilled hope and confidence in African Americans. As a soldier stationed in Georgia noted, "I have found out the only way that our evolution problems can be solved is by organization and I think the NAACP is the one who should see the job through."[5] The soldier's vision was widely shared. When Mary Smith of Philadelphia received her niece's letter describing the appalling treatment of black Wacs at Fort Devens, she turned to the NAACP for help.[6]

The NAACP played a pivotal role in the case from the beginning. Carolyn Moore, the executive secretary of the Philadelphia branch to whom Smith entrusted Warfield's letter, immediately alerted Thurgood Marshall, the chief lawyer of the LDF, about the circumstances at Fort Devens. After the strike, the NAACP contacted the legal head of its Boston branch, Julian Rainey, to secure civilian representation for the defendants, and its Assistant Secretary Roy Wilkins corresponded with Stimson on the Wacs' behalf. Meanwhile, its affiliates across the country sprang into action to assist and complement the national organization's efforts.[7] Back at Fort Devens, local activists investigating the circumstances of the strike were reporting their findings to the NAACP.[8]

The NAACP did not lack for outside partners in the high-profile Wac case, as other organizations and individuals also eagerly took up the cause. The United People's Action Committee in Philadelphia, the American Civil Liberties Union, the American Legion, and the Workers Defense League volunteered their services, as did others who also pressed the nation's leaders to intervene. Chicago's John Brown Organization of America implored President Roosevelt, "will you inform us, show us, by giving these four Colored women their Freedom?" More brazenly, the Negro Youth of Greater Boston assured Stimson that "the whole policy of Jim Crow race discrimination and segregation make a sham and mockery in so far as Negroes are concerned."[9]

African American women's organizations came out in force on behalf of the black Wacs. Black women had a long history of providing vital support for each other, particularly through the empowering collective agency of clubs. The National Council of Negro Women (NCNW) kept especially close tabs on the case.[10] Its president and black Wac mentor, Mary McLeod Bethune, apprised Eleanor Roosevelt of the situation, and both women tried to meet with the WAC director, Colonel Oveta C. Hobby, to discuss it. In ill health brought on by exhaustion, Hobby referred the First Lady to her trusted staff officer, Lieutenant Colonel Westray Boyce.[11] Bethune kept in regular contact with the NAACP, the War Department, and local Bostonians who were investigating the circumstances. She also financially backed a trip to the area by Charles Houston—dean of the Howard University law school, former special counsel to the NAACP, and Thurgood Marshall's mentor— who volunteered his immense skills to locally investigate the incident.[12] Rebecca Stiles Taylor, a Bethune ally in the NACW, contextualized the case in the struggle of all black women. Writing in her *Chicago Defender* column that "the cause of our four WACs belongs to the entire group [of black women]," she predicted that their "names also will be handed down as martyrs for the cause of justice to black women." Jane E. Hunter, president of the Ohio State Federation of Colored Women, urged Stimson to look into the circumstances behind the strike and ensure justice for the convicted Wacs.[13] Regardless of their social status, African American women knew well the indignities of compounded racial and gendered discrimination.[14] From New York to California, leaders of women's organizations followed the case, and so did the women they collectively represented, through membership or in spirit.[15]

African American women responded to the strike action with a sense of urgency, beginning with Carolyn Moore and Mary Smith. Moore was the energetic twenty-nine-year-old executive secretary of the Philadelphia NAACP branch, whose militant strategies often brought her into conflict with the city's black male leaders, while her dedication to ordinary people assured her a popular following among other black Philadelphians. Smith would have known about Moore given her pivotal role in the city's long Transport Workers Union strike and its recent successful conclusion, so when her niece, Harriet Warfield, wrote to her about the treatment of black Wacs at Fort Devens, Smith knew to whom she could entrust the letter. Sensing its importance, Moore immediately fired off a two-page report to Thurgood Marshall and urged expediency in the matter.[16] Soon, ordinary African American women were marshaling their resources to do their part. In Boston, Bessie Hipkins sent Anna Morrison a letter and a dollar. In

Chicago, Ruth M. Apilado closely followed the case and would soon pen a poem to the four. Across the country, others raised the case with officials and funds for the Wacs with the sense that this was their fight, too.

As another pivotal arm of the civil rights movement, the black press published accounts of the Fort Devens strike and court-martial. Without its coverage, the case likely would not have found its way into the main-stream press—and certainly not within a favorable light if it had. In the 1940s, the mainstream press rarely mentioned African Americans outside of crime reports and racial disturbances. The black press filled the void by devoting its pages to African American issues from African American per-spectives.[17] Determined to inform and inspire its readers, editors published stories of individual achievements and collective contributions to the war effort and to the civil rights movement. Their early solidarity around the Double V campaign indicates that while marketplace competitors, they stood united in the battle against racial injustice. Taking the cue from its readers' increasing impatience with white Americans' tolerance of racism, the black press struck a militant tone, often in hard-hitting commentaries. Among the boldest, and hence the most popular of these newspapers, were the *Pittsburgh Courier* (whose editor, Percival L.Prattis, initiated the Double V campaign), the *Chicago Defender*, and the *Afro-American*. Sales soared, as did the number of publications, so that by the early 1940s each major black metropolitan area could boast its own newspaper. As copies made their way to small towns across the nation, readers from coast to coast learned about African Americans, civilians and those in the military, and the risks that these otherwise ordinary citizens took to protest racial discrimination.[18]

In this manner, the black press picked up the story of the Fort Devens strike, widely disseminated updates on the case, championed the Wacs who had resisted discrimination, and rallied national support for the women. Indicating the case's significance to the movement, editors occasionally headlined new developments, and commentators featured the strike in col-umns that railed against racial discrimination. The *Pittsburgh Courier* cited the army as culpable in the affair because it was working against the same principles for which it is fighting. *Chicago Defender* commentator "Charley Cherokee" accused the army of goading the women into insubordination. He argued that the Wacs "got so mad over race prejudice, that they refused to obey orders," thereby doing "just what whites want them to" and getting court-martialed.[19] Such passionate commentaries exonerated the Fort Devens Wacs and castigated their officers.

The rising influence of the black press alarmed many white Americans who objected to its views and feared it as a destabilizing force of radicalism. The FBI regularly monitored its staff while Secretary of War Stimson, interpreting the black press's challenges to the military's segregation policies as a threat to national security, tried to block its newspapers' distribution at military installations.[20] Some white service personnel did their part by warning black troops that these papers "distorted facts to the detriment of the Negroes themselves."[21] Personal experiences convinced African Americans otherwise. Alice Young's scrapbook clippings of her court-martial includes nineteen articles. All appear to be from black publications, and none from the mainstream white press.[22]

The civil rights movement was at its core a grassroots movement in which, as the Fort Devens case demonstrates, ordinary citizens formed its foremost pillar by laying the foundations for nationwide campaigns. In March 1945, these included the Fort Devens Wacs who resisted discrimination and countless African Americans who supported them. In Boston, a locally prominent pastor, the Reverend Kenneth Hughes, delivered a sermon that compared the Wacs to Queen Esther and honored them as "strong and courageous defenders willing to stand up for their rights and the rights of others."[23] Strangers sent money to aid the Wacs' appeal, and a few wrote poems exalting the Wacs' courage. Others contacted their local organizations about the case; the Baltimore NAACP affiliate reported that "our office has been flooded with letters and telegrams urging that something be done about this injustice."[24] African Americans wrote their national civil rights leaders and organizations and requested that they use their high-level contacts to resolve the matter. Many sent their concerns directly to President Roosevelt, precipitating a meeting at the White House with Hobby to discuss the matter. Ordinary citizens flooded Stimson's office with letters demanding justice for the women. Local activists monitored events on the ground, while others further afield encouraged members of their religious congregations, veterans' organizations, civic groups, union locals, and college fraternities and sororities to take action. Held incommunicado and unaware of this vast network of support, the Fort Devens Wacs nevertheless greatly benefitted from the array of individual and collective interest in their case and the wealth of resources and seasoned strategies this involvement lent to their cause.

The collaborative mix of civil rights activists and organizations, the black press, and ordinary citizens unleashed a wellspring of popular support for the Wacs. By the end of March 1945, the *Chicago Defender* acknowledged this grand synergized spirit in an article titled "Notables Demand Probe in Conviction of Wacs." Though providing an extensive list of the prominent individuals and organizations, it managed to name just a fraction of those involved.[25] Ultimately, the article's title failed to capture the full breadth of the campaign, in which each pivotal arm of the civil rights movement, working in unscripted tandem, inspired and fueled the actions of the others. In the Wac case, extensive grassroots efforts provided the local structure and funds on which prominent leaders and national organizations depended. National leaders, in turn, wielded this massive outpouring of citizens' action as a mandate to keep the pressure on high-level persons to whom ordinary African Americans did not have access. Additionally, their prominence brought widespread attention to the campaign, which stimulated other grassroots actions and facilitated coordinated efforts. Meanwhile, the black press was reporting it all—local and national efforts—keeping the story fresh, relevant, and in the public eye.

The confluence of African American actions over a case featuring female soldiers soon attracted the attention of the mainstream press. In contrast to African Americans' fulsome support of the convicted Wacs, the mainstream press found little to excuse in the defendants' insubordination. Commentators generally praised Miles for his patience, focused on the women's willful violation of an order, and accepted Lawson's and Stoney's testimony that white and black Wac orderlies performed the same duties. Some papers suggested that the female defendants were unsuited for military service, as did the *Atlanta Constitution* when it pointed out that Lovell Hospital cared for "hundreds of soldiers who have been wounded overseas." The inference was clear: the defendants had abandoned injured men who had fulfilled their duties under far more dire circumstances than those that the women were protesting. The *Washington Post* proposed that "the tradition of unquestioning obedience has not yet been developed among our women soldiers." Likewise, the *Boston Herald* observed that "of course, these are women and Wacs really aren't soldiers, but discipline is discipline and there is no color line in the oath of allegiance."[26]

Despite the mainstream press's pro-army slant on the case, many of its white readers voiced support for the black Wacs based on the facts it revealed. In a letter to the *Evening Gazette* in Worchester, Massachusetts, a white reader cited "disgust" with the verdict, arguing that the Wacs had every right to expect equal treatment. "Are not our boys fighting and dying to ensure that individuals, all over the world, whatever their race or color, be assured of equality in the sight of Man?" Others bristled to learn of Crandall's alleged "dirty work" remark. In a letter to Secretary of War Stimson, a white man took issue with the notion that the only question in the case was the defendants' refusal to obey an order. "That statement is false," he insisted, "if Crandall said Negro WACs were supposed to do 'the dirty work.'" A man from Rhode Island asked President Franklin Delano Roosevelt to intervene, noting that "I'm not a colored person, but am very sympathetic with the colored people's aspirations."[27]

The trial of African American women in uniform therefore managed to transcend racial boundaries as Americans, black and white, contrasted the nation's democratic reasons for fighting the war and the army's discriminatory treatment of black Wacs. A white man from Oregon wrote Stimson: "I don't blame the Wacs for refusing to obey orders. Their disobedience then was all that they could do to protest an unfair un-American, pro-Hitler statement." A white woman asked the president "are we going to be as cold and inhuman in our practices as Hitler?"[28] The distinguished African American minister, the Reverend Hughes, compared American racism to the "Nazi race doctrine which we fight."[29] A Boston area book club (the race of its members unknown) likened the attitude of Crandall and Miles to fascists and Nazis.[30]

As civilian support for the Wacs intensified and diversified, it provoked speculation among those Americans who, convinced that the army did not racially discriminate, assumed that subversive connections existed between the Wacs' supporters and radical elements of society. *Time* magazine ominously reported that the sentence had provoked protests by "Negro and radical leaders." The *Boston Herald* also recognized radical intentions: "The basic charge was discrimination—the familiar anti-unity red rag." To the surprise of many, the usually liberal-leaning *Christian Science Monitor* took a similar stance. In his lengthy exposé of the case, commentator R. H. Markham claimed that "when the case became public, some Negro groups, without investigating the facts, set up charges of persecution and discrimination."[31] Along with threats of racial integration, the case fueled for many fears of communist infiltration.

The Wac strike also drew the interest of several elected officials, three of them members of Congress from New York City. Each hailed from a minority segment of the city's diverse population: Adam Clayton Powell was African American, Vito Marcantonio an Italian Catholic, and Emanuel Celler Jewish. In a joint statement sent the day after the court-martial's verdict, Powell and Marcantonio called on Stimson to supply them with the trial transcript. "It is unbelievable," they announced, "that in times like these that the colonel in charge of the Lovell General Hospital refused to let Negro Wacs assist in nursing back to health our soldiers by forbidding them to take temperatures and ordering them to do 'all the dirty work.'" Celler corresponded directly with Miles, "whose responsibility it will be to review the court-martial and sentence," candidly noting that Crandall's statements were "unseemly" and that the sentence the Wacs received "extremely severe."[32]

Another member of Congress, Pennsylvanian William T. Granahan, had been in contact with Fort Devens before the trial. Warfield, whose letter to her aunt had notified the NAACP about the tense situation at Fort Devens, had also written to Granahan, her representative. The congressman had many questions about the women's treatment, and for reasons that the U.S. public did not know then nor would learn about until years later. During February and March 1945, four members of the black WAC detachment at Fort Devens attempted suicide. The first, Beulah Sims, did so three weeks before the strike. After the strike, three others attempted the same, all within the space of just eight days. Lucille G. Edmonds tried to take her life on March 10, the day Miles ordered her detachment to return to their duties at the hospital. Edmonds had complied, though it took coaxing from Alice Young for her to remain on her ward. That evening, she swallowed a bottleful of sleeping pills. Two days later, Private Grant Gilliland ingested Lysol. On March 18, the day before the trial began, Private Charlene Cook tried to hang herself. Despite the rash of suicide attempts, it took Granahan's request to learn if the attempts were connected to the Wacs' treatment at Fort Devens to spur a War Department inquiry. (After its investigation of the strike, the army told Granahan that it had not found a connection.)[33]

Aside from Granahan's inquiry, interest in the strike rarely translated into interest in the black Wacs' experiences as women in uniform that

had led to the strike. Instead, followers of the case folded the Wacs' grievances into those of black male soldiers. Consequently, they generally placed
Young, Green, Morrison, and Murphy as stock characters in well-worn
debates over race and military policies—albeit with a gendered twist. For
instance, a white Californian woman, unsettled by the notion of hard labor
and a prison sentence for female personnel, pleaded with Roosevelt, "can't
there be a way out of carrying out that sentence?"[34] A Cleveland, Ohio, black
legionnaire group petitioned the government to allow special consideration
to the four Wacs because "we do not wish to believe that the Army has
lowered itself to the handling or dealing with women, regardless of race,
the same way that we deal with or handle men." In a nationally coordinated
drive by black legionnaires, a Washington, D.C., chapter sent a similar mis-
sive: "whereas, women being more frail, impulsive and sensitive than men,
with extreme difficulty overcame these known facts when enlisting . . .
succumbed to an emotional, natural and irrepressible outburst."[35] Though
well-meaning, such concerns mirrored the women's attorney's arguments
at their trial and therefore missed, as did Julian Rainey, the reasons for the
strike. Morrison, Young, Murphy, and Green had opted for a court-martial
not due to female frailty but because of military policies that marginalized
them as both African Americans and as women.

The intensity of the civilian interest in the case put the spotlight on Fort
Devens and the pressure on General Sherman Miles, the chief officer of the
First Service Command, to provide answers. Immediately after his April
10 meeting with the Wacs, Miles ordered his assistant inspector general,
Lieutenant Colonel William J. White, to learn the circumstances that had
led to the strike. The two-day investigation revealed numerous administrative inconsistencies in the treatment of black Wacs at Fort Devens, leading
White to concede that the detachment's complaints "are in general justified."
This was not a ringing endorsement of the defendants, whom he labeled
"recalcitrant girls who refuse to perform their duty," but rather a recognition
that extenuating circumstances had contributed to their reasons to strike.
White stood clear of indicting the army's segregation policies, focusing
instead on Crandall's poor handling of the situation. He advised Miles to
transfer the colonel from Fort Devens, and Miles agreed, though he would
do so discreetly. The NAACP, Bethune, ordinary citizens, and the black press
were clamoring for the colonel's removal, yet Miles was unwilling to openly
concede to civilian demands over military matters. Ultimately, he did just

that, though through the thin mask of a planned leave of absence as cover for Crandall's unceremonious departure.[36]

To counter public accusations of racial discrimination, the First Service Command, likely with Miles's approval, released news of a white Wac who it had also court-martialed for refusing to work, found guilty, and sentenced—as it did the Fort Devens defendants—to a year of hard labor, forfeiture of pay, and a dishonorable discharge.[37] Unknown to the public, the comparisons between the two cases ended there. Private Carolyn G. Kaniuk, a driver stationed in Boston, had repeatedly missed work. Assigned additional duty as punishment, she failed to appear. Confined to her room, she escaped. AWOL for twenty days, she turned up in a New York City hotel room, where she was living, drinking, and occasionally brawling with a male companion.[38] Like most military tribunals, Kaniuk's had been a closed hearing, so the public knew only that the wayward Wac had failed to report for duty. At least two officers in the First Service Command, however, were well-acquainted with the finer points of the Kaniuk court-martial: Major Leon E. McCarthy, who prosecuted the case, and Miles, who as the command's chief officer would have reviewed the verdict. The circumstances leading to the two trials were very different, and these two men would have known that.

Regardless of the differences in the two cases or the civilian outrage over the army's treatment of the four Wacs, Miles believed that the trial had been fair and the verdict valid. He felt that he had done everything in his power to ensure justice for the Wacs, including personally laying out the consequences of pursuing their work stoppage, offering to investigate their grievances, clearly articulating his order to return to work, and insisting on a fair trial for those who opted for the court-martial. As Miles explained later, "I naturally wanted to be very sure that I would not have a miscarriage of justice through any legal technicality."[39] The verdict was his to review, and Miles intended to uphold it.

On March 29, the NAACP announced that Thurgood Marshall, the lead attorney for the LDF, had agreed to represent Young, Green, Morrison, and Murphy in their appeal. The decision highlighted the wartime significance of the case for the civil rights movement. Deluged with thousands of petitions for legal assistance, the LDF had to be brutally selective, accepting only cases that would "boldly challenge the constitutional validity of segregation."[40] According to Marshall, he had such evidence of "discriminatory policies practiced against Negro Wacs" at Fort Devens. He may have been alluding to reports from locals who had learned that Crandall's neglect of his black female troops was generally known, and that even enlisted white soldiers were aware that Fort Devens was a "hell-hole" for black Wacs. Furthermore, Crandall's absence at the court-martial due to a supposedly planned thirty-day leave fooled no one, least of all Marshall. When it became apparent that this pivotal figure would not be present at the appeal, either, Marshall remarked that the sudden leave of absence seemed to "justify our position in the matter."[41] Marshall could count also on an unprecedented level of public interest in the case. Though the majority of white Americans barely took notice of the thousands of black servicemen sentenced to years and even decades to prison, they were proving less willing to accept courts-martial and prison sentences of any length when the defendants were female.[42] With the nation's most famous civil rights lawyer at the helm, black and white Americans awaited the appeal.

The civil rights movement's various contingents had galvanized massive support for the Wacs, though in reality the movement was rarely so unified as divisions within even the popular Wac strike demonstrate. The most obvious fissure in the campaign was the controversial Julian Steele, a Harvard graduate, president of the NAACP Boston affiliate, and Miles's confidante for race issues in the First Service Command. Steele's public statements expressed at best halting support for the Wacs, which caused an uproar among African Americans. Furthermore, he dismissed local activists' investigations that uncovered rampant discrimination at Fort Devens, defended Miles for his patience with the orderlies, and insisted that the case was about insubordination, not race.[43] On March 21, the *New York Post* confirmed Steele's position when reporting his reaction to the verdict, heading the article "NAACP Leader Calls It Fair."[44] More surprisingly, the usually fiery Prattis, editor of the *Pittsburgh Courier*, also criticized the Wacs for taking part in a strike. He agreed that the women had legitimate complaints but not "the right to refuse a direct order."[45] Insisting that change was slow, the same editor who had boldly launched the Double V campaign three years earlier to symbolize African Americans' immediate demands for rights used the case of the black Wacs to urge African Americans to be patient.

Steele's and Prattis's critiques of the Wac strike call attention to the rifts within the civil rights movement—and the likely juggernaut behind these rifts. As in any cause, clashing personalities and conflicting strategies often proved divisive, yet the civil rights movement also contended with government surveillance that naturally bred internal distrust.[46] Leery of moles in their operations, locals investigating the circumstances at Fort Devens agreed to supply information, though only under the condition that their names "must not be disclosed." One cautioned, "please don't mention my name," adding that "Steele may have some friends and he is afraid of the general." Another confirmed that "Too much caution cannot be used in concealing the source of this information. Intelligence is already on the march, particularly to learn if any organizations are involved in getting information to and from the post."[47] Inevitably, concerns over government spies in their midst took its toll. In the larger context of the movement, these concerns made it difficult for African Americans to know whom to trust, thereby hampering actions and causing cleavages.[48] In the case of the Wac strike, fear of clandestine surveillance impeded the collection of evidence verifying discrimination at Fort Devens, though it did not halt it. The groundswell of African American support for the Fort Devens black Wacs ensured that the movement's fault lines remained relatively minor in this case and that overall solidarity held firm. This solidarity, however, also guaranteed government monitoring of the African American community and its efforts on the Wacs' behalf.

In late March, Isadore Zack, an officer of the U.S. Army Counterintelligence Corps, filed three confidential reports to the War Department, each describing the local African American response to the Fort Devens Wac strike. According to his "undercover colored agents," Zack informed his superiors that "indignation swept throughout" Boston's African American communities as locals blamed the army's racial practices for the strike and viewed the women as "martyrs for a great cause." Zack also passed on his informers' personal conversations with *Pittsburgh Courier* reporter Leotha Hackshaw and the former chairman of the Boston NAACP chapter (and rival of the then-chairman Julian Steele), Ray W. Guild. Both supported the Fort Devens Wacs and were liberal in their views, leading Zack to suspect possible communist links to the case.[49] Though the strike involved patriots in the armed services protesting their jobs, not communists seeking to open a red front, the army found reason to surreptitiously monitor Boston's African American community's responses to the case.[50]

Owing to the civil right movement's cohesive framing of the strike around the democratic reasons for the war, most Americans focused on the army's treatment of the women rather than any risks that these women or their champions posed to national security. Through its various components, the civil rights movement had effectively rallied black and white citizens into taking action. The court-martial's unusual female defendants triggered interest in the Fort Devens incident, yet the movement's loose coalition of organizations, leaders, the black press, and grassroots efforts gave this interest form, substance, and teeth. Within three weeks, their joint initiatives had gained the attention of their intended target, the Secretary of the War. The clear majority of letters pouring into Stimson's office supported the four Wacs. Both prominent and ordinary citizens denounced the verdict, demanded the black Wacs' release, clamored for Crandall's dismissal, requested investigations, and questioned the army's treatment of black Wacs. The War Department received so much correspondence about the case that on March 27, Stimson ordered his staff to prepare a form letter to respond more efficiently to inquiries.[51] The strike and the civilian response to it illustrate the ideal prototype of the civil rights movement during World War II, when its various arms, united in their dedication to the values of democracy and justice, brought national attention to the cause thereby prompting high level action.

Miles had intended to see the Wac case through to its end, yet after the trial, it had begun slipping out of his purview and into Stimson's hands. By the end of March, circumstances required the expertise of those more experienced in dealing with the public than Miles, with his by-the-book approach. Stimson's assistant judge advocate general, Colonel William A. Rounds, took the lead in resolving the matter. Consequently, while Marshall, Bethune, the black and mainstream presses, and Americans around the country were gearing up for the second trial, Rounds was working with Miles to reduce the spotlight on the incident.[52] The intensity of the civilian reaction to the Fort Devens court-martial featuring black Wacs compelled the U.S. Army to take a different course of action than it normally did when prosecuting black male troops. Typically, it dug in its heels to justify convictions and, after long and hard-fought legal battles, offered piecemeal sentence reductions to discourage similar behavior among black soldiers.[53] In contrast, a week after the Fort Devens verdict, the War Department sought a way to bring the case of the black Wacs, and scrutiny over its treatment of them, to a close. In an unusual move, the army attempted to assuage the public outcry through a compromise solution.

6
Military Protocol

Easy Way Out
—Headline, *Time*, April 16, 1945

Within two weeks of the Fort Devens strike, the case had spiraled out of the control of the three military parties embroiled in the incident: War Department officials who were dealing with prominent civil rights officials, several members of Congress, and the public, all of whose debates over the guilty verdict going into the appeal had only intensified; lower-level military personnel with administrative and supervisory positions over Fort Devens black Wacs, who were facing uncomfortable questions about their actions before the strike; and the four convicted servicewomen at the center of the controversial case. Confined in Lovell Hospital North rooms awaiting their appeal, Mary Green, Alice Young, Anna Morrison, and Johnnie Murphy were reeling from the trial, guilty verdicts, and sentences of a year of prison and dishonorable discharges. By late March, all three of these groups were seeking ways to extricate themselves from the affair, and soon, they would find them. Solutions varied, though ultimately each depended on demonstrable adherence to army policies and measured dissemblance behind military protocol. Because the military's hierarchal structure demanded conformity from all personnel, concealing the full extent of personal attitudes would prove a useful strategy for the three military parties involved in the Fort Devens case.

Concealing individual views and motivations could not have been otherwise given army policies that on one hand officially prohibited racial discrimination while on the other hand assumed inherent racial and gender deficiencies among its African American Wac troops. The resulting contradictions rendered invalid genuine and open discussions in military circles of the case's core issue, namely, the treatment of personnel who were both black and female. Personal views that did not fit neatly into conversations that the military was willing to have were best hidden or otherwise disguised as consistent with army dictates. According to the War Department, army policies and disciplinary protocols assured uniform, fair, and impartial treatment for all personnel. In reality, they just as easily provided a convenient cloak to hide what could not be said. Each group—War Department officials, the four Wacs, and the women's supervisors and administrators—used this cloak to cover the full truth of their thoughts and actions.

From the vastly different vantage points of the three parties emerged three distinct dissembling strategies. The War Department turned to the *Manual for Courts-Martial* for regulations that would allow it to quickly dispatch the case without injury to its authority or concessions to the defendants' charges of discrimination. It also ordered an investigation of the incident that, while extensive, contorted the findings to exonerate the military and fault the Wacs. Lower-level military personnel involved in the case hid personnel biases behind army policies and protocols to deflect their failure to meaningfully employ black Wacs and attend to their advancement and morale. Morrison, Young, Green, and Murphy also hid the full truth. By April, they began stepping back from their bold assertions of racial discrimination that had opened them to a volley of assaults against their character. Instead, to varying degrees, they attested to their satisfaction with their treatment in the U.S. Army. In the aftermath of the court-martial, all three military parties sought to protect themselves by conforming to military protocol and its incumbent expectations.

With the appeal looming and the public's interest intensifying, the War Department desired an end to the controversial case. In late March, its judge advocate's office consulted with Major General Sherman Miles, who, as commander of the First Service Command, was responsible for reviewing verdicts in court-martial cases. Eager to avoid the appeal, the officers referred Miles to the *Manual for Courts-Martial*, Article of War 8: "When any such commander is the accuser or the prosecutor of the person or persons to be tried, the court shall be appointed by superior competent authority." Because Miles was the accusing officer, they argued, he had not been in a position to convene the original court-martial. On this basis, they proposed that Miles nullify the verdict against the Wacs and dismiss the case.[1]

Miles was hard-pressed to hold back his irritation. He insisted that he had intervened only after his subordinates had "failed to break, what was, a mutiny." Also citing from the courts-martial manual, Miles asserted his right to review the case: "action by a commander which is merely official and in the strict line of his duty cannot be regarded as sufficient to disqualify him." Miles was certainly acting in "line of his duty" when he broke the strike, since no one else under his command had been able to do so. Furthermore, once he handed the case to his judge advocate, he had not been part of the proceedings as either the accuser or as the prosecutor. Obviously uncomfortable relying on what he considered a technicality to dispose of the controversial case, Miles strongly defended his actions. Nevertheless, he diplomatically added, he felt "constrained to request advice on the matter in order that the provisions of Article of War 8 may be satisfied."[2] This was hardly the sentiment of one genuinely seeking advice. Clearly the whole procedure was distasteful to the straight-talking general.

The War Department's assistant judge advocate, William A. Rounds, responded that "nowhere have we found a suggestion that an officer can play so vital a part in the origination of the charges and still sit in judgment upon them." He advised Miles that further proceedings against Morrison, Green, and Young were "legally insufficient" and recommended that he declare the defendants' sentences null and void. In addition, he endorsed setting aside Murphy's case, predicated on disobeying an order by Lieutenant Victoria Lawson rather than by Miles, "in the interest of uniformity."[3]

Evidently, Secretary of War Henry L. Stimson desired a dismissal. His superiors and the public would hold him, not Miles, responsible for the appeal no matter the outcome. Stimson was no stranger to racial controversy. His department prosecuted hundreds of black soldiers in other high-profile cases, yet this court-martial, featuring women in the dock, had proven especially, and needlessly, difficult. Stimson likely saw little point in making an example of defendants whose corps was slated to dissolve six months after the war. Invoking Article 8 fit the circumstances and made judicial sense. Most importantly, it gave the army grounds to release the four Wacs, a move certain to appease the women's supporters. Miles had little choice but to concede to Rounds's recommendation and on April 2 revoked the sentences.[4] Two days later, Young, Morrison, Green, and Murphy returned to duty at Lovell Hospital South.[5]

Reaction from the public was immediate. In general, the mainstream press expressed displeasure, contending that the dismissal sent the message that

African Americans could expect special treatment. *Time*'s update on the case, "Easy Way Out," typified the reaction when it accused the War Department of retreating from the case to "hold the lid on its simmering race problems." Commentators charged black leaders with maneuvering a dismissal rather than working with the standard rules and procedures under which white personnel operated. *The Christian Science Monitor* reminded readers that a white Wac (Private Carolyn Kaniuk) had received the same sentence without fanfare, yet in the case of black Wacs, "some Negro groups, without investigating the facts, set up charges of persecution and discrimination."[6] In contrast, the black press decried notions of favorable treatment. The *Boston Chronicle*'s Marty Richardson insisted, in all capital letters, that the Wacs "never should have been tried in the first place." He and others expressed relief that the women they considered heroes were free. A banner headline extending across the *Philadelphia Afro-American* rejoiced, "4 Wacs Cleared," though in fact the army had not exonerated them. "Noblesse oblige!," cried out Harry Keelan from his *Afro-American* column. "The courage of these four girls is the spark which shall ignite the tinder into a flame from which real, effective leadership shall be foraged by hammered blows of war both at home and abroad." Many sensed a promising breakthrough in the military's treatment of black service personnel when, days after the Wacs' release, the navy reversed fourteen seamen's 1943 dishonorable discharges. "New Hope for Race in Rulings Favoring Negroes," boasted the *Arkansas State Press*. An image of a soldiers' cemetery in the *People's Voice* commemorated these victories with the caption "they did not die in vain."[7]

Nearly all who followed the case agreed on at least one thing: the behavior of the Lovell Hospital's commanding officer Colonel Walter Crandall warranted a War Department inquiry. Veteran activist Horace Cayton observed in the *Pittsburgh Courier* that "conditions must have been pretty bad to make [the Fort Devens Wacs] make this desperate attempt to assert their womanhood." A *Washington Post* commentary conceded that an investigation of Crandall would improve morale between the races.[8] Americans understood that the colonel had a responsibility to consider the welfare of his troops and that he had sorely neglected this duty.

Crandall was not the only officer who had neglected to take responsibility for the black Wacs at Fort Devens. Ward men, the nurses, and other officers at Lovell Hospital South admitted that they knew that the black Wacs were unhappy in their jobs, yet they faulted the women's presumed low skills, lackadaisical attitudes, and testy temperaments. They denied

that racial discrimination was an issue at Fort Devens. According to Chief
Nurse Major Eileen Murphy, black Wacs preferred to gripe rather than
take action to improve themselves. Most of the women's officers acknowledged the growing disenchantment of Lovell Hospital's black Wacs yet also
expressed surprise at how upset they had grown over their assignments.
Major Ethel M. Aikens remarked that while the orderlies "were not receiving any education advantages . . . we didn't know that it was causing any
conflict." First Lieutenant Andrew Cunningham admitted that even he, the
hospital's intelligence officer, had no idea that the women would strike. He
noted that he dutifully reported to Crandall "if something had occurred . . .
like an attempted suicide or smuggling liquor on the post," yet otherwise,
"there was nothing definite" to piece together the extent of the problems.[9]
Despite his intolerance for the insubordinate Wacs, Lieutenant Colonel
William J. White, Miles's assistant inspector general and the author of the
First Command's investigation of the strike, conceded that widespread officer neglect of the black Wac orderlies had created the circumstances that
sparked the strike.[10]

Nevertheless, White singled out Crandall for having been particularly
careless. After faulting the colonel's bungled treatment of the black Wacs,
he characterized his interactions with other personnel as uncooperative
and his administrative abilities as inadequate.[11] As described by White,
the officer with twenty-six years of military service was an accident waiting to happen. Following the report's condemnation of Crandall, the army
unloaded much of the strike's baggage on this lone officer's shoulders.[12]

Whether the army heaped blame on Crandall as a purposeful strategy to
excuse army policies and other military personnel of complicity in the strike
or out of a genuine belief that the black Wacs would have been content if not
for this one officer, the effect was the same: the army had an explanation
for the strike, and that explanation did not involve discrimination against
black Wacs. By extension, Crandall's abrupt departure soon after the strike,
poorly disguised as a thirty-day leave, seemingly vindicated the actions of
other personnel linked to the Wacs though they, too, had failed to attend
to the enlisted women's training, assignments, ratings, and morale. With
the army plainly, if not openly, faulting the colonel, the Wacs' supervisors
and Lovell Hospital South administrators were freed from examining how
their treatment of the women and their lack of interest in their concerns
may have contributed to the strike.

Despite the civilian outcry over Crandall's role in the strike and White's damning assessment of the colonel's leadership in his investigation's report, the army had no intention of disciplining the hospital administrator. When this became apparent, *Courier* commentator Cayton vented his frustration with the army's rush to court-martial African Americans while consistently exempting the white officers involved from prosecution. "Maybe this act [the dismissal of the Wac case] was supposed to indicate the great liberality of the Army's part," he surmised, "and then again maybe it was done to avoid an investigation."[13] As Cayton suspected, the army had been going to some lengths to protect Crandall's actions from scrutiny. Indeed, when White advised Miles to immediately remove the offending officer from the post, he recommended that the transfer take place quietly, and "should not in any way be regarded as punitive or disciplinary. Miles agreed, and on March 15 he privately informed Crandall that he would soon be relieving him of his duties.[14] Shortly afterward, the First Service Command announced that Crandall's request for a thirty-day leave of absence—which, in fact, Crandall had not requested—had been approved. Thereafter, Miles and War Department officials repeatedly denied that the colonel's untimely departure, just before the trial, was in any way related to the Wac case.[15]

Such precautions barely disguised Crandall's ouster from Fort Devens, yet the army considered the pretense necessary. Miles was determined, as White had cautioned, to avoid "the impression that the members of the Detachment by their action" had led to the abrupt changes in the officer's career.[16] Thus, the army was not shielding the long-serving officer out of collegial sympathy, but because, as Cayton had understood, genuine deficiencies existed at Lovell Hospital South that the army did not want exposed. Whether or not these deficiencies were all the fault of just one man, they nevertheless indicated that standards of military protocol at Fort Devens had serious flaws.

The army conducted two investigations of the strike, the First Service Command's in March and the War Department's through the month of April, and both uncovered extensive failings in the administration of black Wacs at Fort Devens. The detachment operated under a Byzantine chain of command in which no one claimed responsibility for its members' training, duties, promotions, and morale. Officially, Lieutenant Lawson was in charge of all Wacs at Fort Devens. The WAC, however, expected its black units, staffed by black officers, to function more or less on their own. Therefore, according to

Lawson, her subordinate Lieutenant Tenola Stoney, the black detachment's commanding officer, could have acted independently of her and taken issues regarding her troops directly to Crandall. Stoney seemed unaware of, or at least uncomfortable with, this chain of command deviation and her prerogative to use it. Furthermore, both lieutenants left the orderlies in the hands of the hospital's officers, ward masters, and even civilian nurses, who gave the enlisted women orders yet recognized no other responsibility to them. As Major Eileen Murphy, Lovell Hospital's principal chief nurse, explained, "I did not feel they were my responsibility—I mean, I don't like to step out of line and take someone else's job." She then added, "they have a C.O. [commanding officer]."[17] Over the five months before the strike, the Fort Devens Wacs' chain of command had broken down—that is, if it ever existed.

As the various deficiencies came to light as a result of the strike, Miles began instituting changes, of which his removal of Crandall was only the first. On March 20, 1945, the day the army convicted the four Wacs, Miles disbanded the entire WAC Detachment SCU 1127, which had consisted of a black unit of a hundred women and a white unit of nearly twice that number of personnel. Miles reorganized it into three new units, the Second, Third, and Fourth WAC Hospital Companies, a move that ironically least affected those whose strike action had prompted the change.[18] Black Wacs remained in their same segregated unit though under its new name, the Fourth WAC Company.[19] Miles also replaced Stoney as commanding officer with the experienced Captain Myrtle Anderson, one of the highly qualified women that Director Oveta Culp Hobby had recruited for the corps' first officer training program. Stoney stayed on as assistant company commander, a new position that Miles created for her. Miles assigned Lawson to lead the Second WAC Company, thereby removing her from the black Wacs' command structure. He also modified the orderly assignment descriptions that Crandall had posted, for the first time, just before his departure. The revisions relieved Wac orderlies at Fort Devens, black and white, from the more strenuous duties of pushing heavy food carts and scrubbing down trashcans as well as washing dishes and cleaning walls. By mid-April, Miles implemented a Wac orderly training program. While Miles's attention to ensuring proper protocols addressed several administrative problems discovered as a result of the strike, it failed to address limited job assignments for and discriminatory treatment of black Wacs.[20]

The War Department hoped that the dismissal of the case, the restoration of the women to duty, and the changes implemented at Fort Devens would quell criticism of its treatment of black Wacs, yet given the widespread interest in the high-profile case, inquiries continued. The NAACP acting secretary Roy Wilkins requested a full investigation into the causes of the strike given that "there still remain some significant and unexplained aspects of the situation." Mary McLeod Bethune also called for a review of the circumstances that led to the strike, warning the army that, despite the dismissal, "the case doesn't end there."[21] The inquiries by several congressmen added impetus for an investigation. Lastly, the War Department had questions of its own about the causes of the strike, and it wanted answers.

On April 2, the War Department ordered an in-depth investigation of the incident "to include all of the circumstances leading up to and concerning the refusal to work."[22] It assigned two white officers to the case, Lieutenant Colonel Milton S. Musser and Major Ruby E. Herman. By May 4, 1945, the day that Musser signed off on the report, he and Herman had interviewed more than 120 people. Four of them were the women whose actions had sparked the nationally publicized court-martial.

On April 11, 1945, Musser and Herman sat down with Anna Morrison. The recently released private repeated her earlier grievances. She criticized her officers for telling the black Wacs that if they did a good job, "you might get something better." It was an empty promise as far as Morrison was concerned, for though she and the other enlisted black orderlies kept "on slaving and slaving and slaving," nothing changed. She deeply resented Stoney's lack of initiative on their behalf, noting that "later we found out that half of the things we told her never got any further." Morrison expressed her frustrations with maid duties, an especially bruising ordeal given the army's shortage of Wacs for specialized military assignments. "We are not helping by washing dishes and doing that type of work." At this point, Musser asked, "The wards had to be kept clean. You agree with that, don't you?" Morrison concurred, but asked in return, "why should they put all of the filthy work off on us to do? Why couldn't we do something better than that?"[23] Morrison suggested hiring civilians for orderly work, and Musser moved on to his next point.

Musser and Herman probed Morrison about her role in the strike on March 9. Regarding the specific circumstances of her involvement, Morrison insisted that she could not remember. Already into their second week of interviews, the investigators by then knew that she had been among the most vocal proponents for some action. How forcefully was uncertain, though witness accounts and her own guarded responses suggest that she had actively urged solidarity, and not always as amicably as she described to investigators. Had she tried to enlist support, Musser and Herman asked? Morrison responded that her message that day was, "whatever we do, we don't want to fight among ourselves." Asked about threats against those who did not join the strike, she recalled two incidents, claiming that neither was serious. She agreed that some of the Wacs told Lula Johnson that if she went to work, "something will happen to you," while others who clearly planned to honor the strike had gathered around Tessie Mitchell as she dressed for work. Morrison dismissed both as jokes because, she said, everyone thought it hilarious that either Johnson or Mitchell would abandon them during a strike action. Besides, she added, "nobody would have gotten hurt."[24] It was an odd remark given that later that day, a large group of Wacs cornered one of its members, Ruby Pierce, and repeatedly punched her for speaking to Crandall after the meeting.

Convinced that Morrison had tried to rouse support for the strike, the investigators continued to question her about her actions on the morning of March 9. Musser asked if she had visited the other barracks that day. Morrison said she couldn't remember. Did she go to other rooms in her barracks? Since everyone was moving to different areas in the building, she agreed that the probability existed. Did she swear at Crandall? "Not at the Colonel," she replied. Was she part of the group who attacked Pierce after she spoke to Crandall? No, she said, and then described how she had tried to escape the melee when someone aiming for Pierce hit her in the shoulder. "I had to crawl through there to save my own self," she told the interviewers. Invoking a sort of survival mode mentality, Morrison explained that she did not have a chance to see who was involved so could not name names.[25]

Morrison also spoke of her relationships with other Wacs and her white coworkers at Fort Devens. A little over a month before the strike, an argument between her and Queen Brown, another Wac on her ward at the time, had escalated to violence. Morrison held out her arm to show the investigators the scar Brown allegedly caused after attacking her with a (fortunately dull) butcher knife. This led to a brawl in the kitchen and her transfer to a different ward. Otherwise, Morrison claimed that she and her new ward man, John Froias, had a good relationship and that she got along with most of the other Wacs, ward men, nurses, and patients at the hospital.[26]

Interested in whether recent changes had affected the attitude and conditions of Lovell Hospital's black Wacs, the investigators asked Morrison if she currently had any complaints. She responded, "everything is going all right now." Nevertheless, when Herman asked her if she experienced discrimination, she said, "Ma'am, that is what caused the whole thing." She then recounted the "dirty work" her detachment still performed while "all the time the white Wacs were working the dispensary and lab." She also complained that black Wacs continued to do KP while white Wacs remained exempt from such duties. Despite these ongoing frustrations, at no point did Morrison attempt to modify her earlier claim that "now that we are not doing the same thing[,] I am perfectly satisfied." Certainly, Miles had alleviated some of the more physical tasks, yet Morrison was still an orderly doing much the same work for which she had risked a court-martial a month earlier to protest. During the interview, however, she expressed contentment with her situation. At one point, she volunteered without prompting, "I am getting along all right."[27] Musser and Herman were left with trying to make sense of Morrison's change of heart without a significant change of duties.

Mary Green was far more guarded than Morrison when she spoke to Herman (who interviewed her without Musser). She was also exceedingly cooperative, responding positively to all questions and speaking highly of her duties. Did she like her present work? She did. Would she be "happy and contented to continue doing the work you are doing now?" She would. Was she treated well at the PX? Yes. Did she have complaints about Lieutenant Stoney? "As much as I can say about her—she has been very nice." Did she have any complaints about other immediate superior officers? "No." Throughout the interview, Green was agreeable to all. So positive were her responses that Herman expressed astonishment: "How did you happen to get involved in this court-martial, Pvt. Green," she asked, "with an attitude like that?"[28]

According to Green, she left her ward on March 10 in violation of Miles's order, not in protest of her duties, but because she was hungry. On pass when the strike began, Green had shuttled between Fort Devens and its nearby towns and presumably missed meals. She returned when her detachment members were restricted to their barracks so could not visit the mess hall for dinner on March 9. While others had breakfast the next morning, Green claimed that she did not know that Stoney had released them for chow. Following orders, she said, she stayed in her barracks, thereby accounting for why she told her ward man, Sergeant Rhoyd Heath, that she was too hungry to work. Green said that Heath then directed her to return to her barracks and report to her commanding officer. Once again, the private professed to following orders, explaining that when she saw Lawson in the dayroom, she reported to her as the ward man had instructed. Green denied that she returned with Young and Morrison, saw Stoney, or had been in her office on her arrival, or nodded to anyone that she would take the court-martial. Instead, she claimed that she first saw Lawson who, for reasons that she did not immediately understand, asked for her name and serial number and ordered her to pack. Green said that when another Wac informed her that she had volunteered for a court-martial, she returned to Lawson and asked to be taken off the list. At this point, her account merges with Young's, Morrison's, and Lawson's versions of events that afternoon. Green told Lawson that she could not do the ward work because she might be pregnant. Herman asked her if she was pregnant. Two months after first reporting to Stoney that she might be, Green could only respond that she "was still in doubt about it." The interview ended on another positive note as Green insisted that she was currently happy with her duties and content to continue working as a ward orderly.[29]

A probable explanation for Green's agreeable responses and denial that she had knowingly volunteered for the court-martial may relate to the young woman's mounting personal difficulties. These included serious health issues. Before the strike, Green had had three pregnancy tests. The first two were negative but the last, confirmed on the day of Miles's meeting, tested positive. Even if Green had not learned of the results then, she had cause to be concerned over the physical nature of her work. She suffered from a number of other ailments, including a cervical infection, and was likely in great pain during her court-martial and throughout her incarceration. "I stay pretty sick most all of the time," she told Herman.[30] Moreover, she was under considerable stress. The strike and court-martial had taken its toll on all four of those on trial, yet Green was also the single mother of two. At twenty-one years of age, she was possibly pregnant again, though not with the father of her children—both causes for automatic expulsion from the WAC. Given her situation, Green may have seen little benefit in calling attention to herself or testing the boundaries of the WAC's code of conduct. She needed the army's free health care and the $50 monthly paycheck.[31]

Though Green explained that her violation of military protocol was due to hunger pangs, suspected pregnancy, and a misunderstanding of why Lawson asked for her name and serial number, she readily admitted her sympathy with the strike and the reasons for it. (On pass during the first day's actions, she took part only on the second day of the strike.) She told Herman that she had been upset over the long hours orderlies worked, the KP duty black Wacs pulled, Stoney's lack of initiative to correct these problems, and the treatment from civilians who "didn't like colored people."[32] As these were problems in the past, Green added, in different wards and before the shift in command and modification of duties, she said that she had no further complaints and was satisfied with her orderly duties.

The same day that Herman interviewed Green, Musser spoke with Johnnie Murphy. It was not a long conversation, as Musser's questions were pointed and Murphy's responses succinct. He asked her about her duties. She listed them. He asked about her work hours, a well-documented fact. She answered, as would others, 7 a.m. to 7 p.m., with two hours off for lunch. He asked her to describe what she did on March 10 after her release from Lovell Hospital North and her return to the barracks. Due to Murphy's brief replies, each point required follow-up questions. "You reported to the day room?" Murphy nodded, "Yes, sir." Where was Stoney? "In the orderly room." What did Stoney tell her to do? "She didn't tell me anything to do. Just said 'O.K.'" "Then what did you do?" Murphy said she went to the barracks. "Then what happened?" Murphy said that she went to the dayroom. The interview slogged along in this fashion, with little of substance asked or given. Musser turned to Murphy's previous court-martial on January 20, 1945. Murphy admitted that she had used "vile language" against Stoney after a barracks inspection turned up a whisky bottle cap among her things and that this had cost her thirty days on restriction and half a month's pay.[33] Musser asked her if she got along with Stoney and Lawson. These and other inquires produced simple "yes" and "no" answers, and that is what Murphy gave.

The topic that Musser seems to have steered clear of until late in the interview was Murphy's powerful declaration that she would take death before returning to work. This had been one of the most widely reported and provocative comments of the strike, yet Musser did not seem eager to enter this territory. Only in the last several minutes did he broach it, asking Murphy how she had responded to Lawson's order to go to work. She replied, "I said [it] like this. I said, 'I'll take death.'" Murphy's attempt to be precise in this instance suggests that she was open to discussing her statement. If so, the opportunity was lost when Musser asked why she felt this way about her work. The strike had never been simply about the actual work, nor was

Murphy's statement confined to her circumstances at Fort Devens. Rather than explain the moral outrage behind her declaration to take death before injustice, Murphy treated Musser's question with a flat, "I don't know the reason." Musser then picked up on an earlier line of questioning that concerned her duties. "Your work wasn't that hard, was it?" Apparently as ready as he to end the session, Murphy agreed: "well, maybe not."[34]

Neither Musser nor Murphy tried to connect with the other. Early in the session, the lieutenant colonel asked the private if the civilian orderlies with whom she worked scrubbed the floors. Murphy said that one did and presumably was about to note that another one did not when Musser cut her off mid-sentence, switched gears, and asked whether she scrubbed floors on her hands and knees. This occurred just once, and was surely inadvertent, but it was in sync with the overall tenor of the discussion. The interview was a formality they both needed to perform. By the end, it dissipated to mainly yes and no questions and responses. Was she satisfied with her current situation? "It's all right." Did she have any complaints about it? "No, sir." Was she satisfied with her work? "Yes, sir."[35]

Young was more forthcoming than Murphy and Green in an interview that, given her varied roles in the strike, promised unique insight. Young had asserted more adamantly than the others her right to train and work as a medical technician. She was also at the center of the temperature-taking incident in which Crandall allegedly announced that black Wacs were at the hospital to perform the "dirty work," and it was during her questions about transportation school that Crandall used the term "black Wacs." Her comments were essential to the investigators' report, and Young was eager to tell her side of the story.

Musser was curious as to why the young private had been so certain that the army would train her as a medical technician. Young began by noting that her recruiter told her that with her nurses' training background, she qualified. At Fort Des Moines, two officers in particular, Lieutenant Wildman and Captain Dukes, singled out her and Ruby Pierce as medical technicians. Officers also told Young and the other recruits, in response to why their transfers were taking so long, that the army was holding them back until it had enough black Wacs to send for medical technician training. She, like the others in her unit, arrived at Fort Devens under the impression that they would soon be training and working in this field. When replacing white Wac orderlies, Young assumed that if she worked hard, she would be noticed and selected to move into an advanced medical role. At least two Lovell Hospital South officers suggested that that time was near. Major Arnison said he would recommend her for a promotion and for medical technician school, and a nurse, Lieutenant Newman, had tapped her and another Wac, Private McCord, "to take the white Wacs' place" and teach other black Wacs how to take temperatures.[36] Young's detailed response underscored her stalwart pursuit of the training she had expected to secure when she enlisted. A secretary recorded it all, and Musser moved on.

Young still wanted to salvage what was left of her chances for medical training, and during the interview tried to do so by demonstrating her cooperative nature and patriotic desire to provide medical services at the hospital. When Musser asked her if she faced discrimination on post, she said that she did not, with the exception of Crandall's earlier comment that black Wacs were there for the "dirty work." Otherwise, she said she got along well with the whites at the hospital, including the ward men, whom she listed by their first names: "Gene, Al, and Jimmy, have been very nice to us." Did she face discrimination at the PX? No, she said, "I just wait my turn." As the session was coming to a close, Young made a last effort to plead her case. When Musser asked if she had any complaints about her present assignment, she replied, "no, I have no complaints at all," only to quickly follow up, "I was just mainly interested in medical technician's school." Perfunctorily, Musser asked about her military occupation specialty (MOS) before returning to his closing line of questions. Did she have any further information that might inform the investigation? "Not that I know of," she began, before once again stressing her desire for medical training. "There isn't anything; no more than what I could ask you, if I could, if there is a chance of me going to medical technician's school. Will I get it?" Musser said he did not know. Sensing that this was her final chance to interest an official with possible leverage to intervene, Young persisted. "I'm just interested in going to medical technician's school. That's all. I feel that if somebody should get very sick in the ward, I would want to be doing something temporary [prior] to the doctor taking over." Musser heard her out and then asked, "were there any other statements?" At that point, Young replied "no." Herman reminded her that the interview was confidential and that she did not need to discuss her responses with anyone, and with that, the session ended.[37] Like her cohorts, Young would serve out her time in the WAC as an orderly at Lovell General Hospital South.

During their interviews, all four orderlies—who a month before had risked a court-martial to protest their jobs—expressed satisfaction with their jobs and treatment at Fort Devens. Despite some modification of duties, however, little had changed during the women's absence. Since the dismissal of their case, Murphy, Morrison, Green, and Young were once again cleaning hospital wards and running errands for the staff and patients in the same job assignments that still afforded little opportunity for advancement or promotions. Furthermore, they and other black Wacs continued to perform KP duty whereas white Wacs still did not and to suffer racial discrimination on their wards and at the PX. Nevertheless, the four told Musser and Herman that they were not experiencing discrimination at Fort Devens.

At this stage, such accord was not necessary, a point Musser and Herman made explicitly clear. They began each interview with a statement that all comments were confidential, and they assured interviewees that their purpose was to understand "the alleged irregularities [at Fort Devens] with respect to the administration of the WAC Detachment." Morrison, Green, Murphy, and Young could speak freely. They were not on trial. Their case had been dismissed, and the army had no desire to revisit it in court. Moreover, Musser and Herman specifically asked them whether they experienced racial discrimination. This was, of course, the reason they had given for taking part in the strike and suddenly they were at liberty—unlike during their court-martial, which dismissed discrimination as a viable defense—to fully detail to high-ranking officials the discrimination they experienced. In fact, they did describe it—and then they didn't, all four eventually defaulting during their interviews to "Everything is fine."

As Wacs, the four enlisted women were entitled to the same rights as other service members, yet military protocol did not typically reach so far as to offer African American Wacs the full protections of those rights. When Morrison, Green, Murphy, and Young protested the inequities of their situation, few listened. When they persisted, they faced a court-martial. Though their trial had given them a forum to present their case, it had also exposed their candid explanations to ridicule. Between the prosecutor and their defense attorney, they heard themselves described as lazy, overly emotional black women who held unrealistic notions about their abilities. For all their efforts, each had earned a year in prison, forfeiture of pay, and a dishonorable discharge. No doubt relieved when Miles voided the charges and restored them to duty, Young, Green, Morrison, and Murphy nevertheless understood that the army had not vindicated them or validated their grievances.

After their release, the four seem to have reassessed their situation. They had tried cooperating with army officers—white and black; male and female—yet virtually all of them had proved incapable of recognizing (or acknowledging) even the most blatant discrimination that the women suffered. By the time Morrison, Young, Green, and Murphy sat down with the investigators, they obviously saw little purpose in continuing to expose the truth as they experienced it. Clearly, the army valued cooperation more, so they reported that their situations were good and that everyone was nice. They would tell the authorities what they wanted to hear and keep their real thoughts inside, where they and the truth of their courageous resistance to the status quo could not be attacked.[38]

Even as the four Wacs attempted to compartmentalize the strain of discriminatory treatment by presenting their current circumstances as satisfactory, their interviews reveal its existence in their daily lives. Asked if she experienced racism at the PX, Morrison replied that she did not, though her explanation indicates that she did. "Lots of times I go in there and the girl won't wait on me and I just walk out. I mean, I never have any trouble with them because I leave."[39] The incongruity of Morrison's response was lost on the investigators. Similarly, Green's extraordinary turnaround—from disliking her job enough to risk a court-martial to fully enjoying it just a month later—might have given the investigators pause. Murphy's transformation from an angry radical to a morosely content orderly and Young's stated satisfaction of her job followed by none too subtle pleas to train as a medical technician also failed to alert Musser and Herman to the inconsistencies of the Wacs' statements of satisfaction and their experiences.

Other members of the new Fourth WAC Company conveyed similar contradictions during their interviews, in part due to the situation then in flux. Midway through the investigation, training sessions began for all Wac orderlies stationed at Fort Devens. Consequently, when Private Lois Floyd was asked if she was satisfied with her work, she answered, "I wouldn't say I was satisfied, but it so happens we are going to school now, and the future looks brighter. I mean, if preparations are made for things to be better for

us, there's no use complaining." Another responded effusively: "I have never
had any dull days on my job since I have been here." Many offered a flat
"yes" when asked if they were currently satisfied with their assignments.
Did they experience discrimination? Many replied no only to, as did Morrison, describe clear examples of discrimination. "Sometimes I would wait
about an hour [at the PX] and would have to turn around and walk on out
because I wouldn't get waited on," said Private Ellsworth Manuel. She then
added, "I don't know whether you would call that discrimination or not."[40]

The War Department's investigation was in almost every aspect a genuinely
exhaustive project, even if it was not penetrating or discerning. Musser and
Herman spent a month checking into multiple strands of possible causes
for the strike. They interviewed the four Wacs at the center of the case,
members of their detachment, other enlisted personnel at Fort Devens,
and officers throughout the First Service Command. They reviewed the
investigation that General Miles had ordered, relevant internal memoranda,
and compiled data comparing the working conditions and AGCT test scores
of white and black Wacs. They investigated whether racial discrimination
was a factor in the women's work assignments, the KP roster, and their
treatment at the PX. They considered the chain of command structure, the
reassignments of the three medical technicians, and motor pool training
programs for black Wacs. The final report was a massive seven-hundred-
page document with over forty attachments. The summary and conclusion
alone filled forty-one pages. Given this enormous effort, the War Department could have reasonably expected the investigation to unveil the precise
circumstances of the strike. Indeed, it did. Contemporary interpretations,
however, failed to grasp them.

The investigators considered the AGCT scores in order to determine if
the imbalance between white and black Wac assignments demonstrated
racial discrimination. First they needed fresh scores, so on April 17, 1945,
the Fort Devens Wacs, black and white, took the test.[41] According to the
raw data, "80 percent of the white enlisted women had AGCT scores of 90
percent or above as compared with only 11 percent of the Negro enlisted
women." (See table 2.)

A review of AGCT data calls attention to three overlooked factors that
disadvantaged the black women's cumulative test scores. First, given Crandall's requisition for orderlies, the WAC most likely sent him personnel who

Table 2. Comparison of White and Black Wacs' AGCT Scores, Fort Devens, April 17, 1945

Grade	1 (130 and above)	2 (110–29)	3* (90–109)	4 (70–89)	5 (69 or below)
White Wacs (drawn from March 9, 1945, roster)	4%	33%	43%	17%	3%
Black Wacs (drawn from March 21, 1945, roster)		1%	10%	61%	28%

* Medical technicians required a minimum score of 90.
Source: Compiled data from summary, 30, WDI.

had tested in Grade V. Conversely, his earlier requisitions for white Wacs for skilled assignments required Wacs who scored in the highest grades. Second, the tests were given on April 17, 1945, just two weeks after Young, Morrison, Green, and Murphy returned to duty. Still reeling from the court-martial, Young, who Howard University had admitted and her recruiter and several officers considered medical technician material, earned 5 points fewer than the 90 percent cutoff point for medical technicians. Post-strike apathy apparently took its toll. One black Wac scored just 5 percent and another received a zero. Several women did not take the test. Green sat for it but did not turn it in.[42] Such laxity calls into question how properly the army administered and monitored the test, and how seriously the black Wacs took the exercise. Third, Musser and Herman did not address the fact that the army relegated to orderly duty even the black technicians—Harriet Warfield, Inez Baham, and Thelma Allen—whose MOS indicated higher scores. An overriding disadvantage of the AGCT scores was the gravity that they were given in assessing the intelligence of personnel. "Right now," offered Wicks in reference to the test results, "I believe there are two girls with IQ's of over 90 on the wards."[43]

To compare black and white Wac orderly duties, Musser and Herman interviewed white enlisted orderlies. Private First Class Ruth Cone, who said she had attended surgical technician school, affirmed that she mopped floors, cleaned latrines, and served meals. She also pointed out that she and the other white Wac orderlies were always on time—a noted problem with many of the black orderlies. Private Helen Bugar said that she scrubbed floors, though only when the civilian workers were on vacation. Asked if white Wacs had expressed dissatisfaction with their orderly jobs before the black Wacs took over for them, Bugar recalled that there had been some "discussion to that effect" because most felt they were overqualified for these tasks. Cone, Bugar, and other white Wac orderlies insisted that they liked their jobs and did not know why the black Wacs went on strike.

Musser and Herman accepted the white Wacs' responses as evidence of the equal treatment of white and black orderlies at Fort Devens, an assessment that overlooked the differences in circumstances. Cone and Bugar stated that civilians typically freed them from some of the less desirable orderly jobs. This had not been the case for black Wacs until after the strike. Bugar volunteered that the white Wacs (who the black Wacs had replaced) had grumbled about orderly work, yet there would be no replacements for black Wacs who also protested. Throughout their interviews, the white orderlies' responses readily conformed to the prevailing view at Fort Devens that white Wacs were more cooperative than black Wacs.[44] These comments negated, at least to the inspectors' satisfaction, the African American Wacs' charges of racial discrimination.

As Musser and Herman learned during their investigation, not all white Wacs took so well to orderly duties. Prior to the arrival of the black WAC detachment, far more had worked at Lovell Hospital where they had "expressed their distaste for [orderly work]," apparently in stronger terms than some grumbling. According to Captain Jacob H. Bauer, director of military personnel at Fort Devens, those who were medical and surgical technicians complained so much about their duties that their effect on morale "created a problem for the hospital." When pressed, Sergeant Wicks admitted that white Wacs sometimes arrived late, "got tired" of scrubbing and washing down the wards, and "complained to everybody in general." As Bauer, Wicks, and other personnel described the problems with white Wacs, they assured the investigators that the women did not behave as poorly as the black Wacs. Then again, their officers had taken steps to stem the problem. Given the complaints, the First Service Command reassigned twenty to twenty-five of the technicians who had been the most vocal in their protests. Shortly afterward, they transferred many of the others to other locations. The wave of removals alleviated much of the friction, and complaints declined though did not end. Wicks, who after the court-martial moved from supervising black Wacs at Lovell South to supervising white Wacs at Lovell North, shrugged off the problems he continued to have. "There's bound to be a little trouble," he said, adding that the white Wacs' officers "disciplined the girls over there."[45]

Musser and Herman reviewed the psychiatric evaluations of the four women who had recently attempted suicide, Beulah Sims, Lucille Edmonds, Grant Gilliland, and Charlene Cook. In each case, psychiatrists acknowledged the psychological burden of the women's orderly assignments and treatment at Fort Devens. They also revealed the personal circumstances of each, citing, for instance, the recent death of Edmonds's grandfather and her alleged emotional immaturity.[46] These latter explanations gave army investigators context to argue that the four were mentally unstable, thereby allowing the women's personal circumstances to take precedence over their experiences at Fort Devens in determining the cause of their suicidal intentions. This was the explanation that the army sent to Congressman Granahan in response to his inquiry into the attempted suicides. In their confidential report, however, Musser and Herman acknowledged that the three attempts occurring after the strike "serve to indicate the extent to which at least some of the Negro enlisted women became upset over the manner in which they considered they were being treated."[47]

The investigators looked into the numerous black Wacs' complaints over their treatment at the PX. In one incident, a black Wac recalled that a clerk served a frankfurter to the white Wac before her in a napkin in the usual manner, and then inexplicably put hers on wax paper. In another, a black Wac had tried to buy Kleenex moments after a white Wac had made the same purchase, only to be told that the PX did not have any others to sell. Most commonly, the Wacs complained that PX clerks ignored them, forcing them to wait for lengthy periods to make a purchase. After inquiries, Musser and Herman deemed each incident unavoidable and in no way indicative of racism. According to the PX officer, Captain Thomas A. Flynn, the snack bar clerk had run out of napkins, the remaining supply of Kleenex were for patients, and during busy periods, whites also had to wait to be served.[48] The investigators once more concluded that the complaints reflected the *appearance* of discrimination rather than actual *evidence* of it.

Musser and Herman's investigation of the motor transport school illustrates the gender biases black Wacs' encountered at Fort Devens and the acceptability of such biases. Contemporaries discussed the case in terms of race, yet society's connection of African American women to service work severely limited black Wacs' opportunities to qualify for anything else. Prompted by Young's requests to train as a driver, the officers looked into whether the motor pool accepted black Wacs into its courses. According to its commanding officer, Captain Barney H. Edwards, it did not. Recollecting his conversation with Young, Edwards said that he had informed her that while permissions were normally required for a transfer, in her case he did not have a course for her to take. The investigators would soon learn why.[49]

At the time of the strike, the light truck drivers' school was the only transportation course at Fort Devens for African Americans, and it was reserved for male personnel to train as "truck drivers for overseas combat and supply units."[50] Black Wacs were ineligible for this course on two accounts: the army's restriction of all Wacs from combat areas, and the WAC's restriction of black Wacs—aside from those in the 6888th Postal Battalion only recently sent to Europe—from overseas duty. The army did train Wacs in this needed specialty. Caroline Kaniuk, the white Wac discovered AWOL in New York, had worked as a driver in the First Command's headquarters in Boston. The person who advised Young to consider the motor pool was a black Wac driver, while a white Wac driver had informed her that the motor pool was seeking servicewomen for a new training course.[51] This course, however, was open to white Wacs, not black Wacs. Such restrictions effectively blocked black Wacs from all post motor pool training programs, though Musser and Herman did not see it this way. From their perspective, the fact that the motor pool offered training to African Americans and to Wacs discounted claims of discrimination.[52]

In the summary report, Musser and Herman conceded that the Wacs had some legitimate grievances, mainly regarding the confusion of their chain of command. Not surprisingly, they blamed Crandall, though they concluded that the fault lay in his way of dealing with the women rather than "any special bias toward Negroes." Stoney also came under criticism for displaying weak leadership, yet Musser and Herman declared her otherwise "a sincere and a capable officer." The two investigators could see why the KP issue remained problematic for the black Wacs, though they marked that down to perception rather than reality. Because white Wacs had once pulled KP (until the arrival of the black detachment), they felt that charges of discrimination over the matter were unwarranted.[53]

In their final analysis of the Fort Devens black Wac strike, Musser and Herman concluded that "there had been what can justly be termed a mutiny, based upon some real and some fancied grievances." When "considering equal rank and comparable classification," they asserted that there were no differences in duties between white and black Wacs. Consequently, they determined, "the primary basis for most of the complaints was a clash of personalities."[54] With some exceptions given the noted shortcomings of Crandall and Stoney, the investigating team reasoned that the strike was not the fault of the women's officers or a result of their assignments. Instead, it occurred because the orderlies' intellectual deficiencies impaired their understanding of the seriousness of their actions: "To persons of their limited mentality," Musser concluded, "it has doubtless appeared for reasons beyond their power of analysis that breaches of discipline on their part will not necessarily involve punishment and may result in advantages to them."[55] During the trial, Rainey had argued that the women's misunderstanding of the military and their place in it had caused them to disobey a direct military order. Musser and Herman apparently accepted this notion in its entirety.

The findings of the intensive investigation repeated many of the critiques that the women's detractors had argued: the Wacs' jobs were not difficult, the women were not qualified for other work, and there is no excuse for insubordination in the military. Musser's and Herman's conclusions also reflected the stereotypes of African American women that had shaped the predominant WAC and War Department assumptions: black Wacs had low abilities, poor values, and an exaggerated sensitivity to race issues. Throughout their summary, the investigators questioned the intelligence of Fort Devens's black Wacs and their competence to carry out their duties. Responding to these women's expectations for specialized training, the report noted that the "low mentality of the majority of the colored Wacs would encourage a belief that such promises had been made."[56]

Musser and Herman were able to substantiate that racial discrimination was not a contributing factor in the strike through a selective gathering of evidence. For example, they focused on the conditions of black Wacs' orderly duties and how they compared to those of white Wacs' orderly duties rather than consider the lack of opportunities that black Wacs had to obtain other military positions. They disregarded the significance of statements that directly linked racial discrimination to the strike action. Murphy, not Musser, injected her defiant "I'll take death" statement during the interview, whereas neither Musser nor Herman probed Morrison's reasons for declaring that she would take a court-martial "if it will help my people." They ignored Young's vigorous pursuit of training and Green's about-face position regarding her interest in her duties. The investigators did not find these points compelling nor the repeated concerns by nearly all of the black orderlies they interviewed matters worth exploring. On the other hand, Musser and Herman put stock in the assurances of the orderlies' officers and ward men that they treated black orderlies as they did other personnel and yet the enlisted women still performed poorly. Sergeant Wicks was adamant that the black Wacs did not have "just cause" for the strike, "not after the work that the white Wacs did here." Fed up with their complaints and tardiness before and after the strike, he told the investigators, "Nobody seems to care if they are here or not. If they go, they go, and there is nothing lost."[57]

Rather than dig deeper, Musser and Herman used the responses to their superficial questioning in the course of their investigation as further justification for the African American women's reputations among white military personnel as unfeminine and prone to unconstrained volatility. Even before the strike, Murphy was on record for using foul language when addressing her commanding officer. Morrison and Queen Brown had not only fought with their fists, but brought a butcher knife into the fray. An argument between a black Wac and a white civilian also exploded into a fight, the incident that led to the plan to separate black Wac and white civilian orderlies which touched off the strike the next day. Many of the black Wacs described the heightened anxiety and "hysterical" crying among the members of their detachment during the strike. At times, these emotions transgressed into appalling behavior. Some cursed Crandall and brutally attacked Private Ruby Pierce for speaking to him. For a month, Musser and Herman listened to and reported descriptions of unrestrained emotions among black Wacs and the violence that occasionally erupted as a result.

From the vantage point of the two white investigators, the black Wacs at Fort Devens could be living up to their stereotyped images: they assumed abilities they did not possess—a point that a fresh round of AGCT scores seemingly validated—and demonstrated more loyalty to their race than to the military and their country. Indeed, they abandoned their posts to complain about racism and refused to name those who had encouraged the strike. According to the Lovell Hospital South white staff, black Wacs were moody, chronically late for work, and hard to manage. In some cases, their behavior went beyond the pale of acceptable femininity. Murphy brought whiskey into the barracks and cursed at her officer while Green was obviously having intercourse with a man not her husband. Such deviations from proper womanhood were consistent with the popular perceptions that black women were uncooperative, lazy, and prone to promiscuous behavior.

Caroline Kaniuk, the white Wac dishonorably discharged at an earlier Fort Devens court-martial, herself exhibited all of these problematic behaviors. She was not only late to work but occasionally did not show up for days. Confined to quarters, she went AWOL. Kaniuk disobeyed orders, drank alcohol, and had an affair. When white Wacs breeched the standards of respectable womanhood, they were individually held to account. When black Wacs did, they confirmed the expected character deficiencies of the other women in their detachment and, by extension, of black women in general.

The publicity of the Fort Devens case produced heightened levels of dissemblance within the upper echelons of the military. The War Department voided the case on the grounds of a technicality that rendered it "legally insufficient," though it had, in fact, sought the technicality to avoid a messy appeal. It also launched an extensive investigation of the strike, thereby conceding to its critics' demands, yet, by marking its findings "confidential," released only the evidence it chose to reveal. Meanwhile, Miles's appointment of a new administrator for Lovell Hospital helped mask War Department policies that had led to the strike. With Crandall gone, the problems at Fort Devens could be seen as resolved.

Professing adherence to military protocol also provided cover for other military personnel who in fact, in violation of their duties, had not previously attended to the black Wacs' assignments, ratings, and morale. Once Crandall took the fall, their actions faced marginal scrutiny, as the army subtly consigned the missteps in the incident (not apportioned to the Wacs) to this one man. As a result, there was no reason to assume others were at fault, an assumption that the court-martial verdict and two investigations appeared to corroborate. Thus exonerated, these military personnel had little motivation to question their treatment of the Wacs, reflect on their views of black women, or consider the inequities that led to the strike at Fort Devens. Furthermore, the two investigations gave them opportunities to personally assert that all races were equal, thereby professing their fair treatment of the black orderlies. *Time* magazine had marked the voiding of the verdict as the War Department's desire to take the "easy way out," yet it also provided an easy way out for other military personnel associated with the case.

Morrison, Young, Green, and Murphy also relied on dissembling behind military protocol. During the strike, they had taken a bold stand against the indignities of their treatment. A month later, they were conforming to army expectations and reporting satisfaction though their duties after their release had not substantially changed. All four seemed resigned to the fact that further protest would not be helpful. They would not be able to convince Musser and Herman of the legitimacy of their stance any more than they had the members of the court at their trial. They could, however, confront the condescending presumptions of black women's character. Each defended her actions as just under the circumstances, and, yet, by presenting an accommodating face, also confirmed her status as a cooperative soldier.

Thus, the protocol of military discipline worked with remarkable speed and efficiency to restore conformity among Fort Devens post personnel and bring closure to the case. With the appeal avoided, Crandall removed, Fort Devens military personnel's commitment to equality stated, and Green, Young, Morrison, and Murphy returned to duty, the Fort Devens strike vanished from the public discourse on race and women in the military. Less than two months after the March 9, 1945, action, the public's interest in the case evaporated. There was nothing new to report.

The army's posturing behind military protocol could hide reality, but it could not change it. Morrison, Murphy, Green, Young, and the others at Fort Devens who participated in the strike knew, despite the denunciations from nearly all others around them, that their reasons for the action were valid. On this issue, they never wavered. The War Department did not agree, yet the strike had forced its staff to recognize that the U.S. Army could not completely dismiss African American women in uniform without consequences. The four Wacs' high-profile action at Fort Devens demonstrated, in ways that other lesser known incidents at Fort Des Moines and elsewhere had been unable to do previously, that African American servicewomen had documented rights in the U.S. military, and that they would use them to assert their full entitlements as citizen-soldiers.

Conclusion

A Sociological Laboratory

"It has been often stated," acknowledged Truman K. Gibson, the civilian aide to the Secretary of War on racial affairs, "that the army is considerably ahead of the majority of most parts of the country in its handling of Negroes."[1] When Gibson commended the army in August 1945, he and his War Department colleagues could point to a wartime record of flexibility in handling race and gender issues. Just four months earlier, the army had dismissed the charges against four enlisted Wacs at Fort Devens who had clearly defied its authority and launched an inquiry into their grievances. Throughout the war, the army introduced policies endorsing the equal treatment for its African American troops and the fair and racial equality of its female troops. It was the first U.S. service to establish a women's corps and, for a time, the only one to enlist black women. The army commissioned black men and women officers, appointed the nation's first African American general, trained black pilots, mobilized African American soldiers into coveted combat roles typically denied them, and sent black Wacs to Europe. Only the U.S. Army, with over twelve million troops, offered so many U.S. men and women from all racial backgrounds equal pay according to rank and, with some modifications for Wacs, nearly the same benefits. So profoundly did these measures upset fiercely protected racial and gendered boundaries that many Americans considered them downright progressive.

An examination of the Fort Devens case reveals a different story. Undergirding War Department policies that ordered equitable treatment were stipulations that, in addition to segregation, reinforced the inequities of the status quo. Hence, while the army enlisted men and women of all racial groups, it steered white men toward leadership roles and black women into servile duties. Although the army commissioned African Americans and women as officers, it prohibited them from command positions over, respectively, white and male troops. The army offered black soldiers in Europe frontline combat positions, though only after heavy losses during the Battle of the Bulge necessitated the change.[2] While the WAC transferred black Wacs overseas, it did so only in the last year of the war, two years after it did white Wacs, and then just one unit, the 6888th Postal Battalion.[3] In sum, the national emergency produced by World War II forced the War Department to modify its racial and gender policies, though, in accordance to its historical pattern, only enough to bridge its personnel shortages and secure the cooperation of subordinate citizens. Otherwise, War Department officials regarded most of its African American and all of its female personnel as temporary troops for a temporary crisis, gearing its policies accordingly to maintain prewar societal conventions.

The Fort Devens court-martial illustrates how civil and military policies that upheld white patriarchal and class privilege affected African American servicewomen during World War II. At Fort Devens and elsewhere, these policies funneled the majority of black Wacs into menial labor, thereby reinforcing derisive images of black women's capabilities and lowering morale. Inevitably, these policies increased the propensity of black Wacs to violate military codes of law—not with the intent of breaking with protocol, but to gain the training, assignments, and respect that these protocols were ostensibly designed to provide. If the strike was not an appropriate way to express their grievances over their marginalization, it appeared to the Wacs at Fort Devens to be their best option in a system that failed to adequately recognize them as members of the armed forces. Civilian policies that had historically marginalized African American women also spurred their resistance to exploitation. Faced with similar policies, black Wacs relied on their foremothers' legacy that both inspired and equipped them to carry on the struggle. From the vantage point of their newly acquired military status, three-fourths of the detachment at Fort Devens, and then just four of its members, refused orders that they believed violated their rights as military personnel.

As the United States entered the war in 1941, the War Department roundly rejected racial integration, citing that the army was "not a sociological laboratory."[4] Toward the end of the war, and just a month after the Fort Devens strike, the War Department reiterated its intent to continue its practice of racial segregation. Responding to a proposed congressional bill to integrate the armed forces, Colonel H. B. Sepulveda insisted that segregation had "proven to be wise and equitable over a long period of years," adding that "with few exceptions" African Americans favored it, too. Furthermore, he warned, to use the army as "a laboratory to conduct social experiment[s] is regarded as a dangerous departure that would be detrimental to national defense."[5] Four years after the War Department had explained its opposition to integration, it was repeating, to a word, the same reasons.

Of course, the U.S. Army, which relied on its citizenry to fill its ranks, had always been a sociological laboratory, yet during World War II it reached new heights of social experimentation when it enlisted black women. Bestowing the exalted status of a soldier proudly protecting the nation on a category of citizens that society marginalized into near invisibility propelled army personnel policies into completely unknown territory. The 6,500 African American Wacs who enlisted during World War II represented the army's largest variable in its social laboratory. Though the army launched the experiment, it had not prepared for it and did not have an adequate template, military or civilian, to guide it in its dealings with African American women. The same could not be said for black Wacs, who had a long history of uniting and fighting for their rights. In a fair contest, the army would have been the underdog. This was not a contest of military equals, however, but one of marginalized citizens challenging privileged elites.

Throughout the war, black Wacs' challenges to the army's guarantees of equal treatment frequently boiled over into disciplinary incidents, yet none received the level of publicity that greeted the Fort Devens case. Word of the strike therefore alerted officers far and wide that African American women would take action when they sensed discriminatory treatment. Additionally, the massive civilian interest in the case, spurred by an effective coalition of the civil rights movement's various arms, put them on notice that black Wacs were not without allies. This incident in particular apparently convinced some War Department officials that they could not simply ignore black Wacs—at Fort Devens or elsewhere.

As events at the large Massachusetts post were unfolding, the army was in the midst of preparing a transfer of black Wacs to Chicago's Gardiner Hospital, a military facility near the white residential community of Hyde Park. War Department memorandums regarding the move do not mention the Fort Devens strike, yet their detailed instructions indicate that the well-publicized incident figured heavily into the plans. Just six months before, the army had ordered Colonel Walter Crandall, the commander of Fort Devens Lovell Hospitals, to requisition black Wacs and then left him on his own to manage the new personnel he clearly did not want. The following January, the army ordered Gardiner Hospital's commanding officer to prepare for a company of black Wacs. As had Crandall, the officer protested by citing housing issues, local opposition, and lack of need for women of low-caliber training. In the aftermath of the strike, the army engaged Crandall's counterpart in each aspect of the women's transfer and assignments. This included organizing suitable housing, assuring a balance of orderlies and medical technicians, preparing a proper orientation, clarifying the chain of command, and reminding officers of their responsibility to attend to the proper working conditions and treatment of the new personnel. Apparently eager to avoid the kind of debacle that had occurred at Fort Devens, the army ordered that any "foreseeable problems in connection with housing and utilization of the negro WAC personnel—be identified and reported."[6] Once the new detachment arrived, army and WAC officials closely monitored the situation. These included the commander of the Sixth Command and the new WAC Director, Colonel Westray Boyce, who personally visited the hospital.[7] Years later, the company's commanding officer, Martha Putney, contended that the high-level interest in this experiment no doubt encouraged the commander of the hospital "to do his part to ensure its success."[8] Putney also speculated that the Lovell Hospital strike had encouraged officers to properly utilize the service of black Wacs.[9]

The Fort Devens incident furthermore demonstrates that, despite military policies designed to separate troops, interracial relationships on an equal footing were gradually being forged. Lieutenant Tenola Stoney had a professional relationship with Lieutenant Victoria Lawson and with Crandall, with whom she occasionally dined in the mess hall. Young was on friendly terms with her ward man, Eugene Beale. In fact, most of the enlisted women of the black WAC detachment claimed that they liked and got along with the majority of the white ward men, nurses, patients, and civilians on their wards. Several of their white officers confirmed that the feeling was mutual. At least one officer had endorsed Alice Young for medical training, while another let her and other black Wacs help with medical duties until Crandall put an end to such initiatives. A white Wac officer who was extremely critical of the black Wac orderlies praised her black nurses for their hard work. If her effusive comments about the nurses were designed to counter suspicions of racism toward the orderlies, they nevertheless indicated a willingness to recognize the abilities of at least educated African American women.[10] As the intersections of class identities continued to complicate gender, race, and rank dynamics, relations remained uneasy after the strike, yet also fluid as white and black personnel continued to work together and depend upon each other. After a white male patient treated Private Willie Ruth Williamson rudely, the offended Wac snapped, "I come to do a job and come in to help all the boys out, and this the thanks I get out of you." The man "almost cried," she said.[11] The terrain for black Wacs remained rocky but was beginning to smooth out with frequent travel.

Positive interracial encounters between black Wacs and white personnel occurred elsewhere, too, though often after fitful starts. A southern white officer candidate who vehemently objected to sharing a barracks with Martha Putney at Fort Des Moines, Iowa, days later apologized. Afterward, the two talked and got to know each other. In Chicago, where Hyde Park residents had sought to block the arrival of black Wacs to Gardiner Hospital, other neighbors welcomed the new company. As one woman assured Stimson, "we are more than glad to have these young women in our community."[12] In Europe, a general threatened to place a white female lieutenant over the black female commander of the only black WAC unit serving abroad, the 6888th Postal Battalion. "Over my dead body," retorted Captain Charity Adams, the former black WAC commander at Fort Des Moines. Aghast at her temerity, the general began drawing up charges against his female subordinate when, to his surprise, Adams responded with a countercharge. The move impressed the veteran officer, and before his return to the United States, he sought her out to tell her so. "Working with you has been an education to me," he told Adams, admitting that before encountering her, "the only Negroes I have ever known personally were those who were in the servant capacity or my subordinates in the Army."[13] Despite segregation policies, relationships built on mutual respect were crossing racial and gender lines as opportunities arose.

The WAC's emphasis on segregation assuredly prevented many such chance opportunities between black and white Wacs. Few World War II Wacs mention regular interactions with their counterparts of another race, a reality that severely impeded a sense of female solidarity that would have naturally taken root given their shared experiences as pioneers of the first women's corps. Instead, isolated into different assignments and living in separated housing areas, black and white Wacs' opportunities for collegiality were minimal at best. Different rapports with their officers further divided the women. White Wacs at Fort Devens, for instance, seemed to have been chums with Lieutenant Lawson, the WAC officer who demonstrated little interest in the black Wacs also in her command. Lieutenant Stoney's contacts with white enlisted Wacs were of a chance meeting rather than in a command position, and as the lone black female officer on post, she did not have a club in which to socialize or network with Lawson or the other officers on post. The WAC's and army's resistance to integration greatly hampered the growth of camaraderie between black and white Wacs.

The Fort Devens strike demonstrates the ability of the state to create and divide categories of citizens, and it shows the high price Americans, black and white, paid for this racial hierarchy. Despite the shortage of personnel, the army refused to train or utilize most of its black Wacs for meaningful tasks. After the war, these women attended school, worked jobs, raised families, assisted their communities, and led productive lives. Anna Morrison, for instance, earned a nursing degree, while Alice Young returned to her job at the U.S. Treasury, where she worked as a valued employee for several decades. The costs to the war effort of dismissing the abilities of these troops is immeasurable—as is the trauma suffered by the black Wacs the army marginalized. At Fort Devens, over fifty orderlies risked a strike, four opted for a court-martial, and another four attempted suicide. The supposed beneficiaries of white patriarchal privilege also suffered. The U.S. Army's reluctance to properly utilize the services of its black Wacs and to arm black men for front-line duty guaranteed that white men during World War II fell disproportionately in combat. Nearly three hundred thousand white soldiers died during the war, and countless others lived with the horrors of the battles they fought for decades afterwards. These men paid an especially heavy price for the white privilege of demonstrating heroism on bloody fields.

The army remained committed to segregation throughout the war, though, for a brief moment, the landmark Fort Devens court-martial attracted the nation's attention to the inequities of racial segregation. The case touched off widespread debate about the practice until the War Department curtailed the discussion by dismissing the charges against Morrison, Green, Young, and Murphy. Thereafter, the Fort Devens Wac strike and the heightened clamoring it provoked in protest against segregation faded from the public discourse. The War Department had managed to weather this case as it had others. After the war, even as major reductions in personnel led the navy and air force to prepare plans for integrating their services, the War Department defiantly defended its segregation policies.

Despite its intransience on modifying its racial policies, the War Department was having second thoughts about its plans to dissolve its female force. Claiming that "the war has shown that the utilization of women in times of war is a necessary and accepted fact," it sought to retain the WAC. In 1948, President Harry Truman obliged by signing the Women's Armed Services Integration Act, establishing the WAC as a permanent corps with closer ties to—and, hence, more integrated into—the regular army than it had been during the war. Two years later, the WAC racially integrated, a result of its much-reduced size. With just seven thousand members, down from over ninety thousand three years earlier, segregation was no longer feasible. Four years before the U.S. Army disbanded its last all-black unit, Wacs were training, working, and living together regardless of racial background.[14]

The role of the Fort Devens case played in desegregating the army is illustrative and noteworthy, but not pivotal. Integration of the armed forces occurred when the impracticalities of segregation were too great for a service to manage. The navy and coast guard, and each of their women's corps, integrated during or shortly after the war when massive personnel rollbacks necessitated it. So large was the U.S. Army that even after postwar reductions, it still had the critical mass needed to sustain the practice, at least among its male personnel. Segregation was extraordinarily inefficient, as it called for duplicating facilities and programs and, as the Fort Devens incident demonstrated to increasing numbers of contemporaries, under-utilized its African American personnel. In 1948, President Harry S. Truman appointed a select few of these contemporaries to the postwar Fahy Committee, established by his executive order 9981, to study the impact of segregation in the military. Among the materials that these men surveyed appeared a number of references to the Fort Devens strike. Though usually part of other reports of racial disturbances, these accounts lent further evidence of the inequities and inefficiencies of segregation that led to the Fahy Committee's recommendation to the president to integrate the armed forces.[15] The army continued to resist. Indeed, no one group or event could have on its own dislodged one of the army's most entrenched and defended policies. In the end, it took the full weight of the civil rights movement, a presidential directive, northern Democrats' courting of the black vote, and urgent troop demands for a war in Korea to at last bring down the curtain on formal racial segregation in the army.[16]

Nearly a decade before the final unit of black and white soldiers integrated in Korea, Mary Green, Anna Morrison, Johnnie Murphy, and Alice Young had refused to return to duties in order to make the case that the army had not fulfilled its promises to treat black Wacs with the respect due all members of the armed services. The strike of African American servicewomen and the publicity that surrounded it so confounded the army that, in an extremely rare decision for trials of this kind, it decided to forgo the appeal rather than risk further public scrutiny of its policies toward and treatment of black Wacs. While the case has been largely forgotten since then, the bulk of related court transcripts, interviews, investigations, newspaper articles, civilian and military correspondence, and army memos remain. These documents validate the Fort Devens black Wacs' claims of racial discrimination and exonerate the four who stood trial. The victory was not personal, timely, nor even official given the verdict's dismissal rather than defendants' vindication, yet it was a victory. Morrison, Young, Green, and Murphy had, in fact, proven their case.

What happened to the four women after the trial? Unfortunately, a 1973 fire destroyed many of the World War II Veteran's Administration records stored in a St. Louis facility. Additionally, the women had not been close friends either before the trial or afterward. After their discharges, they went their own ways, thus locating one did not necessarily lead to another.

Mary Green, who had not known if she was pregnant throughout the incident, continued to be plagued by painful medical problems after her release from confinement. Her maladies kept her constantly in and out of Lovell Hospital until her honorable discharge seven months later. In November 1945, Green returned to Conroe, Texas, where she found temporary work at an inn. In March 1946, she secured a divorce from her husband. Green's first year as a civilian seems to have been at least as tumultuous as her last years in the WAC. In addition to employment and divorce issues, she suffered a miscarriage within a year of her discharge. In part due to her access to veterans' health care, her situation eventually stabilized. She found work in the service industry, remarried, and later settled in Galveston, Texas. Surrounded by her large and loving family, Mary Magdaline Amerson Manning died on August 7, 1996.[17]

Johnnie Murphy spent much of the two months following her release convalescing at Lovell North Hospital before returning to duty in late September. She began the new on-the-job training program for Wac orderlies and earned "fairly satisfactory" marks from her supervisors. A month later, Murphy faced a reprimand for tardiness to her ward. Captain Myrtle E. Anderson, the new commanding company officer, tried to discuss the problem with her. Concluding that the private was seemingly indifferent to her situation, Anderson sent Murphy back to duty pending a transfer to another post. Within two weeks, however, Murphy was facing a court-martial after a fight with another Wac in which she pulled out a "weapon characterized as a dagger." On December 18, the chief neuropsychologist of Lovell Hospital, Major Merrill Moore, testified that overall Murphy behaved well and got along with her coworkers, though occasionally she displayed signs of depression and emotional instability that sometimes turned violent. Suggestions that she had a drinking problem filtered through the session. Moore proposed that the enlisted woman's problems stemmed from an inclination to follow others, citing as evidence the defendant's participation in the strike nine months earlier. This was Murphy's third military hearing, the first in January for bringing alcohol in the barracks and arguing with her commanding officer and the second for her participation in the Fort Devens strike. It would also be her last. On January 6, 1946, the army separated Murphy from the service with what was referred to as a blue discharge.[18] At that point she disappears from the public record.

After the rigors of the court-martial, Anna Morrison, anxious to put the traumatic incident behind her, requested a discharge. She was nevertheless the last of the four to leave the service. Following her separation from the WAC on January 12, 1946, Morrison moved back to her hometown of Richmond, Kentucky. Despite her honorable discharge, she was unable to find work other than low-wage maid jobs, so she soon returned to Ohio, where she had enlisted and where race relations and salaries were more favorable than in the South. Morrison worked as a nurse's aide in a Dayton hospital before relocating to New York City, where she lived for nearly three decades. There, in 1972, the woman that the army had judged incapable of profiting from its medical technician training programs graduated with her licensed practical nurse (LPN) degree. Morrison worked as a nurse in New York and then back in Richmond, Kentucky, until her retirement. "I feel I got that much out of it," she later remarked, noting that she would not have pursued employment in the medical profession had it not been for the WAC.[19] At last, Morrison had the decent-paying employment that she had desired as a teenager. Comfortably ensconced in the middle class with veterans' health care and benefits, Morrison bought a house, was active in her church, and traveled extensively in the United States and abroad.[20]

On March 26, 2002, I reached Anna Morrison with the first inquiry in her memory about the Fort Devens strike and her role in it. In her eighties at that time, she initially protested that she could not remember much about the incident but went on to confirm information, fill in gaps, and describe her contemporary reactions to the experience. As the memories flowed forth, however, so did the pain that she had striven for nearly sixty years to put behind her. Graciously answering questions to help out a persistent graduate student, Morrison was pleased that the strike had received positive recognition but found it difficult to revisit her ordeal. She took little personal credit for the strike, citing instead the efforts of her codefendants. Eventually the painful recollections, coupled with her health problems, took precedence over her interest in reliving the incident.

Bitter experiences forged through courage can shift over the years into memories of personal pride if fostered in a positive environment. The rapid fading of the incident from the popular memory of the war, easily interpreted as a sign of its insignificance, removed the space in which Morrison otherwise might have discussed her actions and the reasons for them.

Instead, she put the episode behind her, telling neither friends nor family of her centerpiece role during World War II's struggle for rights. As that struggle pushed into the next decades, she said that no one had asked her about the case, much less linked it to other sit-down strikes and civil disobedience measures of the civil rights movement. In fact, Morrison herself saw little connection, recalling that during the sixties she had wondered, "would I have been as brave as those young people?" It was an astoundingly humble statement from someone who had braved the daunting authority of the U.S. Army at the height of its power and national popularity.

Anna Morrison passed away on February 22, 2009, leaving her photo albums, scrapbooks, and stacks of travel postcards to her good friend Juanih Campbell. Among the treasured keepsakes, Campbell found two curious articles cut out from old newspapers: "Bluegrass Neighbors 'Sick' over Wac Morrison's Plight" and "New Evidence in WAC Case about a Strike at Ft. Devens." They were the first Campbell had heard of a strike at Fort Devens and the court-martial of her friend.

Alice Young made the most of her remaining months in the service, earning a promotion to private first class, as had Morrison, before her honorable discharge on October 31, 1945. The army never did enroll her in a medical technician training course or utilize her nursing skills, so she left the service as a "medical aidman." On her return to Washington, D.C., a hometown newspaper requested an interview. Young agreed to the interview but declined to comment on the Fort Devens incident. The most she would say on the matter was that "I am awfully glad to be out of the Army and back home."[21]

Young would not pursue her earlier plan to train as a nurse. Instead she returned to her former employer, the Treasury Department in Washington, D.C., as she was entitled under the GI Bill.[22] Six months after her separation from the WAC, she married James W. Porter, a civilian she had met while in the service. The couple raised their five children in Alexandria, Virginia, where Young, active in her church, served as a deacon. She eventually retired from the U.S. Treasury.

On December 18, 1997, Alice Young Porter passed away. At her wake, her daughter, Stacie Porter, decided to commemorate her mother's courage as a way to show her respect for her actions during the Fort Devens strike. "I put her newspaper clippings on a poster board and displayed them for the younger cousins and neighbors who didn't know that side of her." This did not please some of her older relatives, including her mother's oldest sister, Jennie Hill, who told Porter that she "shouldn't have put those news clippings out there. I should just let bygones be bygones."[23]

Despite her aunt's urging to take down the reminders of the strike, Porter respectfully declined. Though her older relatives wanted to leave the painful incident in the past, she wanted to delve into it more, share its importance with the younger members of the family, and celebrate her mother's courageous stand against discrimination. In a letter to the author she remarked, "I have always been very proud of my mother's stand—when I think of the Tuskegee Airmen—I think of my mom." She then added an enduring message from her mother that has helped her over the years: "Don't get stepped on."[24]

Young had spoken little about the incident on her return home. Her sister Jennie Hill said that she did not discuss it with any of her siblings or with her children. When her daughters tried to probe her memories about what had happened, Young rebuffed their inquiries with a curt reply that the army "would treat the blacks real bad."[25] Apparently Young, like Morrison, wished to put the painful incident behind her. Without a forum for the African American Wac veterans to air their thoughts on the case and discuss their experiences, neither woman seems to have had the opportunity to put into context their much-publicized role in the military and social history of the United States.

Given Morrison and Young's reluctance to discuss the case, it is reasonable to assume that none of the four women who opted for a court-martial saw their earlier actions as either extraordinary or heroic. Perhaps they focused on personal actions that they later felt did not meet the standards of heroism. Young, for instance, had screamed at her commanding officer after the meeting with him, Morrison fainted after sentencing, Murphy had a history of trouble in her short time in the service, and Green vacillated when explaining why she took part in the strike. With little public examination of the Fort Devens case once it disappeared from the papers, the women may have focused more on perceived personal weaknesses than on their strengths in attempting such a challenge. Although regrettable, this is indicative of the times in which they lived, when the leaders of the civil rights movement seemed larger than life, above reproach, and mostly male. Nevertheless, neither Morrison nor Young—and one can hope neither Green nor Murphy—expressed shame or embarrassment over their role in the strike. As Hill explained, despite her sister's silence on the matter, Alice Young Porter "felt she did the right thing."[26]

The four Wacs in the Fort Devens case contested state policies that upheld the status quo, yet in doing so, they and other African American women inevitably ran afoul of the military justice system. Inevitably, the same policies that allowed officers to isolate black Wacs also provided the prerogative to squelch their protests against their marginalization. Black Wacs nevertheless persisted, and many faced disciplinary action as a result. Army records documenting these challenges to army policies verify the systemic racism and sexism these women experienced.

Despite their failings, army policies also declared the just treatment of troops regardless of race and sex, a precedent that established important opportunities for African American women and ultimately for the nation. The War Department's decision to create a women's corps pierced the once-exclusive masculine domain of the military and provided a space for fostering relationships across race and gender lines in the military. Narrow as this space was during World War II when the army segmented its troops by race and sex, it has widened over the decades as a platform to discuss sexual harassment and assault, the role of women in combat, and gay and transgender rights. Furthermore, the GI Bill entitled all honorably discharged World War II veterans to government-funded training, jobs, health care, and mortgage loans. These and other benefits ushered many black Wac veterans into chosen professions and middle-class stability, where they continued to contribute to the well-being of their families, their communities, and the nation. Indeed, the WAC's promise of these very opportunities had inspired Anna Morrison, Mary Green, Alice Young, Johnnie Murphy, and thousands of other African American women to serve their country in its declared fight for democracy and justice for all. Today, the black women who have followed in their footsteps constitute nearly a third of all female members of the U.S. Armed Forces.

Recognition of black Wacs and their contributions during World War II has been slow and uneven, yet the African American women who served expressed, then and later, pride in being part of the WAC. As black women, they understood the importance of their roles in advancing the stated goals of the war and of the civil rights movement. By rejecting marginalization and asserting their rights, these women acted in concert with the democratic vision that they and people around the globe were fighting for.

As members of the nation's respected armed forces, they also compelled national debates about the rights of society's peripheral persons that, in themselves, underscored society's deep, if troubled, commitment to those values. The four women who resisted subjugation at Fort Devens generated one of the most intensive of these debates during World War II, yet thousands of other black Wacs also contributed to the proud legacy of women of color and the struggle for justice. Their stories and those of other marginalized people around the world are rarely as visible as the experiences of persons more central to the established narrative, yet they too are essential to history. By confounding more than conforming to standard accounts, they illustrate the importance of recognizing all people whose spirits have likewise moved them to fight injustice.

Notes

Abbreviations

FSCI   Lt. Col. William J. White to Gen. Miles, "Investigation of SCU 1127, WAC Detachment, Lovell General Hospital, Fort Devens, Mass.," March 14, 1945, included in the Records of the Inspector General (Army), RG 159, "General Correspondence," NARA

NAACP   Part 9, Discrimination in the U.S. Armed Forces, 1918–1955, Records
Records   of the National Association for the Advancement of Colored People, microfilm

NARA   National Archives and Records Administration, College Park, MD

RG   record group

U.S. v. Young   General Court-Martial, *United States v. Young*, et al. (CM 278502), March 19–20, 1945, Fort Devens, MA, U.S. Army Judiciary, Department of the Army, Arlington, VA

WDI   Lt. Col. Milton S. Musser to the Inspector General, "Investigation of WAC Detachment, Lovell General and Convalescent Hospital, Fort Devens, Massachusetts," May 4, 1945, file 333.9, Lovell General Hospital (2), General Correspondence, 1939–1947, Record Office of the Inspector General (Army), RG 159, National Archives, College Park, MD

Introduction

The epigraph is Col. Eugene Householder, quoted in Lee, *Employment of Negro Troops*, 142.

1. Established in May 1942, the Women's Army Auxiliary Corps (WAAC) existed for just over a year. In July 1943, the Women's Army Corps (WAC) replaced it. In the narration of events, I refer to the corps itself as WAC (occasionally, and as appropriate, WAAC) and its personnel as Wacs (occasionally, and as appropriate, Waac).

2. Pvt. Anna Morrison testimony, *U.S. v. Young*, 128; A. S. Plotkin, "Negroes Given Heavy Work, Whites Spared, Says WAC," *Boston Globe*, March 19, 1945.

3. Pvt. Mary Green testimony, *U.S. v. Young*, 188–92.

4. Pvt. Alice Young testimony, *U.S. v. Young*, 201–12.

5. Pvt. Johnnie Murphy testimony, *U.S. v. Young*, 237–41.

6. To describe the military's propensity to court-martial African Americans, one journalist quipped, "when whites contracted venereal disease they received medical treatment. Blacks received courts-martial." McGuire, *He, Too, Spoke for Democracy*, 72–73.

7. Hartmann, *Home Front and Beyond*, 34–37; Meyer, *Creating GI Jane*, 12–32.

8. Under the WAAC, officers were classified as director, assistant director, field officer, 1st officer, 2nd officer, and 3rd officer. Enlisted personnel were classified as 1st leader, technical leader, staff leader, junior leader, auxiliary 1st class, and auxiliary. Treadwell, *Women's Army Corps*, 19–20, 113–17.

9. Hull, Scott, and Smith, eds., *All the Women Are White*.

10. Moye, *Freedom Flyers*. Two films based on the Tuskegee airman are *The Tuskegee Airmen* (HBO Home Video, 2010) and *Red Tails* (Twentieth-Century Fox, 2012). The Port Chicago Mutiny is another well-known case. See Allen, *Port Chicago Mutiny*. Two films based on this episode are *History Undercover: Port Chicago Mutiny* (A&E, 1998) and *Mutiny* (Trimark Home Video, 1999). Also see Milburn, *Conflicting Interest*.

11. See F. Murray, "Some Mutinies, Riots, and Other Disturbances," in *Negro Handbook, 1946–1947*, 347–60.

12. Anderson, *Wartime Women*; Bruscino, *Nation Forged in War*; Dudziak, *Cold War and Civil Rights*; Frydl, *GI Bill*; Klinkner and Smith, *Unsteady March*; Kryder, *Divided Arsenal*; Mettler, *Soldiers to Citizens*; Shockley, *We, Too, Are Americans*; Escobedo, *From Coveralls to Zoot Suits*. Lemke-Santangelo, *Abiding Courage*; Guglielmo, "'Red Cross, Double Cross'."

13. Over 70 percent of the 16 million military personnel in the U.S. armed forces during World War II served in the U.S. Army.

14. Col. Householder quoted in Lee, *Employment of Negro Troops*, 142.

15. For further investigation into the importance of the military to the struggle for civil rights, see Buchanan, *Black Americans in World War II*; Dalfiume, *Desegregation of the U.S. Armed Forces*; Foner, *Blacks and the Military*; James et al., *Fighting Racism in World War II*; Lentz-Smith, *Freedom Struggles*; Leonard, *Men of Color to Arms!*; MacGregor, *Integration of the Armed Forces*; Nalty, *Strength for the Fight*.

16. Du Bois, "Now Is the Time Not to Be Silent"; Klinkner and Smith, *Unsteady March*, 160.

17. Lee, *Employment of Negro Troops*, 75–76; 421–23.

18. Meyer, *Creating GI Jane*, 62–63, 70. Though the WAC accepted other women of color, its largest segregated contingent remained African American women. See also Treadwell, *Women's Army Corps*, 597–99.

19. Kimberlé Williams Crenshaw, "The Intersectionality of Gender and Race Discrimination" (lecture, Ohio State University, April 2002); Crenshaw, "Mapping the Margins."

20. Harvard customarily granted scholarships to Howard's highest achieving law students yet denied the honor to Pauli Murray due to her gender. Murray went on to publish the groundbreaking *States' Laws on Race and Color*, earn her doctorate from Yale University, and author legal strategies that proved instrumental in the inclusion of gender rights and protections in title 7 of the Civil Rights Act of 1964. She was also a cofounder of the National Organization for Women (NOW). Developing her Jane Crow theory, Murray fought for genuine legal reform that centered black women to ensure that new protections stretched widely enough to cover all Americans, including those on the margins of society. Azaransky, *Dream Is Freedom*, 34–35, 58–68.

21. Hartmann, *Home Front and Beyond*; Putney, *When the Nation*; B. Moore, *To Serve My Country*; Earley, *One Woman's Army*; McCabe and Roundtree, *Justice Older than the Law*; Sims-Wood, "We Served America, Too!"

22. P. Murray, *Autobiography*, 240.

23. Jones, *Labor of Love*, 199.

24. For sources on how whites benefited from the racial economy, see Katznelson, *When Affirmative Action Was White*; Cohen, *Consumers' Republic*; Sugrue, *Origins of the Urban Crisis*; Lipsitz, *Possessive Investment in Whiteness*; Roediger, *Working toward Whiteness*.

25. Hartmann, *Home Front and Beyond*, 60; Jones, *Labor of Love*, 238; also see Anderson, *Wartime Women*; Shockley, *We, Too, Are Americans*; "Negro Maids Lured to War Jobs, Survey Finds," *Chicago Defender*, March 3, 1945; Milkman, "Redefining 'Women's Work.'" For data, see "Percent of Negro Women among Total Employed Workers in Specified Occupational Groups, April 1940 and April 1944," in *Negro Women War Workers*, 16–18. For the experiences of southern black women who migrated west, see Lemke-Santangelo, *Abiding Courage*.

26. From 1920 to 1945, the percentage of the African Americans in the South plunged from 90 to 75 percent, yet African American women remained largely invisible to many white Americans outside of the roles as servants in the North as well as in the South. By 1940, less than 1 percent worked as clerks or saleswomen, and those who acquired professional degrees found their opportunities limited primarily to teaching and nursing in African American communities. Terborg-Penn, "Discontented Black Feminists," 494; F. Murray, *Negro Handbook, 1944*, 15, 195–98. Jones, *Labor of Love*, 143, 162–64; Shaw, *What a Woman Ought to Be*, 136–37.

27. Brown, *Private Politics*; Chateauvert, *Marching Together*; Giddings, *When and Where I Enter*; Hunter, *To 'Joy My Freedom*; Jones, *Labor of Love*; D. McGuire, *At the Dark End*; Shaw, *What a Woman Ought to Be*.

28. Giddings, *When and Where I Enter*, 220–30; B. Moore, *To Serve My Country*, 51–55.

29. First Officer Harriet West, "Investigations of Black Wac Protests, Interim Reports I and II," album 153, Waddy, Harriet West, Personal Papers.

30. See Putney, *When the Nation*, 61–64; Meyer, *Creating GI Jane*, 96–99. With few exceptions, the Ft. Devens strike remains today virtually unknown outside of academia. One example is a dramatic performance based on the case, Jeffrey Sweet, *Court-Martial at Fort Devens* (Playscripts Inc., 2007).

31. The experiences of other races who served during World War II are beyond the purview of this book. For information on the military's role as the melting pot, particularly in terms of diverse European ancestry, see Roediger, *Working toward Whiteness*, and Bruscino, *Nation Forged in War*. According to Suzanne Mettler, the majority of non-European categories—Native Americans, Puerto Ricans, Mexicans, Chinese, Hawaiians, Filipino, and Japanese—accounted for just 1.6 percent of the army's forces during World War II. They, too, have stories. Mettler, *Soldiers to Citizens*, 29. For information on minorities who served in the WAC, see Treadwell, *Women's Army Corps*, 589; B. Moore, *Serving Our Country*; and Judith Bellafaire, "The Contributions of Hispanic Servicewomen," Women's Memorial, www.womensmemorial.org/hispanic-servicewomen, accessed February 3, 2017.

Chapter 1. The Army Diversifies: Fort Des Moines

1. B. Moore, "From Underrepresentation to Overrepresentation," 117–18.

2. *U.S. v. Young*, 197–98. Stacie Porter, interviews with author, 2002–3.

3. Major Merrill Moore, Chief Neuropsychiatries Section, Court-Martial of Johnnie Murphy, Special Order 295, Lovell General Hospital, December 18, 1945, U.S. Army Reserve Component and Personnel and Administration Center, St. Louis, MO (Veterans Administration, Wichita, KS).

4. Juanih Campbell, interview with author, March 19, 2017; Anna Morrison, interview with author, March 26, 2002; Maurice Stephen, "Bluegrass Neighbors 'Sick' over Wac Morrison's Plight," *Pittsburgh Courier*, undated article in Anna Morrison's scrapbook, courtesy of Juanih Campbell.

5. Luzella Richard, interview with author, February 28, 2014, Conroe, TX. Thanks to Richard's niece, Creisha Lewis Cotton, for helping to facilitate this interview.

6. O. J. Cansler, "Conroe Girl Proud of Being in the WAC," *Pittsburgh Courier*, April 7, 1945, 14; *U.S. v. Young*; Mary M. Green, "Enlisted Record and Report of Separation," and "Transmittal of Records," Army Service Forces, Ft. Des Moines, IA, to AAF Regional Station Hospital, Lincoln AAB, NE, September 1945, Department of Veterans Affairs, Robert J. Dole Medical and Regional Office Center, Wichita, KS.

7. In comparison, 22.4 percent of white women worked in this field, F. Murray, *Negro Handbook, 1944*, 195. Also see *Negro Women War Workers*.

8. Gender-based differentiations remained in force. Servicewomen could request benefits for dependents though not spouses, whereas male soldiers' dependents and spouses were automatically entitled to benefits. Furthermore, no woman could command male troops, and only the corps director could rise to the level of a full colonel. Treadwell, *Women's Army Corps*, 220, 264–65.

9. None of the four were of age to enlist in the WAAC in 1942. The minimum age for the women's corps was twenty-one until the WAC lowered it to twenty. The army's minimum age for men to enlist was eighteen or seventeen with parental permission. Treadwell, *Women's Army Corps*, 220.

10. Over 900,000 black soldiers and 140,000 Wacs served in the army during World War II. Lee, *Employment of Negro Troops*, 414; Treadwell, *Women's Army Corps*, 766; Morden, *Women's Army Corps, 1945–1978*, 25.

11. See Foner, *Blacks and the Military*; Leonard, *Men of Color to Arms!*; Nalty, *Strength for the Fight*.

12. Foner, *Blacks and the Military*, 109.

13. Lentz-Smith, *Freedom Struggles*, 8–9.

14. Nalty, *Strength for the Fight*, 139; Klinkner and Smith, *Unsteady March*, 164–65.

15. Memo, Assistant Secretary of War Robert P. Patterson to President Franklin D. Roosevelt, October 8, 1940. Roosevelt approved its release to the Negro Newspaper Publishers Association, quoted in Lee, *Employment of Negro Troops*, 75.

16. Ibid., 76.

17. In 1943, Army Regulation 210-10 desegregated post recreational facilities, and a 1944 follow-up directive expanded the order to include theaters, post exchanges, and post transportation. For all intents and purposes, the matter was left to individual post commanders who often skirted these directives by changing the names of clubs labeled "Negro" to "Number 2" and requiring troops to sit with their units in assigned areas in post theaters and mess halls. Lee, *Employment of Negro Troops*, 304; Dalfiume, *Desegregation of the U.S. Armed Forces*, 88; Foner, *Blacks and the Military*, 157–58.

18. Pvt. Elsie L. Williams interview, 246, WDI.

19. Memorandum, G-1 for Chief of Staff, in response to a recommendation from William A. Hastie to institute desegregation in the army, November 6, 1941. Quoted in Lee, *Employment of Negro Troops*, 140.

20. Lee, *Employment of Negro Troops*, 356–59.

21. Statement, "Testimony of Pvt. Roberta McKenzie," December 23, 1944, attached to letter from Thurgood Marshall to William H. Hastie, January 13, 1945. Series B, reel 12, NAACP Records. For civilian women's experiences with the law during World War II, see D. McGuire, *At the Dark End*, and Brandt, *Harlem at War*.

22. Foner, *Blacks and the Military*, 154–55.

23. Simmons, *African American Press*, 79–81; also see Nalty, *Strength for the Fight*, 164–69.

24. During the Civil War, for example, Dorothea Dix organized nurses for military hospitals, Harriet Tubman guided Union troops through the South, and allegedly freedwoman Elizabeth Bowser, disguised as a slave in the home of Confederate president Jefferson Davis, spied for the Union. Threat, *Nursing Civil Rights*, 13–15; Foner, *Blacks and the Military*, 46.

25. The feminization of office work in the early twentieth century owes much to the nation's increased need for typists and telephone operators at minimal costs,

related machinery that could be quickly mastered for employees considered temporary, and the steady supply of working women as urbanization surged. Holm, *Women in the Military*, 11–12.

26. During World War I, the War Department contracted 5,000 civilian women for clerical duties in Europe. The army also recruited over 20,000 nurses, half of whom served overseas. In all, over 34,000 women served in the armed services during World War I, most as members of the nurse corps. This included eighteen African American nurses enlisted due to the influenza epidemic that ravaged its forces. Holm, *Women in the Military*, 10–14; Threat, *Nursing Civil Rights*, 23–24.

27. Treadwell, *Women's Army Corps*, 24–25, 45.

28. Meyer, *Creating GI Jane*, 16–18.

29. Ibid., 66–69.

30. Putney, *When the Nation*, 51.

31. B. Moore, *To Serve My Country*, 52.

32. Brown, *Private Politics*, 155–59. B. Moore, *To Serve My Country*, 51–54.

33. Chas P. Howard, "Mrs. Bethune Gives Advice to WAAC's," February 24, 1942, *Birmingham World*, folder 2, box 1, series 2, Martha Settle Putney Collection on the Women's Army Corps.

34. According to Dovey Johnson, who worked for Bethune before enlisting, her mentor preempted Hobby's plan to segregate officers' training (with the aid of First Lady Eleanor Roosevelt). McCabe and Johnson Roundtree, *Justice Older than the Law*, 52–53; Hanson, *Mary McLeod Bethune*, 185–87.

35. Meyer, *Creating GI Jane*, 23–24; Lee, *Employment of Negro Troops*, 421–22.

36. The navy established the WAVES and the Coast Guard SPARS in 1942. Neither admitted black women until the end of the war, though, to serve in integrated units. The marines also accepted white women but refused to enlist black women until after the war. MacGregor, *Integration of the Armed Forces*, 86–88; Foner, *Blacks and the Military*, 174–75.

37. Letter, Wac stationed at Fort Des Moines to *Chicago Defender* editor John H. Sengstacke, January 8, 1944, reprinted in Litoff and Smith, *We're in This War*, 76; Morrison interview; Sims-Wood, "We Served America, Too!," 85, 55; and Cansler, "Conroe Girl Proud."

38. B. Moore, *To Serve My Country*, 58; Morrison interview.

39. B. Moore, *To Serve My Country*, 2; Hobby quoted in Putney, *When the Nation*, 29; letter, Dovey Johnson to Major Harriet West, May 13, 1944, reprinted in Litoff and Smith, *We're in This War*, 72.

40. Address, Director Oveta Culp Hobby to the Alpha Kappa Alpha Sorority, Howard University, "The Role of Our Federal Government," July 6, 1942, file 291.2; "Negro, Historical Background and Background Material Relating to the Legislation and Administration of the Women's Army Auxiliary Corps and Its Successor, the Women's Army Corps, 1942–49," box 221, Records of the War Department General and Special Staffs; Lee, *Employment of Negro Troops*, 423. Putney, *When the Nation*, 29; Foner, *Blacks and the Military*, 149.

41. Williams, *WACS*, 17.

42. Treadwell, *Women's Army Corps*, 221–23.

43. Ibid., 498–99; Meyer, *Creating GI Jane*, 68–70.

44. "Accession of Personnel in the Women's Army Corps: 1942–1946," appendix A, table 2, in Treadwell, *Women's Army Corps*, 766.

45. The Slander Campaign emerged during 1943 as rumors spread that women in uniform were adopting male behavior, and that many were homosexuals, tramps, and prostitutes. Parents were appalled, one white father fuming over his daughter's membership in "an organized uniformed group of whores." Meyer, *Creating GI Jane*, 33–41; Treadwell, *Women's Army Corps*, 200–209.

46. At Fort Clark, TX, for instance, a report detailing the actions of African American Wacs who took the lead in a series of peaceful protests against racial segregation at the post chapel, labeled the women ringleaders and the affair a "conspiracy." War Department, MID, Army Service Forces, "Church Attendance of Colored Personnel," May 4, 1944, Headquarters 8th Service Command, Ft. Clark, TX, file 291.2, Security Classified General Correspondence, 1942–46, Office of the Director of Personnel and Admin (G-1), Director of the WAC, box 49, Records of the War Department General and Special Staffs, 165, NARA.

47. In July 1943, Treadwell, who worked closely with Hobby, explained the WAC leadership's reason for recalling African American recruiters from the field: "It was known that the presence of Negro recruiters had caused situations prejudicial to white recruiting." Treadwell, *Women's Army Corps*, 594.

48. Treadwell, *Women's Army Corps*, 599.

49. Meyer, *Creating GI Jane*, 67; *Facts You Want to Know*.

50. Ft. Devens served as a WAAC induction center for black and white recruits until August 1943, when it closed due to low enlistment rates. The five other induction centers accepted white Wacs only: Ft. Oglethorpe, GA; Daytona Beach, FL; Monticello, AR; Camp Polk, LA; and Rustin, LA. Putney, *When the Nation*, 5.

51. Putney, *When the Nation*, 49; Earley, *One Woman's Army*, 19–20; Sims-Wood, "We Served America, Too!," 57.

52. Putney, *When the Nation*, 49–60.

53. Ibid., 56–60. The publicity campaign invited the attention of Mary McLeod Bethune, NAACP president Walter White, and WAC colonel Oveta Hobby. Publicly, Stimson attributed his decision to morale reasons and privately to avoid further publicity and racial confrontations over the matter. See also Tucker, *Swing Shift*, 53–54.

54. Treadwell, *Women's Army Corps*, 591.

55. B. Moore, *To Serve My Country*, 72–73.

56. Many white Waacs also protested the strict segregation of the cooks' and bakers' barracks. "Report of NAACP Investigating Committee on WAAC Complaints," May 12, 1945, file 291.2, Security Classified General Correspondence, 1942–46, Office of the Director of Personnel and Admin (G-1), Director of the WAC, box 50, RG 165, Records of the War Department General and Special Staffs.

57. 1st Officer Harriet West acknowledged in a radio interview that "There were 40 Negro soldiers stationed at Fort Des Moines prior to the arrival of the Waacs, but they were transferred to Camp Dodge within two days after we arrived there." "Radio Broadcast WINX," April 23, 1943, "Negro" file, Historical Background and Background Material Relating to the Legislation and Administration of the Women's Army Auxiliary Corps and Its Successor, the Women's Army Corps, 1942–49, box 221, Records of the War Department General and Special Staffs; Putney, *When the Nation*, 16–18.

58. As late as April 1945, the swimming pool and officer's club situation had yet to be rectified. See letter from unidentified Wac, Ft. Des Moines, IA, to Roy Wilkins, April 4, 1945, series B, reel 25, NAACP Records.

59. The WAC reluctantly, and temporarily, integrated its officers' program when it had too few African American candidates. In Putney's July 1943 graduation class, just five black Wacs received their commissions. Sims-Wood, "We Served America, Too!," 155–57. Morden, *Women's Army Corps*, 16–18; B. Moore, *To Serve My Country*, 71.

60. The army did not specify black Wacs as replacements for black soldiers to whom it rarely issued arms and typically assigned heavy manual labor. Lee, *Employment of Negro Troops*, 422.

61. *73 Questions and Answers.*

62. "Telephoned to White House by Mrs. Hill," November 16, 1943, file 291.2, Utilization of Negro Race, Security Classified General Correspondence, 1942–46, Office of the Director of Personnel and Admin (G-1), Director of the WAC, RG 165, NARA.

63. Treadwell claims that WAC "solutions" ranged from forming menial labor companies for black Wacs to simplifying courses. Treadwell, *Women's Army Corps*, 593–94.

64. Treadwell, *Women's Army Corps*, 175.

65. According to Army Manual M5, nine southern states during the 1939–40 school year spent an average of $18.82 for each black student and $58.69 for each white student. Nationwide, Americans spent approximately $88.09 per student, which gave most northern recruits, black and white, an edge over most southern recruits. *Leadership and the Negro Soldier*, 30.

66. Gilmore, *Defying Dixie*, 396.

67. P. McGuire, "Desegregation of the Armed Forces."

68. Odum, *Race and Rumors*, 67–80.

69. Horne often appeared in films in the role of a singer whose character was peripheral to the main storyline. Such segments were called "specialty sequences," which producers could easily snip out of the versions shown in southern theaters; Haskins, *Lena*, 67–79.

70. Putney, *When the Nation*, 120.

71. Col. McCoskrie to Col. Catron, August 19, 1943, file 291.2, Security Classified General Correspondence, 1942–46, Office of the Director of Personnel and Admin (G-1), Director of the WAC, RG 165, box 49, NARA.

72. Jones, *Labor of Love*, 252. Until 1944, even Bell Telephone, whose operators could not be seen by its clients, refused to hire black women. Hartmann, *Home Front and Beyond*, 81.

73. Giddings, *When and Where I Enter*, 141–42, 232–36; Jones, *Labor of Love*, 215.

74. Commanders also requested white Wacs for traditional kitchen and laundry jobs although requisitions disproportionately included African American Wacs. Meyer, *Creating GI Jane*, 79–81; Weatherford, *History of Women*, 66–67.

75. Harriet West to Director, Control Division, March 1943, "Investigations of Black Wac Protests, Interim Reports I and II," album 153, Waddy, Harriet West, Personal Papers; Putney, *When the Nation*, 72.

76. "Conference with Mrs. Bethune and members of the National Council of Women—Col. Hobby, Col. Catron, Capt. Strayhorn," August 16, 1943, Director's Daily Journal, Historical and Background Material relating to the legislation and Administration of the Women's Army Auxiliary Corps and Its Successor, the Women's Army Corps, 1942–49, Director of the Women's Army Corps, box 200, Records of the War Department General and Special Staffs.

77. Treadwell, *Women's Army Corps*, 599.

78. Earley, *One Woman's Army*, 79; Major George F. Martin to Hobby, "Enrollment and Assignment of Negro Personnel," March 24, 1943, WAAC/WAC, Historical Background and Background Material Relating to the Legislation and Administration of the Women's Army Auxiliary Corps and Its Successor, the Women's Army Corps, 1942–49, box 221, Records of the War Department General and Special Staffs.

79. Putney, *When the Nation*, 40–41.

80. Johnnie Murphy enlisted on May 25, 1944, and arrived at Ft. Des Moines on June 20; Mary Green enlisted on June 22, 1944, and arrived at Ft. Des Moines on June 28. World War II Army Enlistment Records 1938–1946, National Personnel Records Center, Military Personnel Records Division, St. Louis, MO.

81. "Report of Proceedings of Board of Officers," Fourth WAC Hospital Company, Lovell General Hospital, Ft. Devens, MA, December 18, 1945, Department of the Army, Adjutant General, U.S. Army Reserve Component and Personnel and Administration Center, St. Louis, MO.

82. Mary M. Green, "Enlisted Record and Report of Separation," and "Transmittal of Records," Army Service Forces, Ft. Des Moines, IA, to AAF Regional Station Hospital, Lincoln AAB, NE, September 1945, courtesy of the Department of Veterans Affairs, Robert J. Dole Medical and Regional Office Center, Wichita, KS.

83. Cansler, "Conroe Girl Proud."

84. Morrison interview.

85. Alice Young, testimony, *U.S. v. Young*, 197–98.

86. *73 Questions and Answers*, 1.

87. By the end of the war, 140,000 women had enlisted in the corps. Hartmann, *Home Front and Beyond*, 31; "Strength of the Women's Army Corps: July 1942–December 1946," appendix A, table 1, Treadwell, *Women's Army Corps*, 765, 239.

88. "More Wacs Are Needed in Medical Department," *Morning Register*, Sun Sac City, IA, October 5, 1944, World War II Iowa Press Clippings. In a March 9, 1944, letter citing a "serious shortage of WAC personnel," the War Department ordered commanders to reserve all military personnel, male and female, for military duties rather than place them into jobs civilians could do, quoted in Treadwell, *Women's Army Corps*, 249.

89. *Liberty Magazine*, October 9, 1943, quoted in Treadwell, *Women's Army Corps*, 274.

90. Less than a year after the establishment of the corps, the WAAC deemed a third of its total force of black Wacs "unassignable." Putney, *When the Nation*, 120.

91. Mansoor, *GI Offensive in Europe*, 11–12.

92. After the Battle of the Bulge, critical manpower shortages compelled the War Department to engage black soldiers in combat duty. Nonetheless, it imposed a strict cap on how many men and assigned volunteers to segregated units. MacGregor, *Integration of the Armed Forces*, 51–53.

93. B. Moore, *To Serve My Country*, 81–82; Lee, *Employment of Negro Troops*, 422; Treadwell, *Women's Army Corps*, 599.

94. Martin to Hobby, "Enrollment and Assignment of Negro Personnel"; Putney, *When the Nation*, 74.

95. Putney, *When the Nation*, 89.

96. Anna Morrison interview, 558, WDI.

97. Alice Young interview, 551, WDI.

98. Putney, *When the Nation*, 27.

Chapter 2. Fort Devens

The epigraph is quoted in Earley, *One Woman's Army*, 108.

1. Putney, *When the Nation*, 120; the 1944 transfer paralleled the WAAC's 1943 move of African American recruits from Ft. Des Moines to Ft. Devens's induction center to relieve the overcrowding of the Ft. Des Moines black Wac section. Three months later, the WAAC closed the Ft. Devens induction center and returned the women to Ft. Des Moines. Treadwell, *Women's Army Corps*, 593.

2. The War Department's Adjutant General's Office to First Service Command, September 18, 1944, exhibit U, WDI.

3. The number of black Wacs on active duty at any one time peaked at 4,000 in 1945. Treadwell, *Women's Army Corps*, 596.

4. Summary, 4, WDI.

5. Military housing standards that called for isolating black soldiers on the outskirts of bases while safeguarding white Wacs in or near headquarters resulted in contradictory instructions for housing black Wacs. Lee, *Employment of Negro Troops*, 98–100; Treadwell, *Women's Army Corps*, 515.

6. "Edith Nourse Rogers," History, Fort Devens Museum, www.fortdevensmuseum.org/EdithNourseRogers.php, accessed July 25, 2017.

7. Summary, 4, WDI.

8. Col. Walter M. Crandall interview, 414, WDI.

9. Exhibit AA, list of the names and assignments of white Wacs posted at Lovell Hospital North on March 9, 1945, WDI. Crandall relied on cadet nurses to fulfill the role of the departing medical technicians. Col. Walter Crandall, interview, 8, FSCI.

10. Summary, 4, WDI; in January, the army changed Ft. Devens black Wacs' MOS classification from Basics (521) to Aidmen (657) to better reflect the work they were doing; Maj. Elizabeth W. Stearns, First Service Command WAC Commander, interview, 292, WDI; summary, 5, WDI.

11. Tenola Stoney interview, 1–2, WDI. By the time of the strike, the army had promoted Stoney to 1st lieutenant, likely when she took command of SCU 1127th black WAC Detachment.

12. Summary, 5, WDI. In addition to the 39 white aidmen or orderlies, Crandall released "approximately 3 cadre, 11 clerical, 10 hospital technicians . . . 15 drivers, 5 mess personnel, and 5 miscellaneous." Summary, 5, WDI.

13. Interviews, Sgt. Harold Wicks, 35.7, and Pvt. Wanda Blount, 37.6, WDI.

14. Alice Young testimony, *U.S. v. Young*, 208.

15. Interviews, Sgt. Area Bates, 33.18, and Wicks, 35.8, WDI.

16. "Edith Nourse Rogers."

17. A third facility, Lovell Hospital East, was small in comparison and does not appear to have utilized the services of Wacs, black or white. Referenced as the Ft. Devens Reconditioning Center in the hospital's welcome booklet, Lovell Hospital East was part of the consolidation plan that formed Lovell General Hospital. Welcome booklet, *Lovell General Hospital, Ft. Devens, Mass*, undated (probably 1945), New England Telephone and Telegraph Company in collaboration with the Public Relations Office of the hospital, Ft. Devens, MA, 6, 24, and 30.

18. Ft. Devens skating rink, tennis courts, and mess halls were integrated. The bowling alley operated on a rotating schedule to accommodate white and black enlisted personnel. In January 1945, service club 2 burned down, leaving African American personnel a "very tiny one" until the opening of a large replacement club in April. The black WAC detachment's officer, Lt. Tenola Stoney, insisted that her troops could use the white Club 1, though only two members did, and they reported that they had a good time. Putney, *When the Nation*, 18; interviews, Pvt. Elsie L. Williams, 246, and Stoney, 55, WDI.

19. Welcome booklet, *Lovell General Hospital*, 13 and 17.

20. Summary, 21, WDI.

21. The blue smocks were nurse uniforms that the army had declared surplus when it introduced a new uniform style. Once the WAC learned of their no-cost availability, it dispensed them to hospital workers. The Wacs disliked them because of their "outmoded" style, limited sizes, and the fact that civilian hospital workers wore them, too. Treadwell, *Women's Army Corps*, 536–37.

22. Lt. Victoria Lawson interview, 77, WDI.

23. Putney, *When the Nation*, 75–82; Ft. Clark, TX, servicewoman to Mrs. Roosevelt who, omitting the author's name, forwarded the letter to Col. Hobby on May 2, 1943, file 291.2, Security Classified General Correspondence, 1942–46, box 49, Office of

the Director of Personnel and Administration (G-1) Subordinate Offices, Director of the Women's Army Corps, RG 165, NARA.

24. Adjutant General's Office to Commanding Generals and Service Commands, "Recruiting for Army General Hospital Companies (WAC)," January 13, 1946, "Historical Materials of WAAC/WASC 1942–49," Director of WAC, box 189, Records of the War Department General and Special Staffs.

25. Young testimony, *U.S. v. Young*, 200–201; Crandall interview, 428, WDI.

26. Interviews, Crandall, 438, and Stoney, 7, WDI.

27. Welcome booklet, *Lovell General Hospital*, 23–24.

28. Crandall interview, 418, WDI.

29. Interviews, Pvt. Queen Brown, 117, and Crandall, 435, WDI.

30. Summary, 7, WDI; Crandall interview, 435–36, WDI.

31. Stoney interview, 7, WDI.

32. "Telephone conversation between Col. Hobby and Mr. Jonathan Daniels," November 1944, file 291.2, Security Classified General Correspondence, 1942–46, Office of the Director of Personnel and Administration (G-1) Subordinate Offices, Director of the Women's Army Corps, box 49, Records of the War Department General and Special Staffs.

33. Waacs had not been entitled to many of the same benefits of male soldiers, including "extra overseas pay, government life insurance, and veteran's hospitalization." Treadwell, *Women's Army Corps*, 599; Moore, *To Serve My Country*, 80–83.

34. "Report on Protest of the Assignment of Negro Wacs to the Gardiner General Hospital, Chicago, Illinois," April 6, 1945, and "Situation Created by Assigning a WAC Company (Colored) at Gardiner General Hospital, Chicago, Illinois," April 16, 1945, file 291.2, Security Classified General Correspondence, Office of the Director of Personnel and Administration (G-1) Subordinate Offices, Director of the Women's Army Corps, box 49, Records of the War Department General and Special Staffs; Putney, *When the Nation*, 89–95.

35. Treadwell, *Women's Army Corps*, 389; Moore, *To Serve My Country*, 141.

36. Putney, *When the Nation*, 75–84.

37. Telephone conversation transcript, Col. Whitehurst and Capt. Sisson, First Service Command, March 7, 1945, exhibit MM, WDI.

38. Crandall interview, 438, WDI.

39. Lawson interview, 68, WDI.

40. Lee, *Employment of Negro Troops*, 13.

41. Earley, *One Woman's Army*, 107–8.

42. Foner, *Blacks and the Military*, 150–52; P. McGuire, *Taps for a Jim Crow Army*, 31–35.

43. Moore, "From Underrepresentation to Overrepresentation," 118–19.

44. Lawson interview, 68–69, WDI.

45. Interviews, Wicks, 35.23, Lt. Jane T. Chmielewski, 46.3, and Capt. Russell Elliot, 377–81, WDI.

46. Jones, "Writings of Margaret Barnes Jones," in the personal collection of Teresa Barnes.

47. Putney, *When the Nation*, 96.

48. Wicks interview, 35.9, WDI.

49. Carolyn Moore to Thurgood Marshall, March 6, 1945, series C, reel 12, NAACP Records; inquiry, William T. Granahan to Stimson, March 13, 1945, exhibit CC, WDI.

50. Report, Lt. Stoney's account of conversation with Baham, Allen, and Warfield, February 13, 1945, exhibit HH, WDI.

51. Summary, 28, WDI.

52. Lt. Col. Ralph F. Bowers interview, Bowers.4, WDI.

53. Capt. Elizabeth L. Bryan, Mason General Hospital, March 3, exhibit BB, WDI.

54. Stoney interview, 8, WDI.

55. Interviews, Lawson, 89, and Stoney, 466, WDI.

56. Maj. Miller to Col. Putney, "Complaints from Colored WAC detachment at Lovell General and Convalescent Hospital," March 7, 1945, exhibit D, FSCI.

57. Interviews, Lawson, 72, and Stoney, 11, WDI.

58. "Complaints from Colored WAC detachment," exhibit D, FSCI.

59. Summary, 9, WDI.

60. Interviews, Lawson, 72, and Stoney, 15–17, WDI.

61. Interviews, Anna Morrison, 573, and Mary Green, 36.6, WDI. The army likely introduced the courses in order to retain civilians who had other employment options during the war year's labor shortage.

62. Addressing the many complaints by Wacs over orderly duty, Treadwell reveals that by the summer of 1944, the "problem had become one of the Corps' most serious." The transfer of a hundred black Wacs to Ft. Devens shortly afterward infers that the WAC leadership focused on the complaints of white rather than black Wacs. Treadwell, *Women's Army Corps*, 345–47.

63. Summary, 3–4, WDI; Lawson interview, 67–68, WDI.

64. "List of white members, WAC Detachment, SCU 1127," March 9, 1945, exhibit AA, WDI.

65. Crandall interview, 416–18, WDI.

66. Interviews, Morrison, 573, and Stoney, 478, WDI. Stoney said that she could not recall making this statement.

67. Morrison interview, 571, WDI.

68. Interviews, Young, 537–38, Miller, L.6–7, Mae E. Lewis, 195, Amanda McCord, McCord.13, Green, 36.10–36.11, and Pvt. Elizabeth Parker, 254, WDI.

69. Interviews, Lula M. Johnson, 124, and Morrison, 578, WDI.

70. Ruth B. Waller interview, 97, WDI.

71. Interviews, Waller, 104, and Lawson, 78, WDI.

72. Interviews, Pvt. Tommie May Cartwright, 164, Pvt. Lorraine Overton, 16.13, Waller, 96–97, WDI.

73. McCord interview, McCord.14, WDI.

74. Mary E. Johnson interview, 22.7, WDI.

75. Interviews, Miller, L.8, Ola Jackson, 172, and Anna Kelly, Kelly.9, WDI.

76. Interviews, M. Johnson, 22.7, Miller, L.7, Lewis, 195, and Jessie Gaines, Gaines.4, WDI.

77. Clotha I. Walker interview, 277, WDI.

Chapter 3. The Strike

1. "6 WACs Resign: WAC Clerks Decline to Scrub Floors," *Afro-American* (Washington, D.C.), July 10, 1943, folder 2, box 1, series 2, Martha Settle Putney Collection on the Women's Army Corps. See also NAACP files for correspondence between Viola B. Vessup, one of the discharged Wacs, Truman Gibson Jr., Assistant Civilian Aide to Stimson, and Leslie Perry, Administrative Assistant, series C, reel 5, NAACP Records.

2. F. Murray, *Negro Handbook, 1946–47*, 350–55; Allen, *Port Chicago Mutiny*, 126–27.

3. P. McGuire, *Taps for a Jim Crow Army*, 143–63.

4. Green returned to the barracks looking for Alberta Doss, whom she expected to meet in Lowell. Green was not on duty, so not part of the strike action that day. Mary Green interview, 36.12, WDI.

5. Interviews, Pvt. Alice Young, 528, Pvt. Willie Mae Miller, L.4–5, and Pvt. Elsie Williams, 240–41, WDI.

6. Interviews, Anna Morrison, 579, and Tenola Stoney, 21, WDI.

7. Charge Sheets, "Statement of Victoria Lawson," March 13, 1945, included in *U.S. v. Young.*

8. Summary, 22, WDI.

9. Interviews, Victoria Lawson, 78, and Alice Young, 541–45, WDI.

10. Anna Morrison, interview with author, March 26, 2002; Sims-Wood, "We Served America, Too!," 155.

11. Summary, 22, WDI; interviews, Lawson, 78, Area Bates, 33.27, Stoney, 23–26, WDI.

12. Stoney interview, 27, WDI.

13. Ibid., 59.

14. Lawson interview, 78, WDI.

15. According to Crandall and confirmed by Lawson, Pierce told the colonel that she was not involved in the strike and asked for advice as to what she should have done. Crandall responded, "That, young lady, you should have decided for yourself." See interviews, Pvt. Ruby Pierce, 23.10, Walter Crandall, 425, and Lawson, 78, WDI.

16. Interviews, Bates, 33.27–33.30, Stoney, 27, and Clotha I. Walker, 278, WDI.

17. Stoney interview, 32, WDI.

18. See "Complaints Taken at Lovell General Hospital," March 12, 1945, exhibit C, FSCI.

19. Summary, 15, WDI; Wyant coauthored Army Manual M5, *Leadership and the Negro Soldier*. Sherman Miles interview, 327–28, WDI.

20. John Hurd interview, 371, WDI.

21. Interviews, Hurd, 373, and Stoney, 40, WDI.

22. Summary, 15, WDI.

23. Hurd interview, 373–74, WDI.

24. Bates interview, 33.35, WDI.

25. See outline of officer responsibilities to WAC personnel, memorandum, Surgeon General to Medical Department officers, "WAC Personnel Assigned to Hospital Duties," December 26, 1945, file 220.3, 321 WAC Project, Decimal Files 1942–June 1946, G-1 Personnel, box 483, Records of the War Department General and Special Staffs.

26. Stoney interview, 477, WDI. Gay and Stoney fared little better. Their introduction with Crandall lasted "less than ten minutes."

27. Miles interview, 328–29, WDI.

28. Ibid., 329.

29. Summary, 14–15, WDI.

30. Miles interview, 329, WDI.

31. *Manual for Courts-Martial*, 219.

32. Summary, 15, WDI.

33. Morrison; interview with author.

34. Anna Morrison testimony, *U.S. v. Young*, 147–48; Morrison interview, 584, WDI.

35. Mary Green testimony, *U.S. v. Young*, 173–74.

36. Pvt. Alice Young interview, 545–46, WDI.

37. A month later, Wicks expressed little sympathy for the black Wacs, insisting that white Wac orderlies performed the same jobs without complaint. Sgt. Harold Wicks interview, 35.24, WDI.

38. Young interview, 546–47, WDI.

39. Ibid.

40. Ibid., 547–48.

41. Mary Johnson interview, 22.12, WDI. Other servicewomen intended to turn themselves in for a court-martial until friends dissuaded them when they entered the dayroom. In Pvt. Mary Johnson's case, Lawson advised her against it.

42. Anna Morrison testimony, *U.S. v. Young*, 119; charge sheet "Statement of Victoria Lawson," March 13, 1945, *U.S. v. Young*.

43. Young interview, 549, WDI.

44. Green testimony, *U.S. v. Young*, 188–90.

45. Johnnie Murphy testimony, *U.S. v. Young*, 241.

46. Ibid., 237.

47. Morrison testimony, *U.S. v. Young*, 120.

48. Edward R. Dudley to Carolyn D. Moore, executive secretary, Philadelphia Branch, NAACP, March 10, 1945, series B, reel 19, NAACP Records.

49. Meyer, *Creating GI Jane*, 98–99; "Negro Wacs under Discipline, Offered Counsel for Defense," *Christian Science Monitor*, March 16, 1945; report, Isadore Zack, "Refusal of Duty by Certain Member of WAC Detachment (Colored), Lovell General Hospital," March 23, 1945, series 4, Investigative Reports, 1943–1944, Isadore Zack

Papers; "Devens WAC Strike End: Six Face Court-Martial," *Afro-American*, March 24, 1945, series B, reel 19, NAACP Records.

50. Miles's statement to the Negro Enlisted Women regarding the transfers of the technicians, read by Maj. Stearns, February 17, 1945, exhibit W, WDI.

51. Stoney's report on her conversation with Baham, Allen, and Warfield, February 13, 1945, exhibit HH, WDI; Miles interview, 331, WDI.

52. Miles's military career stretched over forty years. A 1905 graduate of West Point, he advanced quickly through the ranks, and in 1941 rose to the position of chief army intelligence officer. Following the Japanese attack on Pearl Harbor, the War Department removed Miles from the post, promoted him to major general, and reassigned him to the First Service Command in Boston, MA. Arlington National Cemetery Website, www.arlingtoncemetery.net/shermanm.htm (accessed April 2016).

Chapter 4. Trial and Verdict

1. Telegrams, March 21, 1945, in "Copies of list [correspondence] received by Negro Enlisted Women who were Court Martialed," exhibit P, WDI.

2. O. J. Cansler, "Conroe Girl Proud of Being in the WAC," *Pittsburgh Courier*, April 7, 1945, 14.

3. Censors initially retained the letter over apparent concerns that its contents were incendiary. Hipkins, for instance, predicted that Morrison's "name shall live when the unjust and evil doer have perished from the earth." She also enclosed a dollar which army censors immediately handed to Morrison. Morrison shot back that if they kept the letter, they could keep the dollar, too. Letter, Bessie Hipkins to Anna Morrison, March 20, 1945, exhibit P, WDI; Anna Morrison interview, 530, WDI.

4. Pvt. Jackie Young to Johnnie Murphy, Camp Myles Standish Sta. Hosp., Stanton, MA, n.d., exhibit P, WDI.

5. D. McGuire, *At the Dark End*, 35–45.

6. Massachusetts Bar Applications for Julian Rainey, courtesy of the Commonwealth of Massachusetts Supreme Judicial Court for Suffolk County, Boston, MA.

7. Lentz-Smith, *Freedom Struggles*, 113–16.

8. John Froias testimony, *U.S. v. Young*, 89–90.

9. Alice Young testimony, *U.S. v. Young*, 223.

10. Rhoyd Heath testimony, *U.S. v. Young*, 97.

11. Julian Rainey, *U.S. v. Young*, 104–6.

12. Leon McCarthy, *U.S. v. Young*, 107–8.

13. Rainey, *U.S. v. Young*, 134, 180, 316–17.

14. Ibid., 133.

15. By prioritizing African Americans' failure to follow orders, military courts gave little credence to extenuating circumstances, including the Port Chicago seamen's

concerns when ordered to load ammunition under the same unsafe conditions that had killed 250 fellow stevedores. Allen, *Port Chicago Mutiny*.

16. Anna Morrison testimony, *U.S. v. Young*, 141.

17. Johnnie Murphy testimony, *U.S. v. Young*, 238.

18. A. Young testimony, *U.S. v. Young*, 207.

19. Ibid., 201–2.

20. Ibid.

21. Mary Green testimony, *U.S. v. Young*, 180.

22. J. Murphy testimony, *U.S. v. Young*, 244–47.

23. Ibid.

24. Ibid.

25. Victoria Lawson testimony, *U.S. v. Young*, 253–73.

26. J. Murphy testimony, *U.S. v. Young*, 250.

27. P. McGuire, *Taps for a Jim Crow Army*, 59–77.

28. A. Young testimony, *U.S. v. Young*, 203–6.

29. McCarthy, *U.S. v. Young*, 165–66, 212.

30. A. Young testimony, *U.S. v. Young*, 197.

31. Alberta Doss testimony, *U.S. v. Young*, 165.

32. Ibid., 159–64.

33. Ibid., 164–66.

34. Ibid., 168.

35. Ibid., 170.

36. Rainey, *U.S. v. Young*, 133, 167.

37. It was a common question among African Americans, and one famously crystallized in a letter to the editor, Cpl. Rupert Trimmingham, *Yank Magazine*, April 28, 1944.

38. Rainey closing statement, *U.S. v. Young*, 312.

39. Anna Morrison, interview with author, March 26, 2002.

40. Klinkner and Smith, *Unsteady March*, 238; Martin, *Brown v. Board of Education*, 143–47.

41. Rainey, *U.S. v. Young*, 321.

42. Ibid., 314–19.

43. Pauli Murray encountered a similar attitude at Howard University, which trained the nation's finest civil rights lawyers, on discovery that her male classmates and professors did not view African American women's struggle with the same gravity as their own. On her first day, laughter erupted after a professor questioned why women would study law. Faculty and students initially sidelined their rare female classmate in class discussions and, throughout her studies at Howard, banned her from the male-only law fraternity. Murray observed that while African American men championed equal rights for the race, they prioritized the rights of their sex. Murray, *Autobiography of a Black Activist*, 183–84.

44. Rainey, *U.S. v. Young*, 312.

184 Notes to Chapters 4 and 5

45. Rainey, *U.S. v. Young*, 134.

46. Morrison testimony, *U.S. v. Young*, 121–22.

47. Ibid., 116–17.

48. A. Young testimony, *U.S. v. Young*, 220–21.

49. Morrison testimony, *U.S. v. Young*, 129.

50. J. Murphy testimony, *U.S. v. Young*, 241.

51. Ibid., 128–29.

52. Roy Wilkins to Henry Stimson, March 15, 1945, series B, reel 19, NAACP Records.

53. Lawson testimony, *U.S. v. Young*, 253–75.

54. Tenola Stoney testimony, *U.S. v. Young*, 276–82.

55. Stoney testimony, *U.S. v. Young*, 287–88.

56. Ibid., 291–92.

57. A. Young testimony, *U.S. v. Young*, 309.

58. Lawson testimony, *U.S. v. Young*, 271, and Stoney testimony, *U.S. v. Young*, 276.

59. Stoney testimony, *U.S. v. Young*, 298.

60. Rainey closing statement, *U.S. v. Young*, 316–20.

61. Ibid., 317.

62. Ibid., 317–21.

63. McCarthy, *U.S. v. Young*, 321–28.

64. Ibid., 328.

65. Ibid.

66. Ibid., 326.

67. *U.S. v. Young*, 328; Eugene Zack, "Notables Demand Probe in Conviction of Wacs," *Chicago Defender*, March 31, 1945; "Wacs Sentenced to Year of Hard Labor," *Boston Herald*, March 21, 1945; "Court-Martial Convicts 4 Wacs; Negroes Allege Discrimination," *Herald Tribune*, March 21, 1945, all series B, reel 19, NAACP Records.

68. J. Murphy testimony, *U.S. v. Young*, 237.

69. P. McGuire, *Taps for a Jim Crow Army*, 146.

70. Foner, *Blacks and the Military*, 229.

Chapter 5. The Civilian Reaction

1. Alice Young to "Hank," May 4, 1945, exhibit P, WDI.

2. Anna Morrison, interview with author, March 26, 2002.

3. Leotha Hackshaw, "New Evidence in WAC Case: Reopening Sought by Julian Rainey," *Pittsburgh Courier*, March 31, 1945.

4. Marty Richardson, "Fort Devens WACS Have Two Day Trial" and "Groups Seek to Pool Their Efforts," both from the *Boston Chronicle*, n.d., series B, reel 19, NAACP Records.

5. PFC Julius R. Primus to the NAACP, October 2, 1945, series C, reel 11, NAACP Records.

6. Between 1939 and 1945, NAACP membership leaped from over 50,000 to over 500,000. Klinkner and Smith, *Unsteady March*, 166.

7. Carolyn Moore to Thurgood Marshall, March 6, 1945; letter, Roy Wilkins to Henry Stimson, March 15, 1945; press release, "NAACP Will Aid in Appeal," New York, March 29, 1945; Thurgood Marshall to L. E. Austin, president of Durham NAACP Branch (and editor of the *Carolina Times*), April 3, 1945, all in series B, reel 19, NAACP Records.

8. Among the local activists working with the NAACP were a Mr. Pope, who had connections to the USO; Jane Parker, who worked with the Red Cross; and Richard Walker, a War Manpower Commission employee. Report, Richard Walker to Mary McLeod Bethune, March 24, 1945; Robert L. Carter to Mr. Wilkins, "Wac Strike in Massachusetts," March 15, 1945, both in series B, reel 19, NAACP Records.

9. Letter from Eugene E. Burns, United People's Action Committee, to Walter White, secretary of the NAACP, Philadelphia, PA, March 25, 1945; letter from Lucile Milner to Thurgood Marshall, March 23, 1945, both in series B, reel 19, NAACP Records. Morris Milgram, Workers Defense League, to Roosevelt, March 23, 1945; Chicago's John Brown Organization to Roosevelt, March 25, 1945; and Negro Youth of Greater Boston to Stimson, March 25, 1945, all in file 291.2, Race, decimal file, 1940–45, box 1063, Records of the Adjutant General's Office.

10. Letter, Bethune to Stimson, March 22, folder 541, box 38, series 5, National Council of Negro Women Inc., record collection 001, National Archives for Black Women's History, Mary McLeod Bethune Council House National Historic Site, Landover, MD.

11. Boyce, who within four months would succeed Hobby as director, was then responsible for the "allotment of grades for WAC general hospital companies." Putney, *When the Nation*, 63–64.

12. Report, Charles Houston to Mary McLeod Bethune, April 26, 1945, series B, reel 19, NAACP Records.

13. Rebecca Stiles Taylor, "Federated Clubs: Four Negro Wacs Call for Justice. Will They Be Heard?," *Chicago Defender* (national ed.), March 31, 1945, 15.

14. Wolfinger, "We Are in the Front Lines."

15. California State Association of Colored Women to Stimson, April 9, 1945, file 291.2, Race, decimal file 1940–1945, box 1063, Records of the Adjutant General's Office. Also see newspaper accounts of the strike and its supporters in file 228_01, box 296, Publicity (1942–1949), United States Army Women's Museum.

16. Moore's prestrike letter states that Warfield noted three suicide attempts, yet army records list only the Beulah Sims case prior to the strike, followed by three others. Moore labeled the three unverifiable because Warfield did not know the names of the women. The timing of the letter infers either talk or unreported attempts of suicide within the detachment. Carolyn Moore to Thurgood Marshall, March 6, 1945, series B, reel 19, NAACP Records.

17. Simmons, *African American Press*, 71–72.

18. By 1940, nearly 340 African American–published news journals, periodicals, and bulletins circulated the country. Approximately 150 of these were newspapers, enough for each major city to boast at least one weekly edition. The largest devoted

most of their coverage—an average of 75 percent of their entire content—to news and editorials and the remaining 25 percent to feature articles on celebrities, sports, and society. Some cities supported more than one black newspaper: Birmingham and Houston each had two, Philadelphia and New York three, and Cleveland five. F. Murray, *Negro Handbook, 1944,* 264; *Leadership and the Negro Soldier,* 66; Buchanan, *Black Americans in World War II,* 8.

19. "Fruits of Jim Crow," *Pittsburgh Courier,* March 31, 1945; Charley Cherokee, National Grapevine (column), *Chicago Defender,* March 31, 1945, 11.

20. Washburn, *Question of Sedition,* 112–13.

21. For instance, at Ft. Des Moines, IA, Captain Stillman reportedly denounced the *Pittsburgh Courier* as "a trouble maker, undependable, and not worth the paper it is printed on." "Investigation of comments made by a Captain of your Command," Ft. Des Moines, August 12, 1942, Records of the War Department General and Special Staffs, file 291.2, Security Classified General Correspondence, 1942–46, Office of the Director of Personnel and Admin (G-1), Director of the WAC, Record Group 165, NARA; Kryder, *Divided Arsenal,* 178–79.

22. Articles from Alice Young's scrapbook, courtesy of Stacie Porter.

23. Rev. Kenneth Hughes, "Our Debt to the Four Striking Wacs," St. Bartholomew's Church, Cambridge, MA, April 3, 1945; the church raised $140 in donations to help fund the NAACP Legal Defense Fund's handling of the case, Hughes to Roy Wilkins, April 3, 1945, series B, reel 19, NAACP Records.

24. Lillie M. Jackson, President of the Baltimore NAACP, to Roosevelt, file 291.2, Race, decimal file 1940–1945, box 1063, Records of the Adjutant General's Office.

25. Eugene Zack, "Notables Demand Probe in Conviction of Wacs," *Chicago Defender,* March 31, 1945.

26. "Wac Denies Charge She Disobeyed: Declares Illness, Not Mutiny, Reason for Not Working," *Boston Post,* March 20, 1945; "Colonel *Voiced* Bias, Colored WAC Testifies," *Washington Star,* March 20, 1945; "Wac Group Confined in Discipline Action," *Atlanta Constitution,* March 12, 1945; "Negro Wacs," *Washington Post,* April 12, 1945; Bill Cunningham, "WAC Decision Unity Threat," *Boston Herald,* April 5, 1945.

27. Letter to the editor, "Protest WAC Verdict," *Worchester (MA) Evening Gazette,* March 24, 1945, 4, Worchester Public Library, Worchester, MA. Arthur L. Crookham, editor of the *Journal,* Portland, OR, to Stimson, March 21, 1945; Ernest G. Adams to Roosevelt, RI, March 21, 1945, both in file 291.2, Race, decimal file 1940–1945, box 1063, Records of the Adjutant General's Office.

28. Crookham, March 21, 1945; Emily Weymer, San Jose, CA, to Roosevelt, March 21, 1945.

29. Hughes, "Our Debt."

30. Letter, Book Lovers' Club to Judge Advocate General, Auburndale, MA., March 26, 1945, included in *U.S. v. Young.*

31. R. H. Markham, "Case of Negro Wacs: An Analysis," *Christian Science Monitor,* April 5, 1945.

32. Press release, "Marcantonio and Powell demand Investigation of Conviction of four Negro Wacs," March 21, 1945; J. S. Qualey, "War Dept. Probe Asked

of Trial of 4 Negro Wacs," *PM*, March 23, 1945; Zack, "Notables Demand Probe"; letter, Rep. Emanuel Celler to Major General Sherman Miles, March 22, 1945, file 291.2, Race, decimal file 1940–1945, box 1063, Records of the Adjutant General's Office.

33. Psychologists' evaluations cited motivations related to the "harsh and derogatory treatment the Negro enlisted women were receiving." They also documented personal strife that the War Department recognized as the motivating factors, citing, for instance, difficult childhoods and, in Edmonds's case, the recent death of her grandfather and her alleged emotional immaturity. Inquiry, William T. Granahan to Stimson, March 13, 1945, exhibit CC, WDI, and summary, 24–26, WDI.

34. Weymer to Roosevelt, March 21, 1945, file 291.2, Race, decimal file 1940 1945, box 1063, Records of the Adjutant General's Office.

35. American Legion Post 94, Cleveland, OH, and American Legion Post 16, Boston, MA, to the Army Judge Advocate, March 23, 1945, file 291.2, Race, decimal file 1940–1945, box 1063, Records of the Adjutant General's Office; "Legionnaires Ask WAC Sentence Mitigation," *Atlanta Daily World*, March 27, 1945.

36. Summary, 5–6, FSCI; Miles gave Crandall a choice to either retire or embark on a tour to inspect prisoner of war camps. Miles chose retirement. Sherman Miles, interview, 334, WDI.

37. "4 Negro Wacs Regain Post at Ft. Devens," *Christian Science Monitor*, April 3, 1945.

38. General Court-Martial, *United States v. Kaniuk, Carolyn G.*, A-310969, *Private*, Service Command Boston Area, Motor Pool, SCU 3127, (CM 262117), August 25, 1944, Ft. Devens, MA, U.S. Army Judiciary, Department of the Army, Arlington, VA.

39. Miles interview, 331, WDI.

40. In 1930, Nathan Margold, the NAACP's lead attorney, drafted the Margold Plan to assist his legal team in the selection process. He proposed investing in a small number of precedent-setting segregation cases to "strike directly at the most prolific sources of discrimination." Due to their limited funds, Marshall and his mentor Charles Houston agreed in principle with the plan to attack segregation head-on. More aware of the racially intolerant climate than Margold, who was white, they had little faith that a few major case victories would explode the concept of segregation. With Marshall at the helm, the LDF expanded its caseload so as to lay a wide foundation for future direct assaults on racial injustice. Greenberg, *Crusaders in the Courts*, 58–59; Martin, *Brown v. Board of Education*, 13.

41. Press release, "NAACP Will Aid in Appeal," March 29, 1945; Thurgood Marshall to Mrs. Isabel Barmore, New York, April 2, 1945; report, Walker to Bethune, March 24, 1945, all in series B, reel 19, NAACP Records.

42. For instance, the army's sentencing of seventy-three servicemen in Hawai'i to between eight and thirty years for similar insubordination received far less attention in the mainstream papers than in the black press. "73 Convicted: Hawaii Troops Sentenced to Long Prison Terms," *Chicago Defender*, February 10, 1945.

43. See Walker's March 24 report to Bethune and his follow-up dated March 26, 1945, series B, reel 19, NAACP Records.

44. Naomi Jolles, "4 Negro Wacs Convicted—NAACP Leader Calls It Fair," *New York Post,* March 21, 1945.

45. P. L. Prattis, "The Horizon," *Pittsburgh Courier,* March 31, 1945; Finkle, *Forum for Protest,* 181–82. Finkle argues that many in the black press denounced the Wacs for disobeying orders. In fact, reporters acknowledged the women's violation of military orders yet prioritized the circumstances that had provoked their refusal to obey their officers.

46. Steele likely sought to steer clear of elements that would bring suspicions of radicalism upon him. Prattis, a leading figure among the militant press and therefore a target of FBI monitoring, may have considered the case of the Wacs, who received relatively light sentences, an opportunity to temper his criticism of the military. Simmons, *African American Press,* 75–83. Also see Washburn, *Question of Sedition,* 166–202.

47. Carter to Wilkins, "Wac Strike in Massachusetts," March 15, 1945; letter, "Dear Ruby," from unknown author seeking anonymity, March 17, 1945; and report, also unsigned and undated, likely from the same person, all in series B, reel 19, NAACP Records.

48. O'Reilly, *Racial Matters,* 12–20.

49. Reports, "Refusal of Duty by Certain Members of the WAC Detachment (Colored)," March 23, 1945, and "Negro WAC Situation," March 28, 1945, both in series 4, Investigative Reports, 1943–1944, Isadore Zack Papers.

50. At Ft. Devens, Intelligence Officer Andrew Cunningham wanted to install a couple of agents in the black WAC detachment but could not find reliable candidates. Andrew Cunningham interview, 341–42, WDI.

51. G. B. Walker to Assistant Chief of Staff, "Court-Martial of Four Negro Wacs at Ft. Devens, Mass.," March 27, 1945, file 291.2, Race, decimal file 1940–1945, box 1063, Records of the Adjutant General's Office.

52. Correspondence, Miles and Rounds, March 28–30, 1945, *U.S. v. Young.*

53. After a bungled investigation in 1944 following a night of mayhem and one death at Ft. Lawton, Washington, the army convicted twenty-eight black soldiers. A 2007 review overturned the convictions. Hamann, *On American Soil;* Rory Marshall, "Army Tosses Out Convictions of Black Soldiers in 1944 Death," *Arkansas Democrat-Gazette,* October 28, 2007, 5A; Foner, *Blacks and the Military,* 149; J. Williams, *Thurgood Marshall,* 128–30.

Chapter 6. Military Protocol

1. Letters, Col. William Rounds to Gen. Miles, March 31, 1945, and Miles to Judge Advocate General of the Army, March 28, 1945; "Memorandum to Colonel William A. Rounds," March 30, 1945, all in *U.S. v. Young.*

2. Ibid.

3. Ibid.

4. Sherman Miles interview, 331–32, WDI.

5. Had the verdict stood, the Wacs would not have served prison time. Instead, the WAC would have immediately and dishonorably discharged them. As noted in

a confidential letter to all commands, the WAC did not have the facilities to confine women. Treadwell, *Women's Army Corps*, 506–7.

6. "Easy Way Out," *Time*, April 16, 1945; "Lessons from Fort Devens," *Christian Science Monitor*, April 5, 1945.

7. Marty Richardson, "It's Like This," *Boston Chronicle*, April 7, 1945, part 9, series B, reel 19, NAACP Records; "4 Wacs Cleared," *Philadelphia Afro-American*, April 7, 1945; Harry Keelan, "Voice in the Wilderness," *Philadelphia Afro-American*, April 14, 1945; "New Hope for Race in Rulings Favoring Negroes," *Arkansas State Press*, April 27, 1945 (American's Historical Newspapers); "What We're Dying For," *People's Voice*, April 14, 1945, Jean Blackwell Hutson Research and Reference Division, Schomburg Center for Research in Black Culture, NY.

8. Horace R. Cayton, "News Items," *Pittsburgh Courier*, April 14, 1945. "Negro Wacs," *Washington Post*, April 12, 1945, 6.

9. Interviews, Maj. Eileen Murphy, Army Nurse Corps, 605; Maj. Ethel M. Aikens, Army Nurse Corps and Assistant Chief of Nursing Service, 306; 1Lt. Andrew W. Cunningham, also Lovell Hospital's officers of its male detachment, 342; also see interview of Maj. Victor Breen, all in WDI.

10. Summary, 5, FSCI.

11. Ibid., 3–5.

12. Others credited Crandall for his effective administration of the Lovell General Hospital. Miles's response to White's report, March 15, 1945, 7, FSCI; summary, 31–35, WDI.

13. Cayton, "News Items."

14. Investigation Report, Lt. Col. William White to Gen. Miles, 5–6, FSCI; Miles's response to White's report, March 15, 1945, 7, FSCI.

15. Letter, Truman K. Gibson to Roy Wilkins, April 12, 1945, series B, reel 19, NAACP Records.

16. Ibid. Also see Gen. Sherman Miles interview, 332–34, WDI.

17. Maj. Murphy interview, 596, WDI.

18. Victoria Lawson, "Historical Report on SCU 1127, WAC Detachment, and 2nd, 3rd & 4th WAC Hospital Companies (Z/I), Lovell General & Convalescent Hospital, Fort Devens, Massachusetts for the period 1 January 1945 to 18 April 1945 Inclusive," April 18, 1945, exhibit S, WDI.

19. As customary in the army, the black detachment fell last in the numerical line and was renamed the 4th WAC Hospital Company.

20. Summary, 35–36, WDI.

21. Letters, Roy Wilkins to Henry Stimson, April 5, 1945, and Wilkins to Gibson, April 19, 1945; Paul Sann, "Ask Probe of Colonel in Wac Case," *New York Post*, April 4, 1945, all in part 9, series B, reel 19, NAACP Records.

22. O. A. Gotschalk to Inspector General, "Request for Supplemental Investigation," April 2, 1945, WDI.

23. Anna Morrison interview, 570–71 and 565–66, WDI.

24. Ibid., 577–78.

25. Ibid., 576–77, 590.

26. Ibid., 562–63.

27. Ibid., 588.

28. Mary Green interview, 36.23, WDI.

29. Ibid., 36.24–36.27.

30. Ibid. Also see Green's medical file, Department of Veterans Affairs, Robert J. Dole Medical and Regional Office Center, Wichita, KS.

31. According to Morrison, the four Wacs did not receive their monthly pay after their conviction. Morrison interview, 590, WDI.

32. Green interview, 36.26, WDI.

33. Johnnie Murphy interview, ek.6–7, WDI.

34. Ibid., ek.12.

35. Ibid., ek.13.

36. Alice Young interview, 527–28 and 551–52, WDI. Musser and Herman did not interview Arnison or Newman.

37. A. Young interview, 554, WDI.

38. Darlene Clark Hine argues that due to the historical absence of protections against racial and sexual abuse, African American women developed a psychological mechanism to defend themselves against the pervasiveness of multiple layers of oppression. Unable to physically escape the negative imaging and degrading and often violent treatment from a hostile society, black women adopted a "culture of dissemblance" by which they could mentally separate from these assaults and mentally rebuild on the grounds of resistance they laid. Hine, "Rape and the Inner Lives."

39. Morrison interview, 589, WDI.

40. Interviews, Lois Floyd, Tommie Cartwright, and Ellsworth Manuel, WDI.

41. Presumably the WAC had administered the test when the women enlisted, yet the records do not mention earlier AGCT scores.

42. Col. Wallace S. Douglas, Director of Military Training to the Inspector General, Ft. Devens, notifying him that "grades obtained in test given April 17, 1945," April 19, 1945, exhibit G, WDI.

43. Harold Wicks interview, 35.11, WDI.

44. Interviews, Ruth Cone and Helen E. Bugar, WDI.

45. Interviews, Capt. Jacob H. Bauer, Director of Personnel, Ft. Devens, 392–93, and Wicks, 35.5, WDI.

46. Final summary, Charlene Cook by Capt. Alice E. Rost, NC, "Neuropsychiatric Service, Mason Hospital," April 4, 1945, exhibit BB, WDI. Charlene Cook said that while she was distressed over her experiences at Ft. Devens, especially after Miles's order signaled no escape from menial labor, she never intended to commit suicide. According to the report, she checked herself into the hospital after the order, attached her pajama belt to her hospital bed, tied the other end around her neck, and flung herself to the floor. She claimed she was mimicking the other suicides at an ill-timed moment, assuring the nurse that she had always been a practical joker.

47. Summary, 24–26, WDI; William T. Granahan to Stimson, March 13, 1945, exhibit CC, WDI.

48. Ibid., summary, 20–21.

49. Ibid., 22–23.

50. Ibid., 40. From April 1944 to March 1945, the motor pool operated just one course for black male soldiers and none for black Wacs.

51. A. Young interview, 542, WDI.

52. Summary, 22–23, WDI.

53. Ibid., 37–39.

54. Summary, 38, WDI.

55. Ibid.

56. Summary, 37, WDI.

57. Wicks interview, 35.26, WDI.

Conclusion: A Sociological Laboratory

1. Gibson concludes with a recommendation that the army move toward integration. Memorandum, Truman K. Gibson Jr. to John J. McCloy, Assistant Secretary of War, August 8, 1945, quoted in Nalty and MacGregor, *Blacks in the Military*, 173.

2. During the Battle of the Bulge, fought from December 1944 to January 1945, the army was so desperate for replacement soldiers that it offered black volunteers combat duty in white infantry companies. Over 5,500 men volunteered for the 2,500 slots available for the project. Overwhelmed by applicants, many willing to suffer rank reductions for the opportunity, the army rescinded the integration aspect of the initiative. MacGregor, *Integration of the Armed Forces*, 52–53; Foner, *Blacks and the Military*, 161–62.

3. Treadwell, *Women's Army Corps*, 599.

4. Col. Eugene R. Householder, Adjutant General's Department to the Negro Newspaper Publishers Association, December 8, 1941, reprinted in Lee, *Employment of Negro Troops*, 142.

5. Col. H. B. Sepulveda, AGD, Acting Director, Opn. & Tng. Div. to Director Control, Div. AGO, April 14, 1945, file 291.2, Race, decimal file 1940–1945, box 1063, Records of the Adjutant General's Office.

6. Col. John R. Hall, Sixth Service Command, Chicago, IL, "Utilization of Negro WAC personnel at Gardiner General Hospital," April 30, 1945, Records of the War Department General and Special Staffs, file 291.2, Security Classified General Correspondence, 1942–46, Office of the Director of Personnel and Admin (G-1), Director of the WAC, RG 165, box 484, NARA.

7. In July 1945, Boyce replaced Col. Oveta Hobby, who resigned due to fatigue and illness. So serious was Hobby's condition that her husband brought a stretcher to assist her departure. Winegarten, *Oveta Culp Hobby*, 49.

8. Gardiner General Hospital to "All Personnel Concerned," July 9, 1945, box 1062, Records of the Adjutant General's Office.

9. Putney, *When the Nation*, 91–93.

10. Maj. Eileen Murphy interview, 607, WDI.

11. Pvt. Willie Ruth Williamson interview, 29.10, WDI.

12. Letters to Stimson, Virginia Spence, Chairman, West Hyde Park Independent Voters of Illinois, June 30, 1945, and Wilma Walker, Dean of Students, University of Chicago, July 2, 1945, file 291.2, Race, decimal file 1940–45, box 1062, Records of the Adjutant General's Office.

13. Earley, *One Woman's Army*, 192.

14. Morden, *Women's Army Corps, 1945–1978*, 32–33, 48, 85–86, 397. The "integration" aspect of the act reflected the WAC's closer connection with the regular army than during the war. The WAC racially integrated in 1950 yet remained separate from the regular army until 1978, when it disbanded. Following the postwar reduction of WAC personnel, segregated training programs, barracks, base facilities, and assignments were too impractical to continue. According to WAC historian Morden, Wacs of all races welcomed the change.

15. Truman issued executive order 9981 in July 1948, thereby establishing the Committee on Equality of Treatment and Opportunity in the Armed Services. Chaired by Charles Fahy, it was commonly referred to as the Fahy Committee. Among its members was Stimson's civilian aide for racial affairs, Truman Gibson. Fahy Committee Documents, box 12, Records of the President's Committee on Equality of Treatment and Opportunity in the Armed Services.

16. Dalfiume, *Desegregation of the U.S. Armed Forces*, 190–202, 218–19.

17. Mary Green, World War II Army Enlistment Records 1938–1946, National Personnel Records Center, Military Personnel Records Division, St. Louis, MO; Julia Levenston, interview with author, February 2014.

18. So-called blue discharges were neither honorable nor dishonorable discharges, yet they carried a stigma of inadaptability that made it difficult for bearers to obtain employment. Court-martial of Johnnie Murphy, Special Order 295, Lovell General Hospital, December 18, 1945, U.S. Army Reserve Component and Personnel and Administration Center, St. Louis, MO, Veterans Administration, Wichita, KS.

19. Anna Morrison, interview with author, March 26, 2002; Juanih Campbell, interview with author, March 19, 2017.

20. Morrison's postcard collection of her travels include sites as far away as France and Singapore. Campbell, interview with author.

21. "Wac and Family Happily Reunited," unsourced and undated article from the scrapbook of Alice Porter Young, courtesy of Stacie Porter.

22. The GI Bill entitled all honorably discharged World War II veterans with at least ninety day in the service to a wide range of benefits. This included the option to return to their previous jobs, government funded training and health care, and subsidized loan guarantees. Congress, however, set a nine-year limit to access these generous entitlements. The timetable was designed for men expecting to seek training and jobs immediately after separation from the service, not for female veterans, most who were in the prime of their childbearing years. Similarly, the

GI Bill offered government tuition and guaranteed mortgages yet allowed schools to deny admittance and banks to turn down loans based on an applicant race and gender. While the GI bill benefitted women and minority veterans, the majority of its endowments flowed to white men. Mettler, *Soldiers to Citizens*, 64–65, 144–55.

23. Letter, Stacie Porter to author, July 31, 2002.

24. Ibid.

25. Ibid.

26. Jennie Hill, sister of Alice Young Porter, interview with author, February 8, 2003.

Bibliography

Archival Collections

Alice Young letters and scrapbook. In the personal possession of Stacie Porter (daughter).

Department of the Army, Adjutant General, U.S. Army Reserve Component and Personnel and Administration Center, St. Louis, MO.

Department of Veterans Affairs, Robert J. Dole Medical and Regional Office Center, Wichita, KS.

Isadore Zack Papers. U.S. Army Counterintelligence Corps (CIC) Materials, 1942–1997. University of New Hampshire Library, Durham, NH.

Margaret Barnes Jones scrapbook and "The Writing of Margaret Barnes Jones" (essay). In the personal possession of Teresa Barnes (great-niece), professor of African History, University of Illinois.

Martha Settle Putney Collection on the Women's Army Corps (WAAC, WAC). Collection 038. National Archives for Black Women's History, Landover, MD.

National Council of Negro Women Papers. National Archives for Black Women's History, Museum Resource Center, Landover, MD.

Records of the Adjutant General's Office. Record group 407. National Archives, College Park, MD.

Records of the National Association for the Advancement of Colored People. Part 9: Discrimination in the U.S. Armed Forces, 1918–1955. Microfilm.

Records of the National Association of Colored Women's Clubs, 1895–1992. Part 3: Board of Directors and Executive Committee Minutes, Executive Director Reports. Microfilm.

Records of the Office of the Inspector General (Army). Record group 159. National Archives, College Park, MD.

Records of the Office of the Judge Advocate General (Army). Record group 153. National Archives, St. Louis, MO.

Records of the President's Committee of Equality of Treatment and Opportunity in the Armed Forces. Record group 220. Harry S. Truman Presidential Library, Independence, MO.

Records of the U.S. Army Service Forces (World War II). Record group 160. National Archives, College Park, MD.

Records of the War Department General and Special Staffs. Record group 165. National Archives, College Park, MD.

Waddy, Harriet West. Personal Papers. United States Army Women's Museum Archives, Fort Lee, VA.

World War II Army Enlistment Records 1938–1946. National Personnel Records Center, Military Personnel Records Division, St. Louis, MO.

World War II Iowa Press Clippings. Iowa Digital Library, University of Iowa Libraries, http://digital.lib.uiowa.edu/cdm/search/collection/wwii/searchterm/World%20War%20II%20Iowa%20press%20clippings/mode/exact.

Newspapers and Periodicals

Atlantic Daily World
Birmingham World
Boston Chronicle
Boston Globe
Boston Herald
Chicago Daily News
Chicago Defender
Christian Science Monitor
Herald Tribune
New York Post
Philadelphia Afro-American
Pittsburgh Courier
Time magazine
Washington Post

Books and Articles

Allen, Robert L. *The Port Chicago Mutiny*. New York: Warner Books, 1989.

Anderson, Karen. *Wartime Women: Sex Roles, Family Relations, and the Status of Women during World War II*. Westport, CT: Greenwood Press, 1981.

Azaransky, Sarah. *The Dream Is Freedom: Pauli Murray and American Democratic Faith*. New York: Oxford University Press, 2011.

Brandt, Nat. *Harlem at War: The Black Experience in WWII*. Syracuse: Syracuse University Press, 1996.

Brown, Nikki. *Private Politics, Public Voices: Black Women's Activism from World War I to the New Deal*. Bloomington: Indiana University Press, 2006.

Bruscino, Thomas. *A Nation Forged in War: How World War II Taught Americans to Get Along*. Knoxville: University of Tennessee Press, 2010.

Buchanan, Russell. *Black Americans in World War II*. Santa Barbara, CA: Clio Books, 1977.

Chateauvert, Melinda. *Marching Together: Women of the Brotherhood of Sleeping Porters*. Urbana: University of Illinois Press, 1998.

Cohen, Lizabeth. *A Consumers' Republic: The Politics of Mass Consumption in Postwar America*. New York: Alfred A. Knopf, 2003.

Crenshaw, Kimberlé. "Mapping the Margins: Intersectionality, Identity Politics, and Violence against Women of Color." *Stanford Law Review* 43, no. 6 (July 1991).

Dalfiume, Richard M. *Desegregation of the U.S. Armed Forces: Fighting on Two Fronts, 1939–1953*. Columbia: University of Missouri Press, 1969.

Du Bois, W. E. B. "Now Is the Time Not to Be Silent." *Crisis*, January 1942.

Dudziak, Mary L. *Cold War and Civil Rights: Race and Image of American Democracy*. Princeton, NJ: Princeton University Press, 2000.

Earley, Charity Adams. *One Woman's Army: A Black Officer Remembers the WAC*. College Station: Texas A&M University Press, 1989.

Escobedo, Elizabeth. *From Coveralls to Zoot Suits: The Lives of Mexican American Women on the World War II Home Front*. Chapel Hill: University of North Carolina Press, 2015.

Facts You Want to Know about the WAC. U.S. Army—Women's Army Corps. Washington, DC: Recruiting Publicly Bureau, 1943. Ohio State University Library.

Finkle, Lee. *Forum for Protest: The Black Press during World War II*. Rutherford, NJ: Fairleigh Dickinson University Press, [1975].

Foner, Jack D. *Blacks and the Military in American History: A New Perspective*. New York: Praeger, 1974.

Frydl, Kathleen. *The GI Bill*. Cambridge: Cambridge University Press, 2009.

Giddings, Paula. *When and Where I Enter: The Impact of Black Women on Race and Sex in America*. Toronto: Bantam Books, 1985.

Gilmore, Glenda Elizabeth. *Defying Dixie: The Radical Roots of Civil Rights, 1919–1950*. New York: W. W. Norton, 2008.

Greenberg, Jack. *Crusaders in the Courts: Legal Battles of the Civil Rights Movement*. New York: Twelve Tables Press, 2004.

Guglielmo, Thomas A. "'Red Cross, Double Cross': Race and America's World War II–Era Blood Donor Service." *Journal of American History* 97 (June 2010): 63–90.

Hamann, Jack. *On American Soil: How Justice Became a Casualty of World War II*. Chapel Hill, NC: Algonquin Books, 2005.

Hanson, Joyce. *Mary McLeod Bethune and Black Women's Political Activism*. Columbia: University of Missouri Press, 2003.

Hartmann, Susan M. *The Home Front and Beyond: American Women in the 1940s*. Boston: Twayne, 1982.

Haskins, James. *Lena: A Personal and Professional Biography of Lena Horne*. New York: Stein and Day, 1984.

Hine, Darlene Clark. "Rape and the Inner Lives of Black Women in the Middle West." *Common Grounds and Crossroads: Race, Ethnicity, and Class in Women's Lives*, special issue *Signs* 14, no. 4 (summer 1989): 912–20.

———, Wilma King, and Linda Reed, eds. *"We Specialize in the Wholly Impossible": A Reader in Black Women's History*. Brooklyn, NY: Carlson, 1995.

Holm, Jeanne. *Women in the Military: An Unfinished Revolution*. Novato, CA: Presidio, 1982.

Hull, Gloria T., Patricia Bell Scott, and Barbara Smith, eds. *All the Women Are White, All the Blacks Are Men, But Some of Us Are Brave: Black Women's Studies*. Old Westbury, NY: Feminist Press, 1982.

Hunter, Tera W. *To 'Joy My Freedom*. Cambridge, MA: Harvard University Press, 1997.

James, C. L. R., et al. *Fighting Racism in World War II*. Ed. Fred Stanton. New York: Monad Press, 1980.

Jones, Jacqueline. *Labor of Love, Labor of Sorrow: Black Women, Work, and the Family from Slavery to the Present*. New York: Vintage Books, 1986.

Katznelson, Ira. *When Affirmative Action Was White: An Untold History of Racial Inequity in Twentieth Century America*. New York: W. W. Norton, 2005.

Klinkner, Philip A., and Rogers M. Smith. *The Unsteady March: The Rise and Decline of Racial Equality in America*. Chicago: University of Chicago Press, 1999.

Kryder, Daniel. *Divided Arsenal: Race and the American State during World War II*. Cambridge: Cambridge University Press, 2000.

Leadership and the Negro Soldier. Washington, DC: U.S. Government Printing Office, 1944.

Lee, Ulysses. *The Employment of Negro Troops*. United States Army in World War II, Special Studies. Washington, DC: Office of the Chief of Military History, 1966.

Lemke-Santangelo, Gretchen. *Abiding Courage: African American Migrant Women and the East Bay Community*. Chapel Hill: University of North Carolina Press, 1996.

Lentz-Smith, Adriane Danette. *Freedom Struggles: African Americans and World War I*. Cambridge, MA: Harvard University Press, 2009.

Leonard, Elizabeth D. *Men of Color to Arms! Black Soldiers, Indian Wars, and the Quest for Equality*. New York: W. W. Norton, 2010.

Lipsitz, George. *The Possessive Investment in Whiteness: How White People Profit from Identity Politics*. Philadelphia: Temple University Press, 2006.

Litoff, Judy Barrett, and Davis Smith. *We're in This War, Too: World War II Letters from American Women in Uniform*. New York: Oxford University Press, 1994.

MacGregor, Morris J. *Integration of the Armed Forces, 1940–1965*. Defense Studies. Washington, DC: Center of Military History of the U.S. Army, 1981.

Mansoor, Peter R. *The GI Offensive in Europe: The Triumph of American Infantry Divisions, 1941–1945*. Lawrence: University of Kansas Press, 1999.

Manual for Courts-Martial: U. S. Army (Corrected to April 20, 1943). Washington, DC: U.S. Government Printing Office, 1943.

Martin, Waldo E., Jr., ed. *Brown v. Board of Education: A Brief History with Documents*. Boston: Bedford/St. Martin's, 1998.

McCabe, Katie, and Dovey Johnson Roundtree. *Justice Older than the Law: The Life of Dovey Johnson Roundtree*. Jackson: University Press of Mississippi, 2009.

McGuire, Danielle L. *At the Dark End of the Street: Black Women, Rape, and Resistance—A New History of the Civil Rights Movement from Rosa Parks to the Rise of Black Power*. New York: Knopf, 2010.

McGuire, Phillip. "Desegregation of the Armed Forces: Black Leadership, Protest and World War II." *Journal of Negro History* 68, no. 2 (spring 1983): 147–49. Accessed from JSTOR.

———. *He, Too, Spoke for Democracy: Judge Hastie, World War II, and the Black Soldier*. New York: Greenwood Press, 1988.

———. *Taps for a Jim Crow Army: Letters from Black Soldiers in World War II*. Santa Barbara, CA: ABC-Clio, 1983.

Mettler, Suzanne. *Soldiers to Citizens: The G.I. Bill and the Making of the Greatest Generation*. New York: Oxford University Press, 2005.

Meyer, Leisa. *Creating GI Jane: Sexuality and Power in the Women's Army Corps during World War II*. New York: Columbia University Press, 1996.

Milburn, Anthony B. T. *Conflicting Interest: The 477th Bomber Group Mutiny, April 1945*. PhD diss., Ohio State University, 1997. Ohio State University Library.

Milkman, Ruth. "Redefining 'Women's Work': The Sexual Division of Labor in the Auto Industry during World War II." In Linda K. Kerber and Jane De Hart-Mathews, eds., *Women's America: Refocusing the Past*, 374–94. New York: Oxford University Press, 1987.

Moore, Brenda L. "From Underrepresentation to Overrepresentation: African American Women." In Judith Hicks Stiehm, ed., *It's Our Military, Too! Women and the U.S. Military*, 115–35. Philadelphia: Temple University Press, 1996.

———. *Serving Our Country: Japanese American Women in the Military during World War II*. New Brunswick, NJ: Rutgers University Press, 2003.

———. *To Serve My Country, To Serve My Race: The Story of the Only African American Wacs Stationed Overseas during World War II*. New York: New York University Press, 1996.

Morden, Bettie E. *The Women's Army Corps, 1945–1978*. Army Historical Series. Washington, DC: Center of Military History, U.S. Army, 1992.

Morehouse, Maggi M. *Fighting in the Jim Crow Army: Black Men and Women Remember World War II*. Lanham, MD: Rowman and Littlefield, 2000.

Moye, Todd J. *Freedom Flyers: The Tuskegee Airmen of World War II*. Oxford: Oxford University Press, 2010.

Murray, Florence. *The Negro Handbook, 1944*. New York: Current Books, 1944.

———. *The Negro Handbook, 1946–47*. New York: Current Books, 1947.

Murray, Pauli. *Pauli Murray: The Autobiography of a Black Activist, Feminist, Lawyer, Priest, and Poet*. Knoxville: University of Tennessee Press, 1987.

Nalty, Bernard C. *Strength for the Fight: A History of Black Americans in the Military.* New York: Free Press, 1986.

——, and Morris J. MacGregor. *Blacks in the Military: Essential Documents.* Wilmington, DE: Scholarly Resources, 1982.

Negro Women War Workers. Women's Bureau, bulletin no. 205. Washington, DC: U.S. Department of Labor, 1945.

O'Reilly, Kenneth. *Racial Matters: The FBI's Secret File on Black America, 1960–1972.* New York: Free Press, 1989.

Odum, Howard W. *Race and Rumors of Race: The American South in the Early Forties.* Baltimore, MD: Johns Hopkins University Press, 1997.

Putney, Martha S. *When the Nation Was in Need: Blacks in the Women's Army Corps during World War II.* Lanham, MD: Scarecrow Press, 1992.

Roediger, David R. *Working toward Whiteness: How America's Immigrants Became White; The Strange Journey from Ellis Island to the Suburbs.* New York: Basic Books, 2005.

73 Questions and Answers about the WAC. U.S. Army—Women's Army Corps. Washington, DC: Recruiting Publicity Bureau, 1943. Ohio State University Library.

Shaw, Stephanie. *What a Woman Ought to Be and Do: Black Professional Women Workers during the Jim Crow Era.* Chicago: University of Chicago Press, 1996.

Shockley, Megan Taylor. *We, Too, Are Americans: African American Women in Detroit and Richmond, 1940–54.* Urbana: University of Illinois Press, 2003.

Simmons, Charles A. *The African American Press: A History of News Coverage during National Crisis, with Special Reference to Four Black Newspapers, 1827–1965.* Jefferson, NC: McFarland, 1998.

Sims-Wood, Janet. "We Served America, Too! Personal Recollections of African American Women in the Women's Army Corps during World War II." PhD diss., Union Institute, 1994. Ohio State University Library.

Sugrue, Thomas. *The Origins of the Urban Crisis: Race and Inequality in Postwar Detroit.* Princeton, NJ: Princeton University Press, 2005.

The Telephone Worker. Women's Bureau, bulletin no. 207. Washington, DC: U.S. Department of Labor, 1946.

Terborg-Penn, Rosalyn. "Discontented Black Feminists: Prelude and Postscript to the Passage of the Nineteenth Amendment." In Darlene Clark Hine, Wilma King, and Linda Reed, eds., *"We Specialize in the Wholly Impossible." A Reader in Black Women's History*, 487–504. Brooklyn: Carlson, 1995.

Threat, Charissa. *Nursing Civil Rights: Gender and Race in the Army Nurse Corps.* Urbana: University of Illinois Press, 2015.

Treadwell, Mattie E. *The Women's Army Corps.* United States Army in World War II, Special Studies. Washington, DC: Office of Chief of Military History, 1954.

Tucker, Sherri. *Swing Shift: All-Girl Bands of the 1940s.* Durham, NC: Duke University Press, 2002.

Washburn, Patrick S. *A Question of Sedition: The Federal Government's Investigation of the Black Press during World War II.* New York: Oxford University Press, 1986.

Weatherford, Doris. *History of Women in America*. New York: Facts on File, 1990.

White, Deborah Gray. *Too Heavy a Load: Black Women in Defense of Themselves, 1894–1994*. New York: W. W. Norton, 1999.

Williams, Juan. *Thurgood Marshall: American Revolutionary*. New York: Random House, 1998.

Williams, Vera S. *WACs: Women's Army Corps*. Oscela, WI: Motorbooks International, 1997.

Winegarten, Debra L. *Oveta Culp Hobby: Colonel, Cabinet Member, Philanthropist*. Austin: University of Texas Press, 2014.

Wolfinger, James. "'We Are in the Front Lines in the Battle for Democracy': Carolyn Moore and Black Activism in World War II." *African Americans in Pennsylvania History*. Special issue, *Pennsylvania History: A Journal of Mid-Atlantic Studies* 72, no. 1 (winter 2005): 1–23. Penn State University Press Stable, www.jstor.org/stable/27778656.

Index

Adams, Charity (later Charity Earley), xvii, 26, 32, 52–53, 79, 156

African American Wacs. *See* black Wacs (Is this helpful or not? I also have indexed black legionnaires and black officers.)

Afro American (newspaper), 116, 129

AGCT (Army General Classification Test), 29–30, 142–44, 149

Allen, Thelma, 55–57, 62, 67, 76, 81–82, 144

Anderson, Marian, 38

Anderson, Myrtle, 54–55, 132, 160

American Civil Liberties Union, 114

American Legion, 114, 121

Amerson, Mary. *See* Green, Mary

Army, U.S., 5, 12, 15, 18, 152. *See also* War Department

Army Counterintelligence Corps, 124

Army General Classification Test (AGCT), 29–30, 142–44, 149

Baham, Inez, 55–57, 67, 76, 79, 81–82, 144

Barnes, Margaret (later Margaret Jones), 14, 54–55

basics (military classification), xix, 43, 61, 177n10

Bates, Area, 65, 70, 73, 77

Beale, Gene, 78, 87, 155

Bethune, Mary McLeod: background of, xvii, 11, 21; and black Wacs, 21–23, 27, 32, 38; and defendants, 115, 121, 125, 133

black legionnaires, 121

black officers: limitations of command, 18, 152–53; in the WAC, 24, 38, 49, 52–55, 131. *See also* Hurd, John; integration of military; Stoney, Tenola

black press: coverage of black military personnel, 18, 27, 41, 66–67, 116, 187n42; growth and influence of, 18–19, 106, 113, 116–17, 185n18; support of Wac defendants, 3, 84, 116–18, 121, 129, 188n45. *See also* civil rights movement; *and titles of specific black newspapers*

black Wacs: challenge to racial and gender norms by, 5–9, 15, 26–28, 155, 164; as considered suited for menial labor, 28–31, 95–96, 109; effective employment of, 37, 50–51, 56, 155; recruitment and enlistments of, 5, 15, 22–24, 33–35; significance of, to civil rights movement, 5–6, 19, 23, 30, 42, 107, 159; testing limits of War Department's personnel policies, 5–7, 22, 41, 49–50, 154–56; and white Wacs, 25–28, 31, 36, 157. *See also* discriminatory treatment of black Wacs black women's collective actions: through clubs and organizations, xx, 10–11, 21, 31; legacy of, 16, 31, 38–39, 63, 153–54; in support of black Wacs, 21, 114–15. *See also* Fort Devens Wac Strike

Boston Chronicle (newspaper), 81, 112, 113, 129

Boston Herald (newspaper), 118, 119

Boyce, Westray, 115, 155, 185n11

Brown, Queen, 134, 149

Camp Breckinridge, KY, 46, 54, 66

Camp Rucker, AL, 46, 55

Cayton, Horace, 129, 131

Cayton, Irma, 27

Celler, Emanuel, 120

chain of command: breakdown of, 42, 53–54, 57, 131–32, 147; as part of orientation, 48, 74, 155

Chicago Defender (newspaper), 115–16, 118

Christian Science Monitor (newspaper), 119, 129

citizenship and military service, 6, 16, 18–19

civilian reaction to Fort Devens strike, Miles Sherman and, 84, 118, 120–22, 125. *See also* black press; media coverage

civil rights movement: as a coalition of forces, 5, 113, 116–18, 125, 154; demands on military, 5, 7, 17, 19, 159; fissures within, 81, 123–24; government surveillance of, 123–24; and local initiatives, 3, 114–18, 123–24; militancy in, 6, 11, 13, 17, 162; and pivotal role of women, 5–6, 31, 114–16, 101–2, 163–64; and promotion of military service, 16–19, 21–22, 38. *See also* black women's collective actions; National Association for the Advancement of Colored People

Coast Guard, U.S., 22, 158

collective actions. *See* black women's collective actions

Congress for Equal Opportunity, New England, 81

Cook, Charlene, 120, 145, 190n46

court-martial. *See* Fort Devens black Wac court-martial

Crandall, Walter M.: actions following strike, 67–71, 132; background of, xvii, 47–48; inquiries into actions of, 102, 119–23, 125, 129–31; leadership of, 47–48, 57–58, 147; and Lovell Hospital transfer, 42–43, 48–50; and marginalization of black Wacs, 41–44, 48, 52, 60–62, 73, 104; post-strike absence of, 121–23, 131, 187n36; and surgical technicians, 57. *See also* Young, Alice: encounters with Crandall

Crenshaw, Kimberlé, 7

Daniels, Jonathan, 49

Davis, Benjamin, Sr., 17

D-Day, xxi, 33, 35–36, 50

discriminatory treatment of black Wacs: in housing, 31–32, 37, 42, 50, 176n5; and KP duty, 32, 45–46, 135, 137, 140, 147; at the PX, 58–59, 140–42, 146; in training and job assignments, 28–32, 37, 41, 51, 103. *See also* black officers; segregation in the military; WAC assignments

disciplinary cases (other). *See* military disciplinary cases (other)

Doss, Alberta, 76–77, 79, 87, 95–97, 106

Double V campaign, 19, 23, 112, 116, 123

Du Bois, W. E. B., 6

Edmonds, Lucille, 59, 78, 120, 145, 187n33

Elton, Sumner W., 75

Executive Order 8802, 9, 17

Executive Order 9981, 158–59

Fahy Committee, 158–59

Fair Employment Practices Committee (FEPC), 1941, 9, 17

First Service Command: assigns black Wacs to Fort Devens, 42–43; and changes implemented in wake of strike, 131–32, 140; initial responses of, to strike action, 71–76, 122; transfers of white Wac orderlies by, 145. *See also* investigations of strike: within military; Miles, Sherman

Fort Clark, TX, 46, 173n46, 177n18

Fort Des Moines, IA, 11, 26–28, 35–38

Fort Devens, MA, 1, 42, 44–45

Fort Devens black Wac court-martial: absence of Crandall and Beale, 87, 102; closing statements, 105–8; as compared to civilian trials, 85; and judicial protocols, 84, 109; and military justice, 84–85, 109; prosecution's arguments, 90–92, 95; psychological defense strategy, 86–88, 97; Rainey's prioritization of race over gender, 91, 99, 109; restricted used of racism as a defense, 85, 89, 105, 108; and stereotypes of black women, 84–85, 109–11; undermining of reasons for strike, 89, 91, 97–102, 105–6, 108; as unusual, 84, 108; verdict and sentence, 107–8

Fort Devens Wac orderly strike: as a cause célèbre, 3–4, 8, 81; events leading up to, 3, 12, 42, 46–48, 55–58, 67; response by Wacs' officers, 71–78, 81; as rooted in civil rights struggle, 4, 8, 15, 101–2, 124. *See also* surgical technician strike at Fort Devens

Fort Huachuca, AZ, 51

Fort Knox, KY, 46

Fort Oglethorpe, GA, 49, 56

Froias, John, 76, 86–87, 134

Gardiner Hospital, IL, 50, 155–56

Gay, Sophie, xvii, 43, 47, 52–54

gender stereotypes: of black women, 28, 49–50, 85, 95–98, 108–11, 148–49; and the ideal Wac image, 4, 7, 19–20, 25–26; of male service personnel, 16, 19, 108

Gibson, Truman K., 152

Gilliland, Grant, 70, 120, 145

Granahan, William T., 56, 120, 145

Green, Mary (née Amerson): arrest and charges, xvii, 75–78, 80–81, 135–36; background of, 10, 14–15, 33–34; grievances and protests by, 60, 65, 80–81; trial testimony by, 2, 85–88, 91–92; after the war, 160, 163; War Department interview of, 135–37

Guild, Ray, 124

Hackshaw, Leotha, 113, 124

Heath, Rhoyd, 77, 86–88, 135

Herman, Ruby E., 133–37, 139–50

Hobby, Oveta Culp: background of, xvii, 20; and Bethune, 21, 24, 32; and black Wac strike, 4, 115, 117; and race, 21–28, 37, 49, 115; as regulating Wac conduct, 7, 21. *See also* WAC

Horne, Lena, 30, 38

hospitals. *See* Gardiner Hospital, IL; Lovell General Hospital; Wakeman Hospital, IN

Houston, Charles, 115, 187n40

Howard University: law school at, 115; and Pauli Murray, 8; and WAAC recruiting, 24; and Alice Young, 34, 84, 94, 144

Hughes, Kenneth, 117, 119

Hunter, Jane E., 115

Hurd, John, 71–74

Hyde Park, Chicago, Gardiner Hospital in, 50, 155–56

integration of military: and Fahy Committee, 158–59; recreational facilities and officer training, 18, 41, 45, 171n17, 174n59, 177n18. *See also* segregation in military

intersectionality, 5, 7–9, 12, 72–73, 110–11, 146–47. *See also* "Jane Crow"

investigations of strike: by civilians, 115, 123–24; within military, xvi, 82, 120–24, 127, 130–33, 142, 147–50

Jackson, Ola, 62, 64

"Jane Crow," 8, 84, 169n20. *See also* Murray, Pauli

John Brown Organization of America, 114

Johnson, Dovey, xvi, 23, 26, 27

Johnson, Lula M., 63, 134

Johnson, Mary, 64–65

Jones, Margaret. *See* Barnes, Margaret

Kaniuk, Carolyn, 122, 129, 146, 149

Kelly, Anna, 64

labor: civilian women in menial jobs, 14–15, 26, 52, 68, 95; racial disparities in, 8–10, 30–31, 170n8; role of state policies, 9, 15, 31, 95, 162–65

Lawson, Victoria: actions during strike, 67–70, 79–80; and black Wacs, xvii, 41, 43, 52–57, 131, 155; trial testimony of, 85–86, 90, 93, 102–3. *See also* chain of command

Leadership and the Negro Soldier (Army Manual 5), 29, 127

Legal Defense Fund (LDF), xix, 114, 122, 187n40. *See also* Marshall, Thurgood

legionnaires, black, 121

Lovell General Hospital, 43–45, 118, 131, 177n17

Mabry Field, FL, 66

Mahon, George H., 27

March on Washington, 9, 31

Marcantonio, Vito, 120

marines, U.S., 22

Marshall, George C., 20, 35

Marshall, Thurgood, xvii, 98, 114–15, 122–23

McCarthy, Leon E., 1–3, 84–88, 90–97, 106–7, 122

McCord, Amanda, 64, 139

media coverage, 3–4, 8, 85–86, 116–19, 125–29. *See also* black press

medical technician: as desired skilled position, 2, 38, 51; duties of, xix; at Fort Devens, 43, 47, 60–62, 89, 145; qualifications for, 143–44; shortage of, 34–36, 47, 176n88. *See also* WAC assignments; Young, Alice

Miles, Sherman: actions to end strike, 71–72, 74–76, 81–82; background of, xviii, 182n52; confidence in military justice, 82, 84–85, 113, 122–23; and Crandall, 121–22, 131; institutes changes in WAC units, 131–32, 135, 150; managing civilian reaction, 84, 118, 120–22, 125; orders black Wac detachment to Fort Devens, 49–50, 74; reviews verdict, 125, 127–28; and surgical technicians, 76, 81–82. *See also* First Service Command

military, integration of. *See* integration of military

military disciplinary cases (other): conditions leading to, 18, 42; of male personnel, 66–68, 188n53; involving Wacs,

54–55, 66, 173n46. *See also* Kaniuk, Carolyn

military service, citizenship and, 6, 16, 18–19

Miller, Willie Mae, 64, 69

Mitchell, Tessie B., 134

Moore, Carolyn, xvii, 114–15

Morrison, Anna: arrest and charges, xviii, 75–81; background of, 10, 14–15, 23, 34; grievances and protests by, 60, 62; trial testimony by, 1–2, 76, 85–86, 90, 99–102; after the war, 161–63; War Department interview of, 140–41, 150–51

motor pool assignments, 68–69, 146–47

Murphy, Johnnie: arrest and charges, xviii, 76, 80–81; background of, 10, 14–15, 33; after the strike, 160; trial testimony by, 3, 85–86, 101, 108; War Department interview of, 137–38, 140–41, 148, 150–51

Murray, Pauli, 8–9, 84, 169n20, 183n43

Musser, Milton S., 133–35, 137–42, 144–50

mutiny: Miles's avoidance of term, 75; Wac strike denounced as, 3, 42, 55, 70, 74, 128

National Association for the Advancement of Colored People (NAACP): growth and prominence of, during war, 11, 113–14; support of black Wacs by, 38, 58, 81, 114–17, 121–24, 133. *See also* Legal Defense Fund

National Association of Colored Women's Clubs (NACWC), xx, 10–11, 21

National Council of Negro Women (NCNW), xx, 11, 21, 115

navy, U.S., 22, 34, 66–67, 129, 158, 172n36

Negro Youth of Greater Boston, 114

New England Congress for Equal Opportunity, 81

officers, black. *See* black officers

officers, response by, to strike, 71–78, 81

officers, white. *See* white privilege: of officers

Ohio State Federation of Colored Women, 115

orderlies at Fort Devens: black and white
Wac duties of, compared, 60–61, 90,
92–94, 103–4; black Wacs as, 46, 68,
110, 133; civilians as, 59–60; white Wacs
as, 60–62, 144–48, 179n62

Petty, Dorothy, 58
Pierce, Ruby, 58, 134, 149
Pittsburgh Courier (newspaper), 19, 113,
116, 123–24, 129, 186n21
Port Chicago Mutiny, 67, 182n15
Powell, Adam Clayton, 120
Prattis, Percival L., 19, 116, 123
press. *See* black press; media coverage
Putney, Martha, xviii, 28, 38, 69, 155–56,
174n59

Rainey, Julian D., xviii, 81–82, 85–91,
96–101, 105–8
Randolph, A. Philip, 6, 9, 31
Richardson, Marty, 112–13, 129
Rogers, Edith Nourse, 19, 44
Roosevelt, Eleanor, 21, 46, 115
Roosevelt, Franklin D., 114, 117, 119, 121.
See also Fair Employment Practices
Committee
Rounds, William A., 125, 128

segregation in military: defense of, 6–7,
16–18, 158; inefficiency of, 17–18, 41,
157–59; of post facilities, 6, 18, 52–53,
174n58, 176n5. *See also* discriminatory
treatment of black Wacs; WAC assignments
segregation in United States, 9, 15, 18,
23, 31
Sims, Beulah, 57–58, 65, 67, 120, 145
Smith, Mary, 56, 58, 114–15
Stearns, Elizabeth W. 43, 71–74
Steele, Julian, 81, 123–24
stereotypes, gender. *See* gender stereotypes
Stimson, Henry L.: correspondence from
public, 27, 113, 119, 125, 156; correspondence with national leaders, 114–15,
120; on racial issues, 30, 117, 128
Stoney, Tenola: actions during strike,
67–70, 76, 79; court-martial testimony

of, 87, 103–4; relationship with Lawson
and Crandall, 48–50, 155; struggles with
leadership, xviii, 43, 52–59, 62–65, 100–
101, 147.*See also* chain of command
strikes. *See* Fort Devens Wac orderly
strike; surgical technician strike at Fort
Devens
subversives and ringleaders, suspicions of,
26, 31, 90, 117–20, 130, 173n46. *See also*
black press; Zack, Isadore
suicide attempts at Fort Devens, 65, 120,
130, 145–46, 185n16
surgical technician strike at Fort Devens,
55–57, 62, 76, 81–82

Taylor, Rebecca Stiles, 115
Time magazine, 119, 126, 129, 150
Treadwell, Mattie, 29
Truman, Harry S., 158–59,
Tuskegee Airmen, 5, 73, 163

United People's Action Committee, Philadelphia, 114

WAAC, 4, 20–25, 28, 44, 66, 168n1
WAC: and personnel shortage, 35–37, 133,
157, 176n88; as platform for full citizenship, 6, 11–12, 15, 22–24, 64; as promot-
ing conventional gender norms, 4, 7,
19–20, 25–26, 108; opposition to, 19–20,
36; racial integration of, 158; racial policies of, 24–28, 32, 34–37, 43, 131; recruitment for, 24–29, 32, 35, 47; strength of,
5, 36. *See also* black Wacs; white Waacs/
Wacs
WAC assignments: as appropriately
feminine, 4, 20, 31; and civilian labor
patterns, 5, 15, 30–31, 46, 52; compared
by race, 32, 46, 50–55, 103; effects of, on
morale, 32, 37, 50–51, 53, 57; and KP, 32,
45–46; to motor pool, 68–69, 146–47;
and overseas duty, 26, 35–37, 46, 49–50,
153, 178n33; racial disparities in, at Fort
Devens, 43–47, 55–56, 59, 93, 103. *See
also* discriminatory treatment of black
Wacs; medical technician; orderlies at
Fort Devens; surgical technician strike
at Fort Devens

WAC Central Postal Directory Battalion, 6888th, 50–51, 56, 153, 156
Wakeman Hospital, IN, 37
Walker, Clotha, 65, 70
Walker, Richard, 185n8
Wallace, Lillian, 59
Walla Walla Air Base, WA, 51
War Department: and creation of WAAC/ WAC, 4, 15, 20; concessions by, to civil rights movement, 17, 22; and employment of civilian women in military jobs, 19; gender policies of, 49, 108, 153; racial policies of, 7, 17, 22, 29, 152–54; resistance by, to racial integration, 6, 158; and utilization of black Wacs, 22, 36–37. *See also* integration of military; segregation in military
Warfield, Harriet: background of, xviii, 55–58; correspondence of, 56, 58, 81, 114, 120, 185n16; and surgical technician strike, 67, 76
West, Harriet, 31–32
White, William J., 82, 121, 130–31
white privilege: cost of, 30, 36–37, 157–58; as embedded in military policies, 101–2, 108–10, 152–53; invisibility of, 9, 31, 69, 85, 107–8; as manifested in civil policies, 5, 8–9; of officers, 20–21, 27, 108, 154; and patriarchy, 8, 99, 108–9, 157, 169n20
white Waacs/Wacs: at Fort Des Moines, 26–27, 36–37, 69; at Fort Devens, 60, 92–93, 104, 157; ideal image of, 4, 7,

25–26; and overseas duty, 36, 49–51, 58, 146; preferential treatment of, over black Wacs, 29, 33, 53, 104, 109, 157; training and assignments for, 36, 43–46, 91–93, 175n74. *See also* discriminatory treatment of black Wacs; Kaniuk, Carolyn; orderlies at Fort Devens
Wicks, Harold, xviii, 44, 54–55, 78, 86–87, 144–45, 148
Wilkins, Roy, 102, 114, 133
Williams, Elsie, 171n18, 177n18, 180n5
Williamson, Willie Ruth, 156
Women's Armed Services Integration Act (1948), 158
Women's Army Auxiliary Corps. *See* WAAC
Women's Army Corps. *See* WAC
Workers' Defense League, 114
World War I: and African Americans, 6, 16, 86, 52; army's utilization of women in, 19, 172n26
Wyant, Lawrence B., 71–74

Young, Alice: arrest and charges, 2–3, 76–80; background of, xviii, 10, 13–15, 34–35; encounters with Crandall, 47, 68–70, 91, 138; grievances and protests by, 47, 58, 62, 94, 138–39; trial testimony of, 85, 90–91, 94; after war, 162–64; War Department interview of, 138–39, 140–41, 150–51, 155

Zack, Isadore, 124

SANDRA M. BOLZENIUS is a former instructor at The Ohio State University and served as a transportation specialist in the United States Army.

Women, Gender, and Sexuality in American History

Women Doctors in Gilded-Age Washington: Race, Gender, and
   Professionalization   *Gloria Moldow*
Friends and Sisters: Letters between Lucy Stone and Antoinette Brown Blackwell,
   1846–93   *Edited by Carol Lasser and Marlene Deahl Merrill*
Reform, Labor, and Feminism: Margaret Dreier Robins and the Women's Trade
   Union League   *Elizabeth Anne Payne*
Private Matters: American Attitudes toward Childbearing and Infant Nurture in
   the Urban North, 1800–1860   *Sylvia D. Hoffert*
Civil Wars: Women and the Crisis of Southern Nationalism   *George C. Rable*
I Came a Stranger: The Story of a Hull-House Girl   *Hilda Satt Polacheck;
   edited by Dena J. Polacheck Epstein*
Labor's Flaming Youth: Telephone Operators and Worker Militancy,
   1878–1923   *Stephen H. Norwood*
Winter Friends: Women Growing Old in the New Republic, 1785–1835
   Terri L. Premo
Better Than Second Best: Love and Work in the Life of Helen Magill
   Glenn C. Altschuler
Dishing It Out: Waitresses and Their Unions in the Twentieth Century
   Dorothy Sue Cobble
Natural Allies: Women's Associations in American History   *Anne Firor Scott*
Beyond the Typewriter: Gender, Class, and the Origins of Modern American Office
   Work, 1900–1930   *Sharon Hartman Strom*
The Challenge of Feminist Biography: Writing the Lives of Modern American
   Women   *Edited by Sara Alpern, Joyce Antler, Elisabeth Israels Perry,
   and Ingrid Winther Scobie*
Working Women of Collar City: Gender, Class, and Community in Troy, New York,
   1864–86   *Carole Turbin*
Radicals of the Worst Sort: Laboring Women in Lawrence, Massachusetts,
   1860–1912   *Ardis Cameron*
Visible Women: New Essays on American Activism   *Edited by Nancy A. Hewitt and
   Suzanne Lebsock*
Mother-Work: Women, Child Welfare, and the State, 1890–1930
   Molly Ladd-Taylor
Babe: The Life and Legend of Babe Didrikson Zaharias   *Susan E. Cayleff*
Writing Out My Heart: Selections from the Journal of Frances E. Willard,
   1855–96   *Edited by Carolyn De Swarte Gifford*
U.S. Women in Struggle: A *Feminist Studies* Anthology
   Edited by Claire Goldberg Moses and Heidi Hartmann
In a Generous Spirit: A First-Person Biography of Myra Page
   Christina Looper Baker
Mining Cultures: Men, Women, and Leisure in Butte, 1914–41   *Mary Murphy*

Gendered Strife and Confusion: The Political Culture of Reconstruction
  Laura F. Edwards
The Female Economy: The Millinery and Dressmaking Trades, 1860–1930
  Wendy Gamber
Mistresses and Slaves: Plantation Women in South Carolina, 1830–80
  Marli F. Weiner
A Hard Fight for We: Women's Transition from Slavery to Freedom in
  South Carolina   *Leslie A. Schwalm*
The Common Ground of Womanhood: Class, Gender, and Working Girls' Clubs,
  1884–1928   *Priscilla Murolo*
Purifying America: Women, Cultural Reform, and Pro-Censorship Activism,
  1873–1933   *Alison M. Parker*
Marching Together: Women of the Brotherhood of Sleeping Car Porters
  Melinda Chateauvert
Creating the New Woman: The Rise of Southern Women's Progressive Culture in
  Texas, 1893–1918   *Judith N. McArthur*
The Business of Charity: The Woman's Exchange Movement, 1832–1900
  Kathleen Waters Sander
The Power and Passion of M. Carey Thomas   *Helen Lefkowitz Horowitz*
For Freedom's Sake: The Life of Fannie Lou Hamer   *Chana Kai Lee*
Becoming Citizens: The Emergence and Development of the California Women's
  Movement, 1880–1911   *Gayle Gullett*
Selected Letters of Lucretia Coffin Mott   *Edited by Beverly Wilson Palmer
  with the assistance of Holly Byers Ochoa and Carol Faulkner*
Women and the Republican Party, 1854–1924   *Melanie Susan Gustafson*
Southern Discomfort: Women's Activism in Tampa, Florida, 1880s–1920s
  Nancy A. Hewitt
The Making of "Mammy Pleasant": A Black Entrepreneur in Nineteenth-Century
  San Francisco   *Lynn M. Hudson*
Sex Radicals and the Quest for Women's Equality   *Joanne E. Passet*
"We, Too, Are Americans": African American Women in Detroit and Richmond,
  1940–54   *Megan Taylor Shockley*
The Road to Seneca Falls: Elizabeth Cady Stanton and the First Woman's Rights
  Convention   *Judith Wellman*
Reinventing Marriage: The Love and Work of Alice Freeman Palmer and George
  Herbert Palmer   *Lori Kenschaft*
Southern Single Blessedness: Unmarried Women in the Urban South,
  1800–1865   *Christine Jacobson Carter*
Widows and Orphans First: The Family Economy and Social Welfare Policy,
  1865–1939   *S. J. Kleinberg*
Habits of Compassion: Irish Catholic Nuns and the Origins of the Welfare System,
  1830–1920   *Maureen Fitzgerald*
The Women's Joint Congressional Committee and the Politics of Maternalism,
  1920–1930   *Jan Doolittle Wilson*

"Swing the Sickle for the Harvest Is Ripe": Gender and Slavery in Antebellum Georgia   *Daina Ramey Berry*

Christian Sisterhood, Race Relations, and the YWCA, 1906–46   *Nancy Marie Robertson*

Reading, Writing, and Segregation: A Century of Black Women Teachers in Nashville   *Sonya Ramsey*

Radical Sisters: Second-Wave Feminism and Black Liberation in Washington, D.C.   *Anne M. Valk*

Feminist Coalitions: Historical Perspectives on Second-Wave Feminism in the United States   *Edited by Stephanie Gilmore*

Breadwinners: Working Women and Economic Independence, 1865–1920   *Lara Vapnek*

Beauty Shop Politics: African American Women's Activism in the Beauty Industry   *Tiffany M. Gill*

Demanding Child Care: Women's Activism and the Politics of Welfare, 1940–1971   *Natalie M. Fousekis*

Rape in Chicago: Race, Myth, and the Courts   *Dawn Rae Flood*

Black Women and Politics in New York City   *Julie A. Gallagher*

Cold War Progressives: Women's Interracial Organizing for Peace and Freedom   *Jacqueline Castledine*

No Votes for Women: The New York State Anti-Suffrage Movement   *Susan Goodier*

Anna Howard Shaw: The Work of Woman Suffrage   *Trisha Franzen*

Nursing Civil Rights: Gender and Race in the Army Nurse Corps   *Charissa J. Threat*

Reverend Addie Wyatt: Faith and the Fight for Labor, Gender, and Racial Equality   *Marcia Walker-McWilliams*

Lucretia Mott Speaks: The Essential Speeches   *Edited by Christopher Densmore, Carol Faulkner, Nancy Hewitt, and Beverly Wilson Palmer*

Lost in the USA: American Identity from the Promise Keepers to the Million Mom March   *Deborah Gray White*

Women against Abortion: Inside the Largest Moral Reform Movement of the Twentieth Century   *Karissa Haugeberg*

Colored No More: Reinventing Black Womanhood in Washington, D.C.   *Treva B. Lindsey*

Beyond Respectability: The Intellectual Thought of Race Women   *Brittney C. Cooper*

Leaders of Their Race: Educating Black and White Women in the New South   *Sarah H. Case*

Glory in Their Spirit: How Four Black Women Took On the Army during World War II   *Sandra M. Bolzenius*

The University of Illinois Press
is a founding member of the
Association of American University Presses.

———————————————————————

Composed in 10.25/14 Chaparral Pro
with Archer display
by Lisa Connery
at the University of Illinois Press
Cover designed by Jennifer S. Fisher
Cover illustration: Capt. Charity Adams drills her company on
the drill ground at the first WAAC Training Center, Fort Des
Moines, Iowa, May 1943 (National Archives, 111-SC-238651).
Manufactured by Cushing-Malloy, Inc.

University of Illinois Press
1325 South Oak Street
Champaign, IL 61820-6903
www.press.uillinois.edu